ORGANIZING THE INSURANCE WORKER

This dissertation was approved by Henry W. Spiegel, Ph.D., professor of Economics, as director, and by Leonard F. Cain and Rev. Vincent D. Mathews, Ph.D., as readers.

ORGANIZING THE INSURANCE WORKER:

A HISTORY OF LABOR UNIONS OF
INSURANCE EMPLOYEES

BY

REV. HARVEY J. CLERMONT, O.F.M. Cap., M.A.

HD
6515
.I4
C55

THE CATHOLIC UNIVERSITY OF AMERICA PRESS

WASHINGTON, D.C. 20017

196034

Nihil Obstat:

BERTRAND SCULLY, O.F.M. Cap., M.A.
LEONARD GLAVIN, O.F.M. Cap., Ph.D.

Hudson, N. H., December 15, 1965

Imprimi Potest:

ADRIAN HOLZMEISTER, O.F.M. Cap.
Minister Provincial

Nihil Obstat:

RT. REV. WILLIAM COLLINS

Nashua, N. H., January 25, 1966

Imprimatur:

+ ERNEST J. PRIMEAU
Bishop of Manchester

Manchester, N. H., February 8, 1966

The writer wishes to thank the following publishers for their permission to use copyrighted material: *The New York Times,* © 1916-1952 by The New York Times Company. Reprinted by permission; "From *Communism in American Unions* by David Saposs, © 1959, McGraw-Hill Book Co. Used by permission of McGraw-Hill Book Company"; "From *Industrial Life Insurance in the United States* by Malvin E. Davis. © 1944, McGraw-Hill Book Co. Used by permission of McGraw-Hill Book Company"; Alpheus Thomas Mason and Willian M. Beaney, *American Constitutional Law: Introductory Essays and Selected Cases,* © 1954. Reprinted by permission of Prentice-Hall, Inc., Englewood Cliffs, N. J.; and Paul G. Kauper, *Constitutional Law, Cases and Materials,* © 1954. Reprinted by permission of Prentice Hall, Inc., Englewood Cliffs, N. J.; *Labor Fact Book, III,* 1936, "By Permission of International Publishers Co. Inc."; *Communism in American Unions"* by Benjamin Stolberg reprinted with permission from *The Saturday Evening Post,* copyright 1939 The Curtis Publishing Company"; Sumner H. Slichter, *The Challenge of Industrial Relations: Trade Unions, Management, and the Public Interest,* Copyright 1947 by Cornell University. Used by permission of Cornell University Press.

Printed by
COLE PRINTING CO., INC.
8 Franklin Street   Nashua, New Hampshire

IV

For my Parents

and

in Memory of

John Fitzgerald Kennedy

35th President of the

United States

INTRODUCTION

In the annals of the American labor movement the industrial life insurance agent stands apart, for the nature of his work is such that he is atypical. In a sense, he is a production worker, yet neither the product nor the work place are comparable to anything that is generally associated with the industrial system. To be sure, the agent pursues a trade, but here again his success or failure depends upon certain, sometimes undefinable, talents that are not usually connected with craft unionism. Moreover, because his salary is as much conditioned by his commissions as by any flat rate of pay, he cannot be thought of as a typical wage earner.

When he sought membership in the labor movement, the insurance man had not only to overcome prejudice occasioned by ignorance and indifference but downright hostility as well. He had, therefore, to seek out the means whereby he might prove that his condition of employment was susceptible to change and that he could achieve the stability on the job that the organized American worker was in some measure assured of. That his goal required enormous energy and perseverance goes without saying, and it is the purpose of this study to examine the various ways in which he banded together with his fellow workers to make the dream a reality. Naturally, not every agent shared this vision, nor was every agent convinced of the worth of a particular technique or of the value of a particular organization. However, the worker in question was able to use changing social conditions so as to obtain sufficient support for social reform and to attract important allies in the labor movement so as to guarantee his efforts. With that much in his favor he secured for himself a niche in the history of the American labor movement.

Because the insurance agent is not a typical wage earner, it is important to dwell upon certain phases of his profession in order to understand why he sought improvement in his working life through a labor organization. The first of these pertains to compensation which at one time was greatly affected by the so-called lapse ratio, that is, the rate of policies that lapse to those in force. The second aspect of his working life followed upon the first. During the time the agents undertook self-organization, turnover rates were high and these responded to the lapse ratio.

The industrial life insurance agent is primarily a salesman. He works a combination monetary-geographic unit called a debit, and the size of the debit and the number of policyholders it includes not only determine his salary but his success as a salesman as well. The work is fiercely competitive, and the agent who can service a debit of between two hundred and fifty and three hundred families is considered average.

By definition the industrial agent sells industrial insurance. The title derives from the fact that the agent sold this type of insurance to the industrial worker, the traditional low income group. Original-ly, the industrial life policy was designed to assist the poor in burying a deceased breadwinner and was collectible on a weekly house to house basis. As time went on, the companies, while preserving this form of insurance, experimented with other types, such as industrial endowment and intermediate life, or monthly debit ordinary, all of which the agent tried to sell in abundance and which increased his earnings.[1]

Computing an industrial agent's compensation is a tricky propo-sition at best, but over the years certain patterns and variations in salary can be observed. In the first place, an agent is paid on a commission basis. Until 1933, the companies offered the commission on a two-fold basis: (1) the size, or the monetary value of the debit, and (2) the net increase in the debit. The latter part of the agent's compensation, one writer explained, is founded on the "amount of premiums issued and reinstated less that terminated for causes other than death, maturity, or other contractual completions of premium payments." The same author stressed the importance of the second part of the commission because it was as necessary for an agent to conserve an existing policy as to sell a new one for the same premium

[1]It should be noted that in 1954 the word "industrial" was deleted from this kind of insurance, and in its place there was substituted the phrase "debit life insurance," which, in the light of the present state of the economy seems more meaningful. Since the agents established labor organizations at a time when the word was in general use, and since much of story of agents' unions pre-dates 1954, the writer has preferred to retain the original designation.

payment.[2] An agent's commission was, therefore, determined by the "size" and the "net increase" of his debit. Since he was obliged to sell to and service his clients on a weekly basis, an agent was compensated each week.

While many agents were successful salesmen, economic conditions played havoc with the vast majority of the men. In 1929, for example, average weekly earnings of agents employed by the Metropolitan Life Insurance Company were at a high of $56.00. With the onset of the Great Depression these earnings began to fall off until they reached a low of $42.00 in 1933.[3] So far as the debit agent was concerned his salary declined because economic conditions made it impossible for the insured to continue their premium payments. In such a situation the policies were lapsing at an enormous rate with the result that the agents were unable to write new business and to service their debits adequately.

To remedy the decline in commissions such companies as Metropolitan, Prudential and John Hancock devised a new method of compensation, which, in the words of the author already cited, "would preserve the intent of the original method of compensation, but would work satisfactorily in both normal and abnormal times."[4] In order to inaugurate the new plan the three firms had to seek the approval of the New York Insurance Department, which, in the absence of a federal insurance law, controlled industrial insurance in the United States.[5] The Department approved and the three companies offered their debit agents a new contract in 1937.

Under the terms of the agreement the agent was paid the same salary for each week for a period of thirteen weeks, and this in turn

[2]Malvin E. Davis, *Industrial Life Insurance in the United States* (New York: McGraw-Hill, 1944), p. 65.

[3]U.S. Congress, Temporary National Economic Committee, *Hearings, Investigation of Industrial Insurance*, Part 12, 75th Cong., 1st Sess., 1939, p. 6235.

[4]Davis, *op. cit.*, p. 66.

[5]New York codified its insurance laws in 1892, and the Armstrong Committee revised the state's insurance statutes in 1906. Davis asserts: "Companies must conform as to their entire business to the standards of the strictest state in which they do business." New York is the strictest state. *Ibid.*, pp. 94-95.

IX

was based on the record of the agent's production for the previous fiscal quarter. The companies adjusted the uniform salary on the basis of what is known as the "first year commission salary" and the "collection service salary." The former is defined as the rate of new business written over the rate of policies that had lapsed; the latter is computed on the basis of the size of the agent's debit and his rate of lapsed policies. In determining his uniform salary a company therefore computed both the "first year commission salary" and the "collection service salary" of the immediately previous period of thirteen weeks and paid the agent accordingly.

At first the Metropolitan and then Prudential and Hancock paid the agents a minimum salary which was graded according to the average size of the agent's debit in the preceding fiscal quarter. If the agent's total salary was less than the company minimum, he was paid a minimum as determined by the company. A new agent, with no record of previous quarterly business, was paid a special rate of salary.

In commenting on the new compensation plan the New York Insurance Department observed that the agent received "a fair income and may look forward to a very good income as his position in the field improves."[6]

An agent's compensation was adjusted still further to conform to the proportion of the individual lapse rate to that of a particular company's national lapse ratio. By preserving the basic fiscal quarter principle one company, the Prudential, determined the individual and national lapse rates by "dividing the agent's lapse rate for the previous 13 weeks' period by the lapse rate of the company or of the division in which the agent works, whichever is the greater."[7]

The industrial agent therefore is paid on the basis of a standard fiscal quarter which in turn consists of a "first year commission" and a "collection service salary." To these figures are added an additional computation which considers the lapse rate of the individual insured and his company's national lapse ratio.

[6]State of New York, *Report on the Examination of the Metropolitan Life Insurance Company, Special Study of Industrial Insurance,* State of New York Insurance Department, December 27, 1937, pp. 55-58.

[7]U.S. Cong., *T.N.E.C. Hearings,* Part 12, p. 5761.

X

In approving the new compensation plan the New York Insurance Department made it clear that an agent's compensation depended to a great extent upon his ability to conserve business on his debit. Since his salary was based on his record of production during a previous fiscal quarter, an agent was of necessity bound to keep all of his policies in force. In a word, the companies endeavored to prevent policies from lapsing by holding their agents responsible for conserving the business.

However, this was easier said than done. When economic conditions are depressed the poor simply cannot maintain their policies, with the result that they lose whatever insurance they possess and the agent suffers a loss in earning power. To prevent lapses it frequently happened that an agent had to dig into his own pocket for the nickles, dimes and quarters needed to cover premium payments of errant policyholders. Many of the debit men began to participate in a procedure known as the "squirrel cage," an operation whereby they hoped not only to keep policies in force but also to recover the money they lost in making premium payments. The "squirrel cage" consisted of a "continual sale and resale of industrial policies to policyholders who lapsed their policies only to take new policies and lapse again."[8] In other words, an agent simply resold a lapsed policy to anyone ignorant enough to purchase it.

The problem of lapses, or the termination of a policy for failure to meet premium payments, occupied the attention of a New York legislative committee and the Temporary National Economic Committee. The data supplied by their separate studies is revealing.

By way of partial explanation the New York legislators offered the following opinion:

> The number of lapses is principally due to the pressure and force employed by everyone concerned with the sale of the industrial policy. The cycle commences with the home office and ends with the agent. Managers' and assistant managers' salaries or income depend in part on increase in premium volume. The increase of premium income is a determining factor whether or not a manager, assistant manager, or agent is promoted or demoted. The very contract which companies have with agents

[8]*Ibid.*, p. 5596.

provides that most of the agents' income shall come from industrial policies.[9]

The Temporary National Economic Committee disclosed that between 1901 and 1938 over $60 billion worth of policies had lapsed. Taking the figures that came closer to the Great Depression, T.N.E.C. reported that between 1928 and 1937 ninety per cent of industrial policies were terminated in the United States by reason of lapse or surrender, and that only a little over four per cent were closed because of death. According to the Committee's survey, the lapse rate alone represented over seventy per cent of the total.[10]

The Metropolitan Life, Prudential and John Hancock were, of course, aware of these figures and tried to preserve as many policies as possible. To this end they offered their agents a new compensation agreement, a point that has already been discussed. But as late as 1938 the Metropolitan sustained a lapse rate of 48.7 per cent, and Prudential had a rate of 54.3 per cent while Hancock had a rate of 62.7 per cent.[11]

The situation demanded reform, and in 1938 New York and Massachusetts decided to do something about the lapse rate. Each state enacted what was called a "lapse law" which was designed to offer relief to a debit agent who simply had the misfortune of possessing a debit on which policyholders were terminating their policies. Prior to the enactment of the laws an industrial salesman was obliged to keep a policy in force for an indefinite period of time. The "lapse laws" attached a stipulation to industrial insurance selling that would hold an agent responsible for a policy for three years only; if a policyholder, for any reason, decided to terminate his premium payments after that time an agent was not to be penalized.[12]

[9]State of New York, *Report of the Joint Legislative Committee on the Revision of Insurance Laws,* Legislative Document No. 101, 1939, p. 20.

[10]U.S. Cong., *T.N.E.C. Hearings,* Part 12, p. 5607.

[11]*Ibid.,* pp. 6172-173.

[12]The laws of both states are similar, and the Massachusetts law reads as follows: "If a policy of industrial life insurance upon which premiums have been paid for three years or more is surrendered to the company for a cash surrender value or paid up insurance or extended term insurance or lapses for non-payment of premiums, the agent shall not be charged with a decrease for said premium, and no deduction shall be made from his commission or salary." Commonwealth of Massachusetts, *Acts and Resolves,* c. 175, sec. 164A, 1938.

These laws afforded industrial agents relief, and in companies such as Metropolitan, Prudential and John Hancock the debit man could anticipate improved earnings. However, there were great numbers of agents employed by other industrial companies, and these men feared the future. Their concern was not unfounded, for in 1939 the Temporary National Economic Committee reported that one company had a lapse rate of 235.0 per cent and that another firm lapsed 361.0 per cent as many policies as it sold.[13] The agents were also anxious because many of the smaller companies did not operate in either New York or Massachusetts and were consequently not subject to the newly legislated "lapse laws."

Lapsing of policies played a large role in turnover rates among industrial insurance agents. Since their commissions depend in great part upon lapse ratios, debit agents could preserve their jobs only if policyholders in their territories were able to continue their premium payments. It has already been observed that an enormous number of industrial lapses occurred in the United States during the first four decades of the twentieth century. There is also sufficient evidence to show a correlation between the lapse ratio and turnover rates among industrial debit agents. For example, the New York Insurance Department furnished data on turnover among agents who worked for Metropolitan Life for the years 1908 through 1936. The Department's report indicates that in 1908 seventy-six per cent of the agents were terminated, while in 1927 the number had dropped to 38.4 per cent. In 1933 twenty-seven per cent of the men lost their jobs, compared to 18.4 per cent in 1936.[14] A similar decline in employment termination can be found among agents of Prudential and John Hancock, although the pattern does not follow from an examination of most of the other industrial companies.[15]

It should be noted that in whole numbers turnover rates for Metropolitan represent 65,000 men who lost their jobs, for reasons other than death, between the years 1926 and 1936. While this figure hides the toll of human misery and disappointment attendant upon loss of work, it also veils the fact the Metropolitan expended

[13]U.S. Cong., *T.N.E.C. Hearings,* Part 12, pp. 6172-173.

[14]State of New York, *Revision of Insurance Laws,* Doc. No. 101, 1939, p. 20.

[15]U.S. Cong., *T.N.E.C. Hearings,* Part 12, various pages.

upwards of thirty-four millions of dollars in training and equipping agents for debit service.[16]

Many agents felt that as long as they had to depend upon the lapse factor for their salaries they might as well sell as much of the other types of industrial insurance as possible. One form of insurance that proved popular with low income families was the industrial endowment policy. This kind of insurance partakes of the characteristics of any kind of endowment policy and can be defined as "insurance payable on the insured if he is living on the maturity date stated in the policy, or to a beneficiary if the insured dies prior to that date."[17] The value of the policy might be as low as $100.00, but to a poor person the amount was substantial enough to offer a loved one a start in life. In 1938 New York forbade the sale of industrial endowment, although the state modified the prohibition during the following year to allow the companies to sell the policy in every state except New York.[18]

The reason behind the ruling concerns agent pressure tactics. Since he collected higher premiums on endowment, he also shared larger commissions, and this in turn prompted the agent to sell endowment to people who could scarcely afford it. According to a New York study, agents sold endowment "at the rate of four to one over industrial life insurance on lives of children" between 1926 and 1930, and again between 1931 and 1935. The same authority added caustically that debit agents were insuring youngsters whose real defense against the vicissitudes of life was an insured father.[19]

The all too familiar theme of lapsing also applied to industrial endowment, but with a peculiar twist. The New York investigation showed that if an endowment policy lapsed before the end of five years, no part of the investment was returned to the policyholder in

16State of New York, *Revision of Insurance Laws,* Doc. No. 101, 1939, p. 20.

17Institute of Life Insurance, *Life insurance Fact Book,* 1963 (New York: Institute of Life Insurance, 1963), p. 117.

18U.S. Cong., *T.N.E.C. Hearings,* Part 12, p. 5891.

19State of New York, *Revision of Insurance Laws,* Doc. No. 101, 1939, pp. 21 & 23.

cash. The same report proved further that at the end of fourteen and one-half years approximately 85 per cent of endowment policies had lapsed.[20] Since the evidence was so overwhelming New York authorities suppressed its sale. The state reconsidered its nation-wide prohibition because of pressure from other states' insurance departments.

The preceding resumé of industrial insurance practices covers a considerable period of time and might very well be academic. When the United States began to prepare for its defense in 1940, sales of industrial insurance almost immediately started to level off and Americans invested in other forms of life insurance. This long term decline in industrial, vis-à-vis ordinary and group life, has continued to the present time.[21]

However, as early as 1906 the Armstrong Investigating Committee of New York concluded that industrial insurance should either be suppressed or permitted to continue to exist with all its inherent evils. Such also was the finding of the Temporary National Economic Committee. And as late as 1941 Sumner T. Pike of the Securities and Exchange Commission critically evaluated industrial insurance in a way that was anything but favorable; he wrote in part:

> Because of their high cost and the selling practices employed industrial policies are rarely kept in force long enough to accomplish their essential purpose . . . . The three largest companies [the Metropolitan, Prudential and Hancock] selling this type of insurance and several smaller companies have partly under the pressure of public opinion and partly at their own volition instituted many industrial reforms. About 50 per cent of the new business is being written by companies not in this category, however, and as to all companies the evils apparently of necessity inherent in industrial insurance remain.[22]

[20]*Ibid.*, pp. 21-22.

[21]Institute of Life Insurance, *op. cit.*, pp. 13 & 20.

[22]Sumner T. Pike, *Statement on Life Insurance, Delivered February 28, 1941, Before the Temporary National Economic Committee* (Washington: U.S. Government Printing Office, 1941), p. 18.

XV

Industrial debit agents formed labor unions during the heyday of industrial insurance selling. They considered themselves as much the victims of the system as the policyholders and decided that mutual interests and shared hardships necessitated their joining together for their own protection.

Sumner Pike's appraisal of the three giants in the field, the Metropolitan, Prudential and Hancock, came too late to influence these companies' agents who had already joined labor organizations. And these men would not have accepted his testimony anyway. They had suffered too much from industrial lapses and the resultant turnover, from what they considered undue pressure from their employer and from the so-called dictatorial policy of the New York Insurance Department. That the latter agency's purpose was the protection of the policyholder more than the debit agent or the company seems never to have entered their minds. After more than half a century of poor working conditions, these professional employees sought refuge in unions of their own choosing.

This dissertation will relate the history of insurance labor unions from the time of the first recorded organization down to the merger of two small unions in 1959. Greatest emphasis will be given the agents' experience in the largest of the industrial life companies — the Metropolitan, Prudential and John Hancock, for it was with these firms that the collective bargaining relationship became significant. While the writer has not relished the idea of having to resurrect the issue of left-wing unionism, he had to decide that any consideration of the organized insurance agents' history would be incomplete without it. The agent achieved a great deal through the left-wing group, the United Office and Professional Workers of America, and it is tragic that the organization had to pursue a policy that the C.I.O. found unacceptable in a free trade union movement. Because the union sought to include much of the nation's white collar force within its institutional framework, with the result that the agent had very little real power, the organized insurance men established their own unions and made them much less comprehensive. During the 1950's the two organizations engaged in a number of bitter conflicts, but in the last year of that decade decided to bury their differences and to merge their forces for the benefit of the insurance worker.

This book is based on public documents, labor union convention proceedings, interviews, newspaper accounts, several works on the American labor movement and much miscellaneous material. The writer has made use of various decisions of the United States Supreme Court and of lower courts as well. Pertinent federal and state laws have been included, along with an examination of the *Hearings* before the Temporary National Economic Committee and the House Un-American Activities Committee; and the *Decisions and Orders* of the National Labor Relations Board and the *Decisions* of the New York State Labor Relations Board. Much valuable information has been found in the *Convention Proceedings* of the following labor organizations: the A.F. of L., the C.I.O., the United Office and Professional Workers of America, C.I.O., the Insurance Workers of America, C.I.O., the Insurance Agents International Union, A.F. of L., and the Industrial and Ordinary Insurance Agents Council, A.F. of L. The author must make special reference to *The New York Times* as this newspaper opened areas of research discovered in only a few other places. The *Times* also served the very useful purpose of enhancing, and sometimes contradicting, certain materials read in a great number of labor union publications.

The writer wishes to use this occasion to express a deep debt of gratitude to His Excellency, the Most Reverend Firmin M. Schmidt, O.F.M. Cap., D.D., Titular Bishop of Conana and Vicar Apostolic of Mendi, Papua, New Guinea; His Excellency was the author's superior at Capuchin College, Washington, D.C. The writer also wishes to thank a former associate at the College, the Most Rev. Giles Staab, O.F.M. Cap., S.T.D., Definitor General, the Capuchin General Curia, Rome, Italy. The following Capuchin superiors, provincial and local, are deserving of the author's deepest gratitude: the Very Rev. Adrian Holzmeister, Minister Provincial, and the Very Rev. ex-Ministers Provincial, Ignatius McCormick and Seraphin Winterroth, along with the Very Rev. Maurice Maurer, the Very Rev. Hugh Morley and the Rev. Laurence Stubbs, all of the St. Mary Province. In addition to these the writer is indebted to the Very Rev. and Rev. Fathers of the St. Augustine Province with whom he resided at the Capuchin College, Washington.

The author is grateful to his teachers at the Catholic University of America, Washington, D.C., and especially to Henry W. Spiegel, Ph.D., Professor of Economics, who, as major professor, rendered invaluable assistance and guided the dissertation to its conclusion. In this regard the writer also wishes to thank Professor Leonard F. Cain and Rev. Vincent D. Mathews, Ph.D., who read the work and offered helpful suggestions.

Gratitude is also due to the author's Capuchin confrères at St. Anthony Friary, Hudson, N.H., particularly to the Very Rev. Bertrand Scully and the Rev. Leonard Glavin who read the dissertation, and to the Venerable Fraters Dismas O'Keefe who typed the manuscript, Alvin Brown who made the arrangements with the printer, and Matthew McHugh and Bertin Rathschmidt. The author would be remiss in his duty if he failed to thank the Capuchin seminarians; he is most grateful particularly to the members of St. Anthony's senior class, past and present, whose patient understanding made the writing of the book considerably less burdensome. And to the Rev. Lanny Blomberg, O.F.M. Cap., St. Francis High School, Los Angeles, the writer owes a special word of gratitude.

It is difficult to thank adequately the many librarians who have been of assistance. The author asks the librarians of the following institutions to read between the lines: the AFL-CIO Library, Washington, D.C., with a special word of thanks to Mrs. J. Edwin Giles, former head librarian; the Library, United States Department of Labor; the Mullen Library, the Catholic University; the State House Library, Commonwealth of Massachusetts, Boston; the Boston Public Library; the Widener Library, Harvard University and the Manchester, N.H., and the Lowell, Mass., libraries.

A word of thanks is also due the officials of the former separate insurance unions, the Insurance Workers of America, AFL-CIO, and the Insurance Agents International Union, AFL-CIO, for their kind permission to use their facilities and their files.

During the course of the writing of this work the author received considerable help from the following persons, and he wishes to thank them now: Walter Maggiolo, Director of Mediating Activity, the Federal Mediation and Conciliation Service; Anne Kerrigan who introduced the writer to the insurance workers; James Brisbane, staff employee, the Insurance Workers International Union, AFL-CIO; W. J. and Helen Voss; Paul J. Fitzpatrick, former Head, Department of Economics, the Catholic University; Martin Raber; William J. Finncran of Shea, Gould, Gallop and Climenko, New York City; Matthew Hogan whose conversation and files were of great assistance; and Leo Martin.

The author also wishes to thank the Rt. Rev. Msgr. William Collins, Nashua, N.H., for reading the manuscript.

Last, but certainly not least, the writer is grateful to his family. Without the constant prodding of his father, particularly, the author doubts that this book would have been written.

TABLE OF CONTENTS

INTRODUCTION vii

CHAPTER 1

INSURANCE AGENTS SEEK A LABOR ORGANIZATION 1
    Bookkeepers, Stenographers, and Accountants' Union,
        Local 12646 4
    United Office and Professional Workers of America, C.I.O. 9
    The A.F. of L. in Insurance 12
    The International Union of Life Insurance Agents,
        Independent 15
    The Metropolitan Life Insurance Company 19
    The New York State "Little Wagner Act" 24

CHAPTER 2

THE AGENTS GRADUATE TO THE 'BIG-TIME' 29
    The U.O.P.W.A. Achieves a 'Nation-Wide' Contract
        with Prudential 32
    The Prudential Election in Ohio 38
    The Compensation Issue 43
    Other Successes 48

CHAPTER 3

CERTAIN AGENTS LAPSE THEIR POLICIES IN A POOR-RISK
ORGANIZATION 50
    How It All Began 50
    The Temporary National Economic Committee
        Investigates Insurance 60
    The Record Speaks for Itself 64
    Reaction Sets In 68

CHAPTER 4

WHEN A VICTORY IS NOT A VICTORY 72
    Negotiating with Metropolitan 75
    An Additional Note on Compensation 76
    Is Insurance Interstate Commerce 78
    Postwar Economics 83
    A Resolute "Smaller" Company 87

CHAPTER 5

THE AGENTS TEST THE "PECULIAR TWIST" THEORY 96
    The Resignation of Lewis Merrill 97
    The Administration of James Durkin 100
    The 1948 Convention of the United Office and Professional
        Workers of America 103
    The Right-Wing Agents Stage a Production of Their Own 110

CHAPTER 6

THE AGENTS PICK UP THE PIECES 120
    The Prudential Hearings 120
    The C.I.O. Convention of 1948 123
    The Prudential Election 126
    The C.I.O. Convention of 1949 129
    C.I.O. Expels the United Office and Professional
        Workers of America 130
    Choosing Up Sides 135
    Three Small Unions Merge 138
    The John Hancock Case 143

CHAPTER 7

THE NEW C.I.O. UNION: A RECORD OF SURVIVAL 147
    The Insurance and Allied Workers Organizing
        Committee, C.I.O. 147
    The Law vs. the Union Contract 153
    The Insurance Workers of America, C.I.O. 157
    The Hancock "Streamlined" Committee 159
    Defeat in Detroit 163

CHAPTER 8

THE A.F. OF L. UNION: A RECORD OF DISSATISFACTION 169
    An International Union at Last 173
    An Unsuccessful Strike 175
    A Schism is Started 178
    The Prudential Strike Aftermath 180
    Another Reverse on the Home Front 185
    A Landmark Decision from the High Court 187

CHAPTER 9

TWO SMALL UNIONS MERGE 190
    A Most Unlikely Occasion for Unity 192
    A Prolonged Series of Fits and Starts 203
    Merger At Last 209
CONCLUSIONS 211
APPENDIX I: Chronological Table of Major Events 219
APPENDIX II: A List of Organizations of Insurance Workers 223
APPENDIX III: Membership Figures in the More Important
    Insurance Unions 224
BIBLIOGRAPHY 225
INDEX 236

XXI

CHAPTER 1

INSURANCE AGENTS SEEK A LABOR ORGANIZATION

Charles H. Sidener represented the American Agents Association at the 1895 convention of the American Federation of Labor. He urged the convention delegates to enact a resolution declaring unfair the industrial insurance debit agents' contracts with the Metropolitan Life Insurance Company and the Prudential Insurance Company of America. To emphasize the insurance agents' predicament Sidener quoted part of the Metropolitan agreement, which read as follows:

> The total amount of weekly premiums in the Life Policy Register, after deducting the total weekly premiums in the Lapsed Policy Register, are to be debited to my account on Monday of each and every week.

> I further agree not to call or attend any meeting or join any combination of agents or policyholders of this or any other company or society, unless such call, meeting or combination be authorized in writing by the president of this Company.[1]

Whether or not the A.F. of L. responded to Sidener's request is unknown. He attended the convention the following year and asked the labor organization to boycott the Metropolitan Life specifically because the company had done nothing to pacify the Agents Association. It seems he succeeded in convincing the convention delegates to establish a list of insurance firms unfair to his small group of agents. However, in 1899 the A.F. of L. voted to disregard the unfair practice resolution, and in the following year it revoked the Association's union charter, asserting that the organization had no "bona fide existence."[2]

Certain insurance men considered the A.F. of L.'s procedure meaningless. A delegate for a group of debit agents calling themselves the Insurance Agents Local Union 8676 of St. Louis ap-

[1]American Federation of Labor, *Report of the Proceedings of the Fifteenth Annual Convention* (New York, N.Y., 1895), pp. 41-42.

[2]*Ibid.*, Cincinnati, O., 1896, p. 80; Detroit, Mich., 1899, p. 151; and Louisville, Ky., 1900, p. 60.

peared at the 1901 convention and claimed that his organization "had succeeded in getting officers of some insurance companies to look with more favor on the formation of unions among agents."[3] The Local obtained the backing of the Nashville Trade and Labor Council, for in 1902 the Council applied to the convention for a charter for the agents. However, the delegates openly and finally rebuffed the industrial debit men. In words that possess a contemporary flavor the delegates resolved:

> Several applications were received from insurance agents' associations. We declined to issue them for various reasons, two of which are that a card as a union member carried by these agents induces workmen's families to become insured for petty amounts, for which in the aggregate they pay large sums, and on the other hand, it defers the time when wage-earners will establish their own protective and insurance features in their own trade unions. There are other obvious reasons unnecessary to record in this report.[4]

The resolution had the practical effect of placing the Federation in the forefront of a growing list of organizations holding suspect certain practices of industrial life insurance companies. Since agents were party to these practices, A.F. of L. officials reasoned, they had to be excluded from Federation membership. Only at a much later date, when the success of the Congress of Industrial Organizations in unionizing debit agents had become a threat to its own structure and prestige, would the A.F. of L. embrace insurance men. And not until 1925 would the union establish its own insurance society, but this will be a case of delivering too little too late.[5]

Groups of agents continued to form labor unions, however. In the Boston area, for example, a group of Metropolitan and John Hancock insurance men attempted to form a union in 1912 and again in 1913. They received no support from the A.F. of L.; they

3*Ibid.,* Scranton, Pa., 1901, p. 48.

4*Ibid.,* New Orleans, La., 1902, p. 58.

5*The New York Times,* July 22, 1925, p. 10. Called the Union Labor Life Insurance Co., it was capitalized at two million dollars.

3

were simply ignored.[6] Yet, in 1916 there was founded an organization that held out to the agents some hope of permanent union membership. In 1916 Harry Lumpkin established the Insurance Mutual Protective Association, and he made it known that his union had enrolled six thousand industrial agents in Boston, Chicago, Philadelphia, Providence and New York. The Association became involved in a dispute with the Prudential Insurance Company of America over a company directive of June 3, 1916, which compelled agents to cover lapsed policies by obtaining new business and to write new policies, both without commission. The conflict worsened when Prudential dismissed fifty agents of the New York metropolitan area for misrepresenting its wage policy by asserting that they received extremely low wages. Prudential protested that weekly rates of pay averaged between $23.00 and $24.00 per agent, an actual increase, the company insisted, of 30 per cent over the preceding five years. When Prudential refused to re-hire the dismissed agents the Association retaliated by striking the company. Lumpkin's group estimated that two thousand of its members engaged in the walkout, while Prudential officials asserted that only two hundred men joined the dispute. The record remains silent as to the length of the strike and its outcome. So does the A.F. of L. During the conflict the press reported that Prudential accused the Association of radicalism. The basis for this assessment seems to lie in the fact that the Association held membership in the Industrial Workers of the World, an organization considered radical at the time.[7]

There is yet another early example of insurance agents joining together. On July 7, 1918, New York State Assemblyman Charles B. Garfinkel, presiding over a meeting of a group of industrial agents he had organized, introduced Charles W. Ervin, Socialist candidate for governor of New York. It was reported that Ervin declared the agents victims of a false mentality: they considered themselves businessmen and not wage earners. This attitude, he reasoned, had deprived them of the benefits of unionism.[8]

[6]Why Should I Join the U.O.P.W.A., the Insurance Agents Union? Here's Why!" U.O.P.W.A., 1944.

[7]*The New York Times,* July 21, p. 9; July 22, p. 5; July 25, pp. 1 & 7; July 28, p. 9; & July 29, p. 10 (1916).

[8]*Ibid.,* July 8, 1918, p. 13.

The observation seems too simple. Although the vast majority of the agents might regard themselves as members of insurance management, a number of complicated factors were at work, all serving to inhibit the growth of unions of insurance agents. In the most general terms, it can be stated that the rise of company unions, the open hostility of insurance management, incentive plans, and the indecision of the A.F. of L. all conspired to keep the industrial insurance agent outside the labor movement.

BOOKKEEPERS. STENOGRAPHERS. AND ACCOUNTANTS' UNION, LOCAL 12646

The history of organizational efforts among industrial insurance agents is intimately connected with a New York City union of office employees called the Bookkeepers, Stenographers, and Accountants' Union, Local 12646. It is partially out of this group that there was formed the United Office and Professional Workers of America, C.I.O., a national union which achieved a degree of success both in attracting insurance agents and in dealing with the industrial insurance companies.

The B.S.&A.U. had a curious history. The 1909 convention of the A.F. of L. records the presence of a delegate from the Bookkeepers' union, although as far back as 1904 a stenographers' union from Indianapolis was listed among the organizations present.[9] In attendance at practically all of the A.F. of L. conventions between 1909 and 1937 — the year of its departure from the Federation — B.S.&A.U., Local 12646, and other white collar locals petitioned the A.F. of L. for a national union charter and for a full-time organizer. The representatives of the same unions considered this necessary, because by 1913, for example, there were federal locals of office employees in the District of Columbia, New York City, Indianapolis, Chicago, St. Louis, Kansas City, Denver and San Francisco. And by 1919 there were in existence forty locals of office workers with a claimed membership of over 2,000 persons.[10] Delegates from these unions reasoned that the potential white collar member-

[9]A.F. of L., *Convention Proceedings* (Toronto, Can., 1909), p. xi; & Ibid., (San Francisco, Calif., 1904), p. x.

[10]*Ibid.*, Seattle, Wash., 1913, p. 233; Baltimore, Md., 1916, p. 213; & Atlantic City, N.J., 1919, p. 250.

ship of organized labor was enormous. Yet each time the question of a national charter was raised at an A.F. of L. convention, the delegates referred the request back to the union's executive committee on the plea of lack of funds and insufficient membership in the locals.

An occurrence at the 1922 convention indicates that the Federation was stalling the B.S.&A.U. and other white collar locals for reasons other than those already stated. At this gathering a resolution was proposed demanding that A.F. of L. member unions hire union office help only. The delegates rejected the resolution and with good reason.[11] During the previous summer Samuel Gompers had instructed Hugh Frayne, an A.F. of L. organizer in New York, to revoke the charter of B.S.&A.U., Local 12646. The official explanation given was that the union had violated its charter by admitting non-qualified persons to membership. In defending his action Gompers wrote:

> The union in question had taken into its membership a great many persons who were not, who never had been, and who never intended to be either bookkeepers, stenographers, accountants, or office workers of any kind.[12]

Newspaper accounts of the incident reflect a different view. *The New York Call,* for example, reported that the Local had been captured by the Trade Union Education League, a Communist organization whose stated purpose was to take over trade unions.[13] *The New York Times* contains the estimate that one-fifth of the membership of the local was Communist tainted and was able to outvote the majority, and it goes on to relate that a B.S.&A.U. delegate to an A.F. of L. convention had attempted to organize a left-wing section within the Federation.

When the A.F. of L. revoked the union's charter, nine members of the B.S.&A.U.'s executive board reviled the A.F. of L. for a "high handed" piece of "starchamber" procedure and asserted that

[11]*Ibid.,* Cincinnati, O., 1922, p. 481.

[12]Samuel Gompers, "Letter to Albert F. Coyle," *The American Federationist,* XXIX (October, 1922), 778-79.

[13]*The New York Call,* July 16, 1922, in Selig Perlman and Philip Taft, "Labor Movements," *History of Labor in the United States,* 1896-1932, vol. 4 (New York: Macmillan, 1935), p. 541.

the action was undertaken "without a trial, a hearing, or even a statement of charges."[14] They also informed Gompers of their intention of remaining within the A.F. of L. This boast was not an idle one, for one week later it was reported that Frayne accused a former excutive officer of B.S.&A.U. of removing the charter, membership cards and seal from the union headquarters at 62 University Place, New York.[15]

While the deposed "radical" element planned a court case to contest Gompers' right to revoke the charter, the A.F. of L. went ahead with forming a new local. On July 24, 1922, the Federation established an organization which retained the old title, B.S.&A.U., Local 12646. Purged members were present at the ceremony demanding affiliation, but this was refused during the meeting. Leonard Bright and Ernest Bohm became the chief officers of the new local.[16]

These accounts appear less diplomatic than the official statement of Gompers. At the 1923 A.F. of L. convention Bohm brought the dispute into the light of day. He stated that the old Bookkeepers' union was "dominated over and controlled by a group whose sole purpose was propaganda for Communist theories."[17]

In 1924 B.S.&A.U., Local 12646, unsuccessfully attempted to organize the New York Trust Company and the Bankers Trust Company in New York City.[18] Yet within a year the Local enrolled twenty clerks in the Bank of Athens in New York, and its protests against the National City Bank moved that institution to increase its employees' salaries, or so the local leadership said.[19]

[14]*The New York Times,* July 12, 1922, p. 2.

[15]*Ibid.,* July 17, 1922, p. 13.

[16]Bright was an "avowed socialist," *The New York Times,* July 12, 1922, p. 10. He was affiliated with the New York Central Federated Union and, after 1921, had been secretary and business manager of the Bookkeepers' Local 12646, cf. Solon de Leon (ed.), *American Labors' Who's Who* (New York: Hanford Press, 1925), p. 119.

[17]A.F. of L., *Convention Proceedings* (Portland, Ore., 1923), p. 212.

[18]*The New York Times,* October 19, 1923, pp. 1 & 36.

[19]A.F. of L., *Convention Proceedings* (Atlantic City, N.J., 1925), p. 154.

During this time the B.S.&A.U. had also signed an agreement with the International Ladies' Garment Workers' Union, Local 22, according to the terms of which the latter would hire only union secretarial help. Shortly thereafter a dispute arose over the Garment Workers' refusal to employ two members of the B.S.&A.U. On June 18, 1925, Julius Portnoy, Secretary of Local 22, locked out the Bookkeepers' union, an action that so aggravated many of the union's members that they authorized a strike against local 22. However, the walkout was averted when the full membership of B.S.&A.U. refused to comply with the strike vote. The dispute was settled when Portnoy restored the two "radical" members to good standing.[20]

The question of radicalism and Communist affiliation simmered during the next two years and exploded again in February 1927, when the A.F. of L. expelled twenty-three members of B.S.&A.U. A newspaper report indicates that these persons belonged to the Trade Union Education League, an organization that the A.F. of L. wanted no part of.[21]

The Bookkeepers first attempted to organize insurance workers in 1927. On October 16 Leonard Bright announced that his union would seek to enroll the ten thousand member office force of Metropolitan Life in New York City. He asserted that the Bookkeepers would demand recognition from the company and the right to bargain collectively. He further claimed that unionization would raise the office employees' minimum wage to $21.00 per week, instead of the $12.00 the company was paying its office workers, most of whom were girls. In this latter pledge he claimed the support and sponsorship of Mrs. Eleanor Roosevelt and Fannie Hurst, the novelist.[22]

Haley Fiske, president of the company, simply denied that Metropolitan paid these low wages. He said that "some may get as low as $12.00 per week during a trial period, but there are no permanent $12.00 a week salaries." He proceeded to characterize the B.S.&A.U. as a union "our people laugh at." He went on to say:

As a matter of fact none of our workers has been approached except by circulars which ask for $1.00 from each worker for

[20]*Ibid.*, pp. 156 & 165; & *The New York Times*, October 8, 1925, pp. 1 & 12.

[21]*The New York Times*, March 1, 1927, p. 28.

[22]*Ibid.*, October 19, 1927, p. 27.

the union. No one in our organization, so far as I have been able to learn, desires to assist this union. It's altogether an outside crowd which has been making false statements.[23]

On October 21, at 4:30 in the afternoon, the union staged a demonstration in front of the Metropolitan Life building on Madison Square to coincide with the time the workers went home. Demonstrators carried placards that reminded the Metropolitan employees that other "professional people" were organized, and that they were deserving of a decent standard of living. One sign proclaimed: "Join the well-paid workers; why work for a starvation wage!" Speakers were on hand to stir up enthusiasm. Norman Thomas, director of the League for Industrial Democracy, reminded the crowd that Fiske himself believed in unions, and Louis Budenz went so far as to call the Metropolitan president a "hypocrite." However, there was no enthusiasm displayed by the Metropolitan office force.[24]

During the Great Depression B.S.&A.U. membership tripled, so that by 1937 the union had 2,500 members, although there was no increase in the number of office employees' locals in the United States. Forty were reported in existence in 1919 and the number remained the same through 1937.[25]

The office workers' unions continued to agitate for a national charter from the A.F. of L. Bookkeepers' Local 12646 president, Lewis Merrill, spoke out at the 1936 convention of the Federation, protesting the union's failure to grant the charter. Merrill said that a resolution for the charter had been brought to the convention year after year and referred to committee year after year. He observed that "the fault lies with the locals themselves."[26] To remedy the A.F. of L.'s alleged lack of interest in the white collar worker, Merrill and delegates from other office workers' unions

[23]*Ibid.*, October 17, 1927, p. 42.

[24]*Ibid.*, October 22, 1927, p. 42. Budenz is listed as a delegate for a Stenographers' local from Indianapolis, A.F. of L., *Convention Proceedings* (Philadelphia, Pa., 1914) p. xiii.

[25]J. Raymond Walsh, C.I.O.: *Industrial Unionism in Action* (New York: Norton, 1937), pp. 150-52.

[26]A.F. of L., *Convention Proceedings* (Tampa, Fla., 1936), p. 578.

formed a National Committee of Office and Professional Workers and planned to meet in Philadelphia in the spring of 1937.[27]

UNITED OFFICE AND PROFESSIONAL WORKERS OF AMERICA, C.I.O.

Lewis Merrill joined the Bookkeepers, Stenographers and Accountants' Union, Local 12646, in 1930 as a result of a strike waged by the local against the New York Credit Clearing House, a firm by which he was employed. He became president of the union in October 1936 by defeating Sam Baron, then president of the Local.[28] After his election Merrill decided to organize the insurance industry. Sometime before the end of 1936, he met with six industrial debit agents to discuss B.S.&A.U. strategy. Two of these men, Leon W. Berney and James Durkin, were put in charge of an insurance organizing committee, and shortly thereafter, agents of the Metropolitan, Prudential and John Hancock offices in New York City enlisted in the group, and agents from New Jersey, upstate New York, Massachusetts and the West Coast were said to have requested information.[29]

The insurance organization gathered such momentum that on April 10, 1937, William Collins, an A.F. of L. eastern regional representative, is reported to have reminded Merrill that the Federation's prohibition against unions of insurance agents was still in effect.[30]

On April 24, 1937, the B.S.&A.U. leaders called a regional conference in New York City. In attendance were delegates from thirteen A.F. of L. white collar locals, representing a proclaimed membership of some 4,000 persons. A press release contained the information that Collins was on hand for the meeting and listened

[27]*Office and Professional News*, July, 1944, p. 5.

[28]*The Ledger*, November, 1936, p. 7.

[29]"Why Should I Join the U.O.P.W.A., the Insurance Agents' Union? Here's Why!" 1944. Both Durkin and Berney were insurance agents. Durkin was employed by the Equitable Life Assurance Society in 1931 and had attended courses in actuarial science at the College of the City of New York, *Office and Professional News*, July, 1947, p. 1.

[30]United Office and Professional Workers of America, C.I.O., *Report of the Proceedings of the Second Annual Convention* (Washington, D.C. 1938), pp. 22-23.

to the office workers accuse the A.F. of L. of refusing them an international charter to operate in such diverse fields as banking, advertising, social service and insurance. A delegate read a telegram from John Brophy, the C.I.O. organizer, in which he stressed the "need for complete organization of white collar workers just [as it is apparent for] workers in basic industries."[31]

On the following day the B.S.&A.U. passed a resolution calling on the A.F. of L. to establish an international union of office and professional workers. The Federation refused the request, and at the same time threatened to expel the organization. It then proceeded to act in an unorthodox manner. On May 6, 1937, the A.F. of L. announced its intention of organizing insurance agents in Hartford, Connecticut.

On May 17 over one thousand members of the B.S.&A.U. met in New York to counter the A.F. of L.'s threat of expulsion. Collins was again present, and it was reported that he said the meeting had been called without the previous knowledge of the entire membership and warned that the local had been engaging in "activities subversive to the policies and aims of the A.F. of L."[32] He also accused the local of failure to buy initiation stamps and to pay the per capita tax to the Federation. After Collins completed his remarks the officers of B.S.&A.U. reportedly called the charge of financial irregularities a "smoke-screen to becloud the real issue, which was the union's stand on the C.I.O." They demanded that the A.F. of L. revoke its prohibition against unions of insurance agents. When Collins attempted to defend the national union he was shouted down. At length the B.S.&A.U. carried out its own plan; members of the union, by a vote of 1,200 to 4, agreed to disaffiliate from the A.F. of L.[33]

On May 30, 1937, the B.S.&A.U. and thirteen other white collar locals of the A.F. of L., along with nine independent organizations

[31]*The New York Times,* May 18, p. 6; & April 25, p. 3 (1937). In attendance were delegates from New York City, Philadelphia, Newark, New Haven, Boston, Buffalo, Montreal, Toronto, Washington, D.C. and Easton, Pa., and also delegates and observers from the independent Social Service Employees' Union.

[32]*Ibid.,* May 7, p. 3; & May 18, p. 6 (1937).

[33]*The Ledger,* June 1937, p. 5.

of office workers, with a stated combined membership of 8,615, convened in Philadelphia. These small unions voted to become a single organization, henceforth to be called the United Office and Professional Workers of America, International. Lewis Merrill was general secretary of the Convention Sponsoring Committee, and under his direction the new union voted "unanimously" to secede from the A.F. of L. and to seek a charter from the C.I.O. The text of the draft resolution to disaffiliate takes note of the inertia of the A.F. of L. in the white collar field and of its policy of hindering any activity other than its own.

At the founding convention of the United Office and Professional Workers of America (U.O.P.W.A.), the new union voted to adopt a temporary constitution, part of which severely restricted its jurisdiction. The record shows that officials of the former Bookkeepers' Union had been in contact with the C.I.O. from the time of an April 12th meeting. Consequently, John L. Lewis and John Brophy had dispatched to the founding convention Len DeCaux, editor of the weekly *C.I.O. Union News Service,* to persuade the delegates to enact a provision in their constitution granting the union jurisdiction only in those industries where existing C.I.O. industrial unions had no provisions for white collar organizations. The C.I.O. further refused to grant the new Office Workers' union jurisdiction in permanent governmental agencies.

The union's constitution provided for a president, a general secretary treasurer and nine vice presidents. The delegates elected Lewis Merrill as the first president of the organization, and Eugene Turner, a professional employee from Phoenix, as the secretary treasurer. One of the vice presidents selected was a Hartford insurance agent whose name was not announced for fear of recrimination. The union newspaper editor was rhapsodic in his praise of Merrill and characterized him as "clear thinking . . . sometimes quiet and forceful, sometimes humorous and forceful, and sometimes fiery and forceful, i.e., always on the alert, always confident, always to be depended upon."[34]

In attendance at the convention were approximately one hundred and fifty industrial insurance debit agents from New York City who had come into the organization prior to the convention.

[34]*Ibid.*

On June 1, 1937, John L. Lewis granted the U.O.P.W.A.'s request for affiliation to the C.I.O. The text of his approval reads in part:

> As Chairman of the Committee for Industrial Organizations, I am pleased to inform you that your request for affiliation with the C.I.O. is hereby granted . . . [U.O.P.W.A.] is accepted as an international union to organize office and professional workers . . . [It is] further understood, as stated in your provisional constitution, that C.I.O. reserves the right to advise with you on calling a convention at some later date at which time a permanent constitution may be adopted by the United Office and Professional Workers of America.[35]

Thus U.O.P.W.A. was established as an all-purpose white collar union, taking into its ranks insurance workers, stenographers, bookkeepers, typists, bank clerks, artists and the like.

THE A.F. OF L. IN INSURANCE

The Committee for Industrial Organizations was no longer the only union interested in insurance workers. In the fall of 1937 the American Federation of Labor announced that it proposed holding a special meeting of office and white collar employees made up of those unions it had chartered and "which have remained loyal to the parent body."[36] The meeting took place, and at its 1938 convention the A.F. of L. granted this group an international charter under the title, "Office Employees' International Council."[37]

Prior to the formation of the Council the A.F. of L. had attempted to charter an insurance agents local in Hartford, Conn., a fact already mentioned. The effort failed. However, the Federation was still able to beat the U.O.P.W.A., C.I.O., at its own game by being the first of the two unions to charter an insurance local. The event took place in Chicago on June 10, 1937, and the local was called the Industrial Insurance Debit Employees' Union. Jack Bradon was

[35]Letter of Approval, *The Constitution of the United Office and Professional Workers of America,* C.I.O., 1937.

[36]A.F. of L., *Convention Proceedings* (Denver, Colo., 1937), p. 308.

[37]*Ibid.,* Houston, Tex., 1938, pp. 81-82. The organization remained an international "Council" until 1944 at which time the A.F. of L. convention delegates granted it a new status and a new title, The Office Employees' International Union. A.F. of L., *Convention Proceedings* (New Orleans, La., 1944), p. 437.

elected the first president of the local, and Peter Bochstahler and John G. McDonald, the financial secretary-treasurer and the recording and corresponding secretary respectively.[38] During that summer the A.F. of L. also granted charters to groups of industrial agents in Boston and New York City.[39]

About a year later the A.F. of L. was able to establish a federal local in Washington, D.C., and its affiliate in this city came into existence in a roundabout manner. In August 1937 Horace C. Young, a Washington attorney, and John Downey, an engineer who had worked in the insurance section of N.R.A., formed an independent organization of agents which they called the National Association of Industrial Insurance Agents. At the time of the group's formation, Young made the remark that the union was not a radical organization, but rather one that would have the highest respect from insurance companies and from federal and state officials.

The agents elected W. L. Bristow, an agent of the Virginia Life and Casualty Co., as president, and chose Downey as secretary treasurer and Young as general counsel. They designated as members of the union's executive board the above mentioned men and George L. Russ, who was also a Virginia Life agent.[40]

Young and Downey did not stay with the Association for long because, in the words of a veteran observer, "they didn't understand the agents and how fickle they could be."[41] After their departure George Russ set his sights on the union's presidency. He had become an organizer for the A.F. of L. in December 1938 and subsequently interested sufficient numbers of agents in the National Association to disband the independent and to join the Federation. Shortly thereafter he became the president of the newly chartered A.F. of L. Washington local, and Ralph U. Boyer, also a paid organizer of the A.F. of L., its secretary treasurer.

Sometime after his election Russ did a curious thing. In an interview with the writer, some two decades after the event, Russ re-

[38]*The Insurance Agent,* December, 1957, p. 2.

[39]U.O.P.W.A., C.I.O., *Convention Proceedings* (Washington, D.C., 1938), p. 23.

[40]*Insurance Agents' Progress,* December, 1937, pp. 2-3.

[41]Interview with Charles Engelbrecht, former treasurer of the National Federation of Insurance Agents' Council, A.F. of L., July 30, 1959.

ferred to a meeting he had with John L. Lewis. Both men discussed the possibility of amalgamating the Washington Local with the C.I.O. As Russ described it, Lewis informed him that the new C.I.O. international, the United Office and Professional Workers of America, was the union he should join, since it had been established for all insurance workers and other white collar employees. Russ objected to the U.O.P.W.A. on the grounds that its structure was cumbersome. Furthermore, he wanted an organization for industrial insurance men exclusively. Since neither participant could agree on a compromise solution, Russ, and apparently Lewis as well, dropped the idea. The Washington Local went on to become the focal point of much of the A.F. of L.'s future activity in the insurance field.[42]

In June 1938 the A.F. of L. established the Industrial and Ordinary Insurance Agents Council (I.O.I.A.C.). At that time there were eleven locals affiliated to the Federation with a membership of about five hundred agents. George Russ became the president of the Council and Ralph U. Boyer its secretary treasurer.[43]

The organizational setup of the Council was unique. The A.F. of L. established autonomous locals of agents which were directly affiliated to the national union and which were subscribing members of the Council. The latter had no power to negotiate contracts, and any dispute that might reach its leadership had ultimately to be resolved by the Federation. Inasmuch as the A.F. of L. never granted the Council a charter whereby it could act as a true labor organization, the locals could establish their own policy. At times this took the form of limiting membership in the locals to agents of a particular company. During the lifetime of the I.O.I.A.C. the American Federation of Labor considered Russ and Boyer as paid organizers only; both men simply presided over a loose association of locals affiliated to the national union.[44]

[42]Interview with George L. Russ, former president of Insurance Workers International Union, AFL-CIO, July 16, 1959.

[43]"The Insurance Agents' Story," *The Electrical Workers' Journal*, August, 1952, p. 38. cf. also, Industrial and Ordinary Insurance Agents' Council, A.F. of L., *Report of the National 1945 Conference*, (Washington, D.C., 1945), pp. 39-41. The "ordinary" agent was included in the Council as a result of the insistence of Jack Bradon, president of the Chicago Local.

[44]*Prudential Insurance Company of America*, 106 N.L.R.B. no. 55, (1953).

15

The International Union of Life Insurance Agents, Independent

While the C.I.O. and the A.F. of L. were vying for the allegiance of the nation's insurance agents, another organization was conducting a similar campaign. Early in 1937 Ed. Rice, a former manager of the Metropolitan Life Insurance Co., founded the International Union of Life Insurance Agents. He contacted a group of agents in Kenosha, Wisconsin, and these in turn interested insurance men of both the Prudential and the Metropolitan in Milwaukee and Racine.[45] During the course of the year all of the Prudential agents in Racine and Kenosha and eighty per cent of that company's agents in Milwaukee joined the union. By 1940 the union had a total membership of approximately six hundred men.[46]

The International Union of Life Insurance Agents proved of great interest to both the C.I.O. and the A.F. of L. After its founding the United Office and Professional Workers of America, C.I.O., attempted to lure the union into the fold. The latter chose to remain independent (as it is to this day) because the leadership disagreed with the organizational setup of the U.O.P.W.A. The Wisconsin-based organization contended that it was formed for industrial insurance agents and clerks exclusively, while the Office Workers' union attempted to cover too much territory.[47]

With affiliation to the C.I.O. approved, the United Office and Professional Workers decided to concentrate its earliest efforts on Metropolitan and Hancock, two of the so-called "Big Three" industrial companies. (Organizing the agents of the Prudential Insurance Company of America, the third of the industrial insurance trinity, was to come later.) Although these institutions are called "combination companies" today (they offer a complete line of life insurance), they sold a tremendous amount of industrial insurance and employed about forty-six thousand industrial debit agents when the unions were formed.[48]

[45]*Our Voice,* May, 1963, p. 2.
[46]U.O.P.W.A., C.I.O., *Convention Proceedings* (Chicago, Ill., 1940), p. 41.
[47]*Our Voice,* June, 1963, p. 2.
[48]U.O.P.W.A., C.I.O., *Convention Proceedings* (Chicago, Ill., 1940), p. 8. According to the union Metropolitan and Prudential each employed about 20,000 agents.

The U.O.P.W.A. chartered its first insurance local in New York City in July 1937. The unit was designated as Local number 30, and Roy Whitman became its first president and Leon W. Berney the general organizer. In October of that same year the union convoked a meeting of about six thousand agents in New York. Berney is said to have told the gathering that Hancock had agreed to recognize the union and that the company's agents, along with those employed by Metropolitan and Prudential, were completely within his union's jurisdiction.[49]

As if to confirm this remark several thousand members of Local 30 staged a demonstration around the Metropolitan Life offices in Manhattan on November 5, 1937. An eyewitness recounts the events of the day:

> One Friday at noontime, when all the workers in the white collar industries around Madison Avenue and twenty-third street were just going out to lunch, lo and behold, there were four thousand people, barking "We sell security; we want security," marching around the home office for one solid hour.[50]

At the rally Berney is reported to have said that the Metropolitan president, Leroy A. Lincoln, had refused to confer with union officials, asserting that the company was not satisfied that the U.O.P.W.A. adequately represented its employees. At the close of the demonstration a company vice president, Charles B. Taylor, issued this statement:

> It is our understanding that a complaint has been filed with the N.L.R.B. and we feel, therefore, that it would be inappropriate to make any comment at this time.[51]

On the day of the demonstration against Metropolitan, the union petitioned the National Labor Relations Board for a nation-wide election in the John Hancock Mutual Life Insurance Company which had about 6,000 industrial agents at the time.[52] Although

[49]*The New York Times,* October 11, 1937, p. 10.

[50]U.O.P.W.A., *Convention Proceedings* (New York, N.Y., 1948), p. 201.

[51]*The New York Times,* November 7, 1937, p. 6.

[52]*The Ledger,* December, 1937, p. 2. The John Hancock Mutual Life Insurance Company was incorporated under the laws of the Commonwealth of Massachusetts on April 21, 1862. It is a mutual company with no capital stock. *Charters of American Life Insurance Companies* (New York: The Spectator Co., 1895); & *Moody's Manual of Investments, American and Foreign* (New York: Moody's Investment Service, 1938), pp. 1763-764.

he exaggerated the company's intent at a recent gathering of the agents, Berney had reason to be optimistic, for Hancock president, Guy W. Cox, was supposed to have said that "he did not take the organization lightly."[53]

The Board delayed hearing the case and the union officials grew impatient. On December 18, 1937, they tried to arouse public opinion. Equipping over 1,500 automobiles with signs addressed to Hancock policyholders, they drove from Fordham Road in the Bronx to the offices of the *Brooklyn Eagle*. And on Christmas Eve union members picketed the New York offices of the company.[54]

Throughout the early months of 1938, the N.L.R.B. postponed hearings on the U.O.P.W.A.'s petition. Thinking they had asked for too much, union leaders decided to amend the petition for an election among the company's agents in New York, New Jersey and Connecticut. The Board did not respond. Finally, in May the U.O.P.W.A. held its second convention and asked Edward Smith, a member of the Board, to address the delegates. The convention record discloses that Smith explained that the Labor Board was not perfectly "sure of its grounds" and could not proceed against Hancock unless it felt "reasonably certain" that the courts would uphold the union's jurisdiction.[55] Smith's response raised a question that will be treated later on in this work: was insurance interstate commerce?

The U.O.P.W.A. officials caught the drift of his words and decided to utilize another approach. On November 23, 1938, the union's New York Local 30 petitioned the New York State Labor Relations Board for an election among Hancock's Greater New York agents. To complicate matters, Local 30 was joined in the petition by the Independent Hancock Agents' Association, a company union, and by the A.F. of L.'s New York Local, number 20920. Both of these groups insisted that they represented the company's debit men. Meanwhile, the N.L.R.B. closed the original case on December 20.[56]

[53]*The Ledger,* December, 1937, p. 2.

[54]*Ibid.,* January, 1938, p. 8; & *The New York Times,* December 25, 1937, p. 28.

[55]U.O.P.W.A., *Convention Proceedings* (Washington, D.C., 1938), pp. 103-05.

[56]*The John Hancock Mutual Life Insurance Co.,* 3 S.L.R.B. 98 (1940).

Hearings on the petition before the New York Board were held almost a year later. In November 1939 the Board admitted into evidence over one thousand application cards indicating membership of Hancock agents in Local 30. An election did in fact occur on May 3, 1940, and Local 30 won it; 511 agents voted for the union, while 483 voted against it. The New York Board then certified Local 30, U.O.P.W.A., as the bargaining agent for Hancock debit men in the Greater New York area.[57]

On October 9, 1940, Hancock and the United Office and Professional Workers of America signed a collective bargaining agreement covering 1,027 agents in New York and in the counties of Westchester, Suffolk and Nassau. The contract specified that the agents were to receive a two week vacation after three years of service with the company and that a grievance committee was to review certain types of dismissals.[58]

At about the time Local 30 asked the New York Board for an election, another U.O.P.W.A. local was using an identical technique in Massachusetts. Local 41, U.O.P.W.A., filed with the state labor board for an election among Hancock agents of the Greater Boston area. The Local won the election when it was held, but the company refused to bargain. Representatives of Local 41 and the national union filed unfair labor practice charges against the company with the Labor Relations Commission of Massachusetts, complaining that Hancock had a company union and that it conducted an anti-union campaign during the time before the election. Hancock management responded to these charges by developing an argument that will be treated in detail later on: insurance agents were not "employees" within the meaning of the Massachusetts' labor act.[59]

Local 41's state board election victory did not result in a contract between company and union. In fact, Hancock's Massachusetts agents would have to wait for a labor agreement until the Office Workers' union won a nation-wide election among the company's debit men.

[57]*Office and Professional News,* May-June, 1940, p. 1.

[58]*Ibid,* October, 1940, p. 1; & *The New York Times,* October 10, 1940, p. 22.

[59]*The John Hancock Mutual Life Insurance Co.,* Massachusetts' Labor Relations Commission, Case No. CR 698 (1943).

The Metropolitan Life Insurance Company

While it was arguing the Hancock case before the labor boards, the U.O.P.W.A. was simultaneously seeking recognition from the Metropolitan Life Insurance Company.[60] In this litigation the union used the services of the New York Board exclusively. The A.F. of L.'s New York Local 20920 again joined the petition.

In seeking certification the U.O.P.W.A. leaders desired clarification on an important issue: what were the geographic limits of the appropriate bargaining unit? The union claimed that the greater New York area would suffice, whereas Metropolitan contended that it would deal with a labor organization, if at all, on a state-wide basis only.[61] The question of geographic limitation assumed a high degree of relevance as the lines of battle were drawn for the agents' allegiance to company and union.

Moreover, the union leaders believed that filing with the New York Board for an election in the company's eighty-three agency offices in the New York City area would "help test the Metropolitan's contention that insurance does not come within interstate commerce."[62] In its brief to the Board the U.O.P.W.A.'s Local 30 also charged that the firm had established a company union, the Employees' Fidelity Organization, and that it had intimidated agents for union activity. Metropolitan management rejected the Local's allegations.

On January 7, 1938, almost two thousand U.O.P.W.A. agents demonstrated against Metropolitan because it had discharged two employees for union activity. The U.O.P.W.A. newspaper reported that Leroy A. Lincoln, the company's president, met with a committee of the agents who told him that one of their fellow workers had been struck by his manager for refusing to join the Employees' Fidelity Organization. Lincoln asked if the agents believed that Metropolitan was sponsoring the association and was assured the

[60]Originally chartered as the National Travellers' Insurance Co. by the State of New York on April 9, 1867, the charter was amended on March 24, 1868, and the institution assumed its present title at that time. The Metropolitan became a mutual company in 1915. The Spectator, loc. cit., & Moody's op. cit., pp. 2072-073.

[61]The Metropolitan Life Insurance Co., 1 S.L.R.B. 129 (1938).

[62]The Debit, January, 1938, p. 1.

agents thought it was. He is supposed to have promised to take the matter under advisement and to further guarantee that no agent would be dismissed without a personal hearing from him. At this point the agents called off the demonstration.[63]

The debit men's cause was enhanced when the New York Board declared agents to be "employes," and not "independent contractors," under the New York Labor Relations Act in a case involving Local 30, U.O.P.W.A., and the Workingmen's Cooperative Association in New York City. The agents had called a four week strike against the insurance firm in protest over working conditions, and the New York Board used the occasion to hand down the historic decision.[64] The Board's ruling in no way affected the thinking of Metropolitan management, however, for Leroy A. Lincoln was quoted as saying: "I have refused and shall continue to refuse voluntarily to give any recognition to any organization of Metropolitan policyholders."[65]

Meanwhile a New York State legislative committee was holding hearings with regard to Metropolitan Life's office practices. On February 11 Benjamin Kline, an assistant manager of the company, told the committee that his "nerves were cracking." His manager, he said, had instituted a program of writing the most business in his district by means of an interstaff contest which lasted six weeks. The manager conducted a board report twice a week, and the assistant manager whose staff reported the lowest amount of business, together with the minimum reporting agent, were obliged to wear dunce caps on which the manager wrote: "I am lousy, I am a louse." Both men were to be booed by the entire staff, after which they were to inform the office personnel about their low production rates. Kline told the committee that when his turn came the office manager told him that he was "through" and demoted him to the rank of agent.[66]

The question of Metropolitan office practices and the relationship between manager and agent had been previously taken up in a

[63]*Ibid.*

[64]*Workingmens' Cooperative Association,* 1 S.L.R.B. 60 (1938).

[65]*The Metropolitan Life Insurance Co.,* 1 S.L.R.B. 129 (1938).

[66]*The Debit,* February, 1938, p. 4.

letter that Lincoln sent to the field force in November 1937. The letter was reprinted in the record of the Temporary National Economic Committee. Part of it emphasized the importance of the manager-agent relationship, and the pertinent section reads as follows:

> In all our discussions with the Managers and Assistant Managers we continually emphasized the importance of good understanding between them and the Agents, wishing to draw more and more to their attention a feeling of common interest on the part of all the Company's representatives in the District Offices. I consider it of the greatest importance that there be mutual respect and good relations with each other and a common purpose of service to the policyholders and to the Company. I propose to see to it that this policy is carried out in every District Office.[67]

The response to Lincoln's letter indicated that Benjamin Kline's experience was not an isolated one. Although one agent wrote that his years of service with the company were "happy" ones and that his relationship with his manager had been "most congenial," he felt bound to report to Lincoln, "very reluctantly," some of the problems he had encountered during the past year. He put it this way:

> Once when I was on decrease, I was greeted by my present Manager, before my fellow workers, with this remark, 'Mr. —, you should come in this office backwards,' to which I made no reply. Three weeks ago, I asked to be excused one Saturday morning from a meeting and my Manager said 'You have a hell of a nerve to ask to be excused with the record you have.' My Manager also said, 'Do you know I am having a hell of a time to keep you on?'[68]

Another writer, perhaps, summed up the situation best of all when he posed the problem in question form:

> Is it possible that during the panic following the depression when every Manager rallied to the call to conserve business, we formed a habit of driving and threatening, like mule skinners, and it has become a regular procedure? Is it not quite

[67]U.S. Congress, Temporary National Economic Committee, *Hearings, Investigation of Industrial Insurance,* Part 12, 75th Cong., 1st Sess., 1939, pp. 6253-254. Lincoln had spent a part of the previous year and one-half visiting company offices in the United States and Canada.

[68]*Ibid.,* p. 6261.

true that men who were promoted to positions of Manager and Assistant Manager at that time still believe that mule skinning methods are proper and right? These methods are in the very atmosphere. They have become habitual in the business. Yet everyone dislikes them, including the Manager.[69]

It was to this very difficulty that Lincoln addressed himself. Metropolitan had sustained a lapse rate of almost fifty percent in 1938, and there is no reason to suppose that the company's lapse ratio was any better during the preceeding year. Managers and assistant managers were forced to maintain certain quotas, and those agents who rejected the company's methods joined the U.O.P.W.A.

Although the Metropolitan management, for all practical purposes, chose to ignore the existence of the labor dispute with U.O.P.W.A., the New York Labor Board did not. It held hearings on the union's and the A.F. of L.'s petitions on February 8, 1938, at which time it consolidated both petitions. The record of the hearings contains the following points. The Board denied Metropolitan's request for dismissal of the petitions. Company counsel then introduced the argument that it was not subject to the New York State Labor Relations Act because it was already subject to the jurisdiction of the New York Insurance Department. The Board replied that this jurisdiction "does not free it from obligations imposed by other state laws." The Board, therefore, found insurance companies to be "within the meaning of the Act," and further contended that agents were not "independent contractors," as the company had supposed. The Board also determined that the appropriate bargaining unit include "all industrial agents who are operating out of district offices located within the five boroughs of New York City, Nassau, Suffolk, and Westchester counties, exclusive of office managers, assistant office managers, and clerical employees."[70]

On March 23 the Board ordered that an election take place to determine whether Metropolitan agents wanted labor union representation. Both the company and the U.O.P.W.A., along with the A.F. of L. New York Local, used all the forces at their disposal to

[69]*Ibid.*

[70]*The Metropolitan Life Insurance Co.,* 1 S.L.R.B. 129 (1938).

win the election. One agent described the Metropolitan offices as a "daily battlefield." He went on to say:

Union members could get no assistance from the company in writing new business or preserving old business. Every effort was made to increase lapses for the best union man. Applications were held up. Sudden and repeated inspections were ordered on our leading members. Every agent in the City, during the several days preceding the election, was mailed 15 pages of persuasive material against the union, including a three page personal letter from the President of the Company.[71]

Other agents were even more descriptive. One man said that his assistant made him "swear by my wife and child that I'd vote against the union." Another claimed that his manager went about the office singing "Never in a Million Years!" And a third agent reported that his manager assured him that "so long as you stay out of the E.F.O. [Employees' Fidelity Organization] you're like a wart on my nose."[72]

The date for the election was set for April 13. Local 20920, A.F. of L., had chosen to withdraw from the race, leaving the U.O.P.W.A. as the sole union on the ballot. The election was held and when the votes were counted, the U.O.P.W.A. won by a narrow margin, receiving 1,277 votes, while 1,242 agents voted for no union.[73]

On April 23 the Board certified Local 30, U.O.P.W.A., as bargaining agent for a period of one year for 2,500 Metropolitan agents in New York City, Westchester and Long Island. The company refused to negotiate and was found guilty of an unfair labor practice under the New York Act. Metropolitan officials then appeared before the Board and challenged the constitutionality of the New York Labor Act and its applicability in this particular case.

After assuming jurisdiction the Board heard evidence "on the merits" and on June 7, 1938, directed the company to cease and desist. Thereupon the company informed the Board that it would not comply. The Board then petitioned the New York State

[71]U.O.P.W.A., C.I.O., *Convention Proceedings* (Washington, D.C., 1938), pp. 24-25.

[72]*U.O.P.W.A. News,* March, 1939, p. 3.

[73]*The New York Times,* April 14, 1938, p. 2.

Supreme Court to enforce the order, and the Metropolitan countered with a motion that the order be vacated.[74]

On July 27 Supreme Court justice, Aron J. Steuer, handed down a "special term entrance" in which he upheld the New York Labor Board. He compared its power to that of the National Board which, he said "in this instance is indistinguishable from the state act." In arguing the company's case, Samuel Seabury, the Metropolitan's attorney, is reported to have said that the New York Act was based on Russian ideas and quoted passages from Lenin, Stalin and the Russian constitution. He is also supposed to have stated that the Board had no power to fix bargaining units. Justice Steuer ordered the company to bargain with Local 30, U.O.P.W.A.[75]

During the next several months the company continued in its refusal to abide by the decisions of the New York Board and of Justice Steuer. On November 18, 1938, the Appellate Division of the New York State Supreme Court upheld the decision of the New York Board.[76] Metropolitan management remained adamant. In December the Board heard each of the chief disputants again, but the sessions were temporarily suspended while application was made to the courts to review the order of the Board. At length the application was taken to the Court of Appeals of the State of New York.

The New York State "Little Wagner Act"

On April 11, 1939, the Court of Appeals of the State of New York, by a four to three decision, upheld the order of the New York State Labor Relations Board concerning the Metropolitan Life Insurance Company and Local 30, U.O.P.W.A. Historically, the decision is of great importance, for the court ruled on the constitutionality of the New York Board, finding that it "did not violate the state constitutional ban on the creation of new state departments," as the Metropolitan had consistently maintained.[77]

[74]*The Metropolitan Life Ins. Co.* v. *The New York State Labor Relations Board,* 280 N.Y. 194 (1939).

[75]*The Debit,* August, 1938, p. 1.

[76]*The Metropolitan Life Ins. Co.* v. *The New York State Labor Relations Board,* Id. 255 App. Div. 840 (1938).

[77]*The Metropolitan Life Insurance Co.* 5 S.L.R.B. 458 (1942).

The decision of the court in fact upheld the constitutionality of the New York Labor Act, which had become known as the "Little Wagner Act." In its decision the court defined insurance agents as "employes" within the meaning of the act, accepting the Board's own definition which reads in part: "It shall not be limited to employes of a particular company, unless the article explicitly states otherwise." The Board had not specified otherwise.

In considering the choice by the Board of an appropriate bargaining agent, the company had argued that this "amounts to a delegation to the Board of the lawmaking power of the Legislature." The court simply stated that the Board "does not have the limitless power the Metropolitan contends in determining the life of the selected representative." The majority decision pertaining to the Board's power reads in part:

> The defined purposes of the Act do not countenance what the Metropolitan assumes is a limitless power of the board to permit employes to change bargaining representatives for any purpose at any given moment.

The decision of the Board in designating Local 30, U.O.P.W.A., as appropriate bargaining agent was concurred in by the court when it restated the Board's own arguments with regard to the territorial unit encompassed by Local 30. The Board had insisted that the agents were "homogeneous . . . [their] activities are distinctive in that industrial insurance is designed for people of small means." The Board further asserted that Metropolitan Life had itself established the five counties of New York, and the counties of Westchester, Nassau and Suffolk as "one of its territories," and that this territory had resulted in "a close relationship among agents operating therefrom." This ruling is of interest because Metropolitan in seeking a state-wide bargaining unit, claimed that its agents were subject to rules that were uniform throughout the state, that the work of agents is the same in all parts of New York, and that the agents could write insurance and receive commissions irrespective of the residence of the policyholder.

The Court of Appeals next took up the question of the Metropolitan's attempt to have the New York State Labor Relations Act declared unconstitutional, since, in the words of the company, the act "violated freedom of contract." Agreeing with the company that the New York State constitution did not have a commerce clause as did the federal Constitution which was the basis on which the United States Supreme Court upheld the National Labor Relations Act, the court, nevertheless, reasoned on the basis of the document's "due process" clause. The majority opinion of the court held that "due process for us is the same due process to which the Federal Congress is subject when it exercises its commerce clause."

The court at last considered the "Special Term" decision of Justice Steuer by which he had ordered the Metropolitan to negotiate "exclusively" with the U.O.P.W.A. Here the court rendered a finding with which neither the New York Board nor the union could agree. The court interpreted the word "exclusively" to mean the following:

> Exclusively means with no other person as a representative of another but not to prevent negotiations between the petitioner and any of its employes each acting for himself.[78]

This interpretation by the court prompted both the New York Board and the U.O.P.W.A. to request that the court strike it out of the text. The Board reasoned that the question of an individual contract was not properly before Justice Steuer when he made his decision, and that, furthermore, no evidence had been taken by the Board which related to individual contracts nor had it made any order with respect to them. The union contended that the court's interpretation was "uncalled for and calculated to create confusion as well as a possible means by which Metropolitan may circumvent the order."[79] The union supported the thesis that if the company drew up a general contract, applicable to all employees and requiring each person to sign individually, the provision would make it difficult or impossible to prosecute for contempt of court.

The New York justices disagreed and made their decision stand, stating that "if the order really needed clarification in this respect the proper procedure was an application to the Supreme Court."[80] The court directed the Metropolitan to carry out the June 7, 1938, order of the New York Labor Relations Board.

[78]*The Metropolitan Life Insurance Co.* 280 N.Y. 194 (1939).

[79]*The New York Times,* May 1, 1939, p. 20.

[80]*The Metropolitan Life Ins. Co.* 280 N.Y. 194 (1939).

Thereupon, the company decided on a new course of action. On April 13, 1939, every Metropolitan debit agent in the designated bargaining unit received a letter from Leroy A. Lincoln, the company president, announcing the company's decision to meet with Local 30. The letter took into account the court's decision regarding individual bargaining and the individual agent's constitutional right to negotiate his own contract.

On April 16 Allan Haywood, an organizer for national C.I.O., together with Leon W. Berney and Roy Whitman of Local 30, met with representatives of the company.[81] Shortly after the session there occurred a "deus ex machina" which fortified Metropolitan management's belief in miracles. During the latter part of April a group of agents who claimed to represent seventy per cent of the company's agency force petitioned the New York Board for an election. They asserted that they did not want an "outside force" representing them, and more importantly, they pointed out that Local 30's certification as bargaining agent had expired. They were correct, for the Local's certification had indeed expired on April 3, 1939, one year after the Board's original decision.[82]

The Metropolitan then pursued a policy of ignoring the union. In November 1939, for example, it was reported that Charles B. Taylor, a vice president of the company, made the Local's decertification the point of a letter to Metropolitan agents. He said that the company would not be coerced into bargaining with an "unauthorized group." No doubt enraged by Taylor's remark, union officials called the letter a "continuation of the same legalistic evasion to which the Metropolitan had continually resorted in order to deny its agents the right to bargain collectively."[83]

In spite of the loss of its certification as bargaining agent for the Metropolitan insurance men in Greater New York, the United Office and Professional Workers of America had become a force to be reckoned with. In 1938 members of the union's Local 30 endorsed a contract with the Golden Eagle Assurance Corp., and

[81]*U.O.P.W.A. News,* May, 1939, p. 1.

[82]The original decision of the New York Labor Board was handed down on April 23, 1938, and was to continue for a period of one year.

[83]*The New York Times,* November 19, 1939, p. 2.

in the following year the union signed nation-wide agreements with the Sun Life Assurance Co. and the Eureka-Maryland Corp. of Baltimore.[84] These contracts, along with the history-making decision of the Court of Appeals of the State of New York, cast the U.O.P.W.A. in a unique role.

[84]*The Debit*, June, 1938, p. 3; & *U.O.P.W.A. News*, June 1939, p. 3.

CHAPTER 2

THE AGENTS GRADUATE TO THE 'BIG TIME'

The United Office and Professional Workers of America, C.I.O., held its second constitutional convention in May 1938. A study of the convention proceedings reveals that the union had a membership of some 45,000 persons, a figure which, if accurate, represented a five-fold increase over the previous year. Within the union's organizational setup there were seventy-seven local affiliates in forty-eight cities in twenty-eight states and Canada. The breakdown of local affiliation is as follows: there were thirty-six "mixed" locals, including all categories of office and professional workers; there were two in publishing, seven in social service and one each of commercial artists and commercial travellers. Of particular interest, there were twenty-eight insurance locals, and these had a "good standing" membership of about 4,600 debit agents.

The convention delegates unanimously re-elected Lewis Merrill as president and designated six members of the organization's insurance division as vice presidents. They also chose Leon W. Berney, the director of the insurance division, as the second vice president.[1]

At the time of the 1940 convention the U.O.P.W.A. had signed over one hundred new contracts. The insurance division had yet to enter a collective agreement with Metropolitan, Prudential or Hancock, the so-called "Big Three" of the industry, but it had concluded pacts with several of the smaller companies. According to a union source, these firms were the Golden Eagle Assurance Corp., the Sun Life Insurance Co., Newport Associates, the Eureka-Maryland Assurance Corporation of Baltimore, Kenton and Campbell Associates, the Equitable Beneficial Life, Health and Accident Co. of New Jersey and the Equitable Beneficial Mutual Life Insurance Co. of Pennsylvania.

[1]United Office and Professional Workers of America, C.I.O., *Report of the Proceedings of the Second Annual Convention* (Washington, D.C., 1938), p. 7. After a lengthy correspondence between the American and Canadian groups the latter agreed to withdraw from the union "lest it further divide the Canadian labor movement." As a result, the U.O.P.W.A. became a "national" union on September 2, 1940. U.O.P.W.A., C.I.O., *Convention Proceedings* (Chicago, Ill., 1940), p. 56.

A union official stated that there were 12,000 agents in the insurance division, more than a two-fold increase since the time of the 1938 convention. He admitted, however, that dues payments had been falling off and attributed this to the poor bookkeeping methods of the insurance locals. He also announced that the U.O.P.W.A. would no longer seek to organize agents in the fire and casualty companies; the union was simply unable to finance the program.

The delegates to the convention re-elected Merrill as president and chose a newcomer, John P. Stanley, as secretary treasurer. The gathering also selected Berney as one of the nine vice presidents and reappointed him chairman of the insurance division.[2]

Because of the decision of the Court of Appeals of the State of New York finding insurance agents 'employes' under the state's Labor Act, the United Office and Professional Workers of America was assured of its right to seek certification under the state law. The union's rivals, the Industrial and Ordinary Insurance Agents Council, A.F. of L., and the International Union of Life Insurance Agents, were thereby legally sanctioned in New York, and their own activities outside New York had further enhanced the legal status of insurance labor organizations. Both unions had sought and won certification in national and state labor board elections. While these precedents placed all three unions under the protection of the law, they raised questions about the extent of the appropriate bargaining unit.

According to the ruling of the National Labor Relations Board and the New York Labor Board, an insurance union could be designated an appropriate bargaining unit for a specified geographic area, for example, Greater New York. Such a ruling, however, placed a union like the U.O.P.W.A. in the enigmatic position of dealing with the remaining agents of a company in Upstate New York. If the case involved either Metropolitan, Prudential or Hancock, an insurance union temporized; a little was better than nothing, and Greater New York was more than a little. While the U.O.P.W.A. and the independent International Union of Life Insurance Agents generally sought a larger geographic unit, the Industrial and Ordinary Insurance Agents Council, A.F. of L., was more circumscribed. Most often the latter confined "its efforts to district offices or to offices of a single company in a single city."[3]

[2]*Ibid.*, Chicago, Ill., 1940, pp. 8, 12, 13, 56, 111 & 125.

[3]*Prudential Insurance Co.*, 46 N.L.R.B. 430 (1942).

Two representative cases arose involving Hancock, and both reflect, on the one hand, the more expansive policy of the U.O.P.W.A. and the independent, and on the other, the more restrictive attitude of the A.F. of L. Insurance Council and the N.L.R.B. In the first instance, an A.F. of L. insurance local in East St. Louis requested that the manager of the city's Hancock office recognize the local as exclusive collective bargaining representative. Upon consultation with the company's home office the manager informed the local leadership that East St. Louis debit agents did not constitute an appropriate bargaining unit. In the second case, a U.O.P.W.A. local urged the manager of the Hancock office in Hoboken, New Jersey, to recognize its jurisdiction. The company refused on the ground that this geographic unit was not appropriate "inasmuch as . . . [a group of] agents in one district office" was not sufficiently large.[4] The N.L.R.B. agreed with Hancock.

In their presentation to the Labor Board the unions held that they should not be denied the right to bargain, as the company maintained, "merely because the unions have as yet not secured authorization from agents in other offices of the Company."[5] In assessing the Board's decision officials of the U.O.P.W.A. stated that a unit larger than a city might "under other circumstances" be considered appropriate. Their position closely paralleled that of the companies. Insurance management indicated that a larger unit would facilitate the labor-management relationship.

However, the National Labor Relations Board insisted on the smaller unit. It maintained that only a city-wide unit should exist in those areas where unions had local affiliates and that there were precedents to prove its position. The Board had certified A.F. of L. insurance locals in Washington, D.C., and Richmond, Virginia, and the New York Board had determined Greater New York appropriate in cases involving the U.O.P.W.A. with Metropolitan and John Hancock. Furthermore, the state labor boards of Pennsylvania and Massachusetts declared U.O.P.W.A. locals in Philadelphia and Boston appropriate and restricted their certification to these cities and the surrounding areas.

[4]*John Hancock Mutual Life Ins. Co.*, 26 N.L.R.B. 105 (1940).

[5]*Ibid.*

Throughout these early years all three unions adopted a pragmatic approach, taking what they could get. The U.O.P.W.A. and the independent Union from Wisconsin favored the wider unit, while the A.F. of L. seemed satisfied with a smaller territory. The N.L.R.B., on the contrary, was even more expedient, for, as the Board expressed its position in one opinion, it "tolerated the city-wide bargaining unit solely on the basis of the limited extent of self-organization among employees affected."[6]

The nature of the insurance business seems also to have persuaded the Board's members to pursue a policy in keeping with the "limited extent" of insurance unionism. Technically and legally insurance was not interstate commerce, and the Board would have to wait upon the decision of the United States Supreme Court to determine that it was.

THE U.O.P.W.A. ACHIEVES A "NATION-WIDE" CONTRACT WITH PRUDENTIAL

The record shows that both the U.O.P.W.A. and the International Union of Life Insurance Agents, independent, attempted to organize agents of the Prudential Insurance Company of America in 1941.[7] The Company was second only to the Metropolitan Life in size and number of employees.[8] A labor board certification for either union would have been a victory of the first magnitude. Prudential reflected the prevailing opinion of the other insurance firms toward the bargaining unit: if it had to deal with a union at all it wanted a nation-wide agreement.

On January 27, 1941, attorneys of the company and officials of the U.O.P.W.A.'s insurance division discussed the possibility of making the union the sole bargaining representative for Prudential

[6]*Life Insurance Co. of Virginia,* 21 N.L.R.B. 37 (1940) & 24 N.L.R.B. 411 (1940); and *Prudential Ins. Co.,* 49 N.L.R.B. 450 (1940).

[7]*Prudential Ins. Co.,* 4 S.L.R.B. 788 (1941).

[8]The Prudential Insurance Company of America was incorporated under the State of New Jersey as "The Widows and Orphans Friendly Society" on April 3, 1873. Its name was changed to the "Prudential Friendly Society" on February 13, 1875, and on March 5, 1877, the company assumed its present name. The company has a capital stock, authorized and outstanding, of $2 million. *The Spectator, loc. cit.,* & Moody's, *op. cit.,* pp. 1770-771.

agents in Greater New York.[9] Because the N.L.R.B. had not yet ruled on the state-wide unit, Local 30, U.O.P.W.A., decided to file for certification with the New York State Labor Relations Board. The Local alleged that it represented a majority of the Prudential agents in the New York City area. The Board held hearings in May of the same year, at which time it granted the A.F. of L. locals in New York permission to intervene.[10] An election occurred in November 1941, and Prudential agents chose Local 30, U.O.P.W.A., as their bargaining representative; 1,579 Prudential agents voted for the U.O.P.W.A., while 78 agents cast their ballots for the Federation and 575 men voted for no union.[11] The New York Board then certified Local 30 as exclusive bargaining agent for 2,400 Prudential insurance men in New York City, southern Westchester County and Long Island.

Prudential's reaction to the Greater New York election was two-fold. In the first place, the company refused to negotiate with the union on the restrictive basis of the metropolitan area wide unit. In the second place, the company expressed its willingness to consider the possibility of a state-wide unit. In this latter instance, Prudential officials were no doubt influenced by the precedent shattering state-wide victory of the International Union of Life Insurance Agents in Wisconsin, where, in July 1941, the state labor board certified the independent union as the exclusive bargaining representative for the company's agents.

Since the U.O.P.W.A. did not possess state-wide certification in New York, it rejected Prudential's proposal and filed an unfair labor practice charge with the New York Board. The Board simply ordered Prudential to negotiate. While it noted the exception of Wisconsin, the Board declared that prior decisions in the insurance field included no area other than the city-wide unit or the metropolitan area wide unit.[12] The Board's reiteration of the principle in no way moved Prudential; it refused to negotiate with the U.O.P.W.A. on the basis of the Greater New York election results.

[9]*Office and Professional News,* February, 1941, p. 1.

[10]*Prudential Ins. Co.,* 4 S.L.R.B. 788 (1941).

[11]*The New York Times,* November 18, 1941, p. 19.

[12]*Prudential Ins. Co.,* 4 S.L.R.B. 788 (1941).

Impatient with the delay, the U.O.P.W.A. authorized a strike on January 15, 1942, and scheduled the walkout for February 2. On January 22, the union raised the dues of its New York Local's membership from $1.50 to $2.00, and, on January 23, the U.S. Conciliation Service entered the dispute. During the latter part of February the national C.I.O. secured the services of the National War Labor Board, and John R. Steelman, chairman of the Board, persuaded union officials to meet with company management. As a result of this exchange, Prudential appealed to the New York Board for a state-wide election. The Board again refused the petition.

Prudential and the U.O.P.W.A. therefore decided to hold a state-wide election by calling upon the services of the Honest Ballot Association. (This technique did not have the approval of the New York Labor Board.) According to a union newspaper, Prudential then informed the agents of its willingness to negotiate a contract if the union won the privately conducted election.[13] The state-wide referendum took place on May 7, 1942, and the U.O.P.W.A. won it by a substantial majority.[14]

The union's recourse to the Honest Ballot Association gave rise to a wave of discontent among many of the New York Prudential agents. However, the union chose to ignore this fact. Instead, it wrote an unsatisfactory contract and went on to seek a nation-wide representation election.

In June 1942 the union petitioned the regional offices of the N.L.R.B. in the states of Michigan, New Jersey and Massachusetts to conduct elections among Prudential agents on a "state-wide" basis. By this time the union was on firm ground as the Board had ruled the state-wide unit appropriate.[15] The company's Michigan agents were the first to choose the union, and, according to a U.O.P.W.A. source, these were followed by the agents in New Jersey and Massachusetts.[16] The record also shows that Prudential

[13]*Office and Professional News,* February 1, p. 1; February 15, p. 2; April 1, p. 1; May 1, p. 1; & June 1, pp. 1-2 (1942).

[14]*The New York Times,* May 20, 1942, p. 30.

[15]*Prudential Ins. Co.,* 46 N.L.R.B. 430 (1942). Without referring to specifics, the Board simply cited two precedents: *Metropolitan,* 43 N.L.R.B. 962 and *Colonial Life,* 42 N.L.R.B. 1177.

[16]*Office and Professional News,* June 1, p. 1 & October 1, p. 1, (1942).

expressed a willingness to permit an election in Kentucky and Washington and that the U.O.P.W.A. had decided to file an amended petition in Pennsylvania.[17]

Meanwhile, the union and the company signed an agreement for the New York agents. Covering 3,850 debit men, the contract came to be known as "Part I" and contained a grievance clause, a provision for paid vacations after one year of service and a modified form of union security. The latter was in fact a voluntary dues deduction of $2.00 and was designed to persist for one year even if an agent withdrew from union membership.[18]

"Part I" contained a hitch. Prior to the New York negotiations the company had promised the agents a wage increase based on the cost of living. The contract made no provision for this, but a company official promised to pay the increase shortly thereafter, or so the union claimed. Yet, when the determined date arrived, neither company nor union had anything to say about the compensation issue. Because of the union's manifest disinterest, many of the agents protested only to discover that the organization's immediate goal was not a rise in compensation but rather a "national contract" with the company. In response to criticism a union official observed that Prudential had a problem; he said that the company could not grant a wage increase in New York and not in the other states.[19] That the agents were upset by the union's explanation is to understate the case. However, the full extent of their grievance and the causes thereof cannot be detailed at this time.

Company and union went into negotiations and, on November 23, both agreed to enter into a nation-wide contract, if Prudential agents around the country, Wisconsin excepted, proved they wanted it. Again their plan was unorthodox, for they decided to enlist the services of the American Arbitration Association, a private group that would conduct a card check of the Prudential membership.[20]

According to a union newspaper, Franklin D'Olier, the Prudential president, sent a letter to all of the company's debit agents

[17]*Prudential Ins. Co.*, 46 N.L.R.B. 430 (1942).

[18]*The New York Times*, July 6, 1942, p. 9; and *Office and Professional News*, July 15, 1942, p. 7.

[19]*Office and Professional News*, December, 1942, p. 3.

[20]*Prudential Ins. Co.*, 47 N.L.R.B. 139 (1943).

in December 1942. He described the method whereby the election would be conducted and added the following word of caution:

> The company takes no position one way or another with regard to the U.O.P.W.A. or any other union. The law is that the employees involved shall be free to choose one way or another without coercion from anyone.[21]

In an interview, the writer was told that sometime before the D'Olier letter was mailed, Leon W. Berney, director of the U.O.P.W.A.'s insurance division, journeyed to Baltimore to advise Matthew Hogan of the card check. (Hogan was president of the A.F. of L. Prudential Local in the city.) Since the U.O.P.W.A. wanted as many of the states on the ballot as possible, and since Maryland might be excluded, Berney questioned Hogan about the "political implications" of taking the Baltimore Local into his union. Hogan told Berney that he would have no part of the deal.[22]

The American Arbitration Association conducted the card check, and the results revealed the following. Instead of checking cards in New York, New Jersey, Michigan and Massachusetts — in these states consent elections had already taken place — the Association decided to add the results of these elections to the nation-wide survey. In the states to be included in the card check, union membership cards were to be counted as "yes" votes, and the difference between the "yes" votes and the number of agents on the company's payroll was to be counted as "no" votes.

The findings of the A.A.A. indicated that in the areas checked 3,645 agents voted for the U.O.P.W.A.; the consent elections in New York, Massachusetts, Michigan and New Jersey added another 3,804 "yes" votes. Therefore, the U.O.P.W.A. received a total of 7,449 "yes" votes. On the other hand, the Association's check included a total of 4,494 "no" votes; in the states where elections had already been held there were 2,211 "no" votes, making a total of 6,705 "no" votes. The U.O.P.W.A. won the election, and the Prudential fulfilled its pledge by negotiating a "nation-wide" contract with the union.[23]

21*Office and Professional News,* January, 1943, p. 1.

22Interview with Matthew Hogan, August 6, 1959. At the time he was also an official of the Industrial and Ordinary Insurance Agents Council, A.F. of L.

23*Prudential Ins. Co.,* 47 N.L.R.B. 139 (1943).

On February 1, 1943, company and union signed the "nation-wide" agreement. Carroll Shanks, the Prudential Solicitor General, and Frederick Groel, an executive of the company, joined with Lewis Merrill, president of U.O.P.W.A., and Allan Haywood of the national C.I.O. in appending their names to the historic document. The contract was a two-year pact and covered the company's agents in thirty-one states, exclusive of Delaware, Maryland, Virginia, Wisconsin, Minnesota and the District of Columbia.[24] The agreement contained a grievance and arbitration clause, a maintenance-of-membership provision with a voluntary dues deduction, and a provision for a $2.50 weekly increase, subject to the approval of the War Labor Board. The contract included a stipulation that the wage clause could be reopened within a year.[25] The new agreement also contained the following provision:

> If the U.O.P.W.A., C.I.O., is certified in any one of the excepted states or the District of Columbia, the agents in such areas shall automatically be covered by the contract.[26]

The War Labor Board approved the wage increase on March 8, and two days later the Prudential agents ratified the contract by a vote of 4,103 to 380.

The U.O.P.W.A. officials did all in their power to add those states excluded by the contract. They referred to their work as "cleaning up some areas" where the N.L.R.B. had temporarily "denied men . . . the wage improvement and other clauses of the contract."[27] The "clean up" got into high gear in February 1943, when the union was granted permission by the Board to intervene in a series of cases involving A.F. of L. Prudential locals in Baltimore, Richmond and the District of Columbia. Spokesmen for these locals argued that Prudential had refused them recognition on the grounds that the company was not subject to the Board and that the geographic unit sought was inappropriate. In all of these instances, the N.L.R.B. determined that the state-wide unit was indeed appropriate, although this ruling in no way aided the

[24]Ibid., 49 N.L.R.B. 450 (1943).

[25]The New York Times, February 4, 1943, p. 19; and Office and Professional News, March, 1943, p. 3.

[26]Prudential Ins. Co., 49 N.L.R.B. 450 (1943).

[27]Office and Professional News, March, 1943, p. 3.

U.O.P.W.A. When the elections were held, the A.F. of L. defeated the Office Workers' union in every area.[28]

The loss of Delaware prompted the U.O.P.W.A. newspaper editor to accuse the A.F. of L. of selling Prudential agents "down the river on the promise of an 'exclusive union' all to themselves, free from Metropolitan men or Hancock men or anything else." He also adverted to his union's failure to get on the ballot in Minnesota. Asserting that the Prudential agents in the state "fell into the trap of isolation there," he went on to write:

> The U.O.P.W.A. entered the election at the last minute solely to bring some concept of the tremendous significance of the national contract to Minnesota agents but it was unable to clarify the issues in the few weeks available.[29]

His was clearly a partisan summation.

THE PRUDENTIAL ELECTION IN OHIO

When the Ohio election occurred the N.L.R.B. recognized the appropriateness of the state-wide unit. The Board declared Ohio wide open, with the exception of Toledo where the Prudential agents had chosen the A.F. of L. Council as their bargaining representative.[30] On April 27 and 28, 1943, representatives of the three unions appeared in Cleveland requesting certification by the Board. At stake were 1,200 Prudential agents. The Board agreed to let the unions fight it out.[31]

The United Office and Professional Workers used as its base of operations the city of Cleveland where it maintained that over one hundred Prudential agents had voluntarily put themselves on a dues paying basis to the union. The Office Workers staged an elaborate campaign: they held policyholders' meetings and victory dinners, they broadcast over local radio stations, and, most importantly, they contacted every Prudential agent in the state. They used as their

28*Prudential Ins. Co.,* 47 N.L.R.B. 139 (1943).

29*Office and Professional News,* May, 1943, p. 1; and June, 1943, p. 2; cf. also *Prudential,* 47 N.L.R.B. 139 (1943).

30*Prudential Ins. Co.,* 46 N.L.R.B. 430 (1942).

31*Ibid.,* 50 N.L.R.B. 689 (1943); and *Office and Professional News,* July, 1943, p. 3.

main selling point the manifold benefits of the "national contract." To insure victory, Leon W. Berney, director of the union's insurance division, assumed personal charge of the pre-election activities. Working under him were the union's midwest regional director, Jerome Shore, and seven organizers from the national office.[32]

Though not as extravagant, the International Union of Life Insurance Agents, independent, sent men from Wisconsin on week-ends and during vacation periods. The A.F. of L. Insurance Council was hampered by lack of funds and organizers, and, according to the minutes of a Council conference, the U.O.P.W.A. tried to take advantage of this development. The proceedings show that Leon Berney met with Albert O'Neill, a Council member, and told him that the A.F. of L. did not "have a chance in Ohio." Their conversation reads in part:

Berney: C.I.O. has it locked up but we don't want a run-off. We will pay you all the money you have paid into this Ohio election since you've been here if you will withdraw.

O'Neill: Berney, that is very generous of you but we have locals that elected A.F. of L. and we can't desert them; we have at least got to go through with it.

Berney: All right, then, will you do this? If there is a condition like I predict and you're off the ballot on a run-off will your organization, in the interest of organized labor, send a letter to your members asking them to support organized labor in the run-off, provided we do the same thing if the table is reversed?

O'Neill: As a representative of organized labor I can do that, will do that![33]

The election was held on July 29 and proved indecisive; the independent union polled 373 votes, while 281 men voted for the A.F. of L. Council and 212 agents cast their ballots for the U.O.P.W.A. The Labor Board ordered a run-off between the first two unions. In the second election the International Union of Life Insurance Agents defeated the A.F. of L. by a vote of 484 to 352.[34]

[32]*Office and Professional News*, May, 1943, p. 1; and August, 1943, p. 2.

[33]Industrial and Ordinary Insurance Agents Council, A.F. of L., *Report of the National 1945 Conference* (Washington, D.C., 1945), p. 146.

[34]*Office and Professional News*, November, 1943, p. 2.

Berney and the officials of the U.O.P.W.A. reacted to defeat in a calculated manner: every Ohio Prudential agent received a letter urging them to vote for either union. Berney's letter was designed principally to reinforce the loyalty of many union members who had come to think of their leaders as crusading spirits, racing about America on behalf of the white collar worker. The letter created the impression that the U.O.P.W.A. officials placed the needs of organized labor above defeat, and to bolster this opinion the leadership scheduled a Prudential conference in Cleveland "to insure the participation of Ohio Prudential agents . . . who are the chief losers."[35]

However, Berney's letter and the calling of the conference betrayed the actions of a group of union leaders who, although secure in office, were taken unawares by the unexpected strength of the opposition. During the Ohio campaign Berney, Shore, James Durkin and others praised the Prudential "national contract" and endeavored to sweep under the rug an incident that, under ordinary circumstances, would have made such an agreement impossible from the beginning. When the first state-wide Prudential contract was negotiated and presented to the agents of Greater New York, sixty-two per cent of the membership voted against it. The men protested the agreement because they believed that Prudential could have granted a wage increase on the basis of the "Little Steel Formula." They also asserted that the union had risked its labor board certification by using the Honest Ballot Association. Greater New York's rejection was a stunning blow, yet the union's officers dismissed the affair by maintaining that the vote among Upstate New York agents was sufficiently large to offset the defeat — an assertion that the New York City agents disputed.

The U.O.P.W.A.'s conduct in ratifying the agreement so embittered Prudential's Greater New York agents that many of them quit the union and sought membership in the A.F. of L. Prudential Local in Manhattan. From their new vantage point they tried to undermine the power of the Office Workers' leadership, but their effectiveness was not tested until the Ohio campaign.

Sometime prior to this event the defecting agents wrote a letter to all the New York City agents, explaining the Prudential contract

[35]*Ibid.*, September, 1943, p. 3.

and their reasons for rejecting it. (Both the A.F. of L. Insurance Council and the independent union used this letter to great advantage in Ohio.) The New York debit men were frank in their appraisal of the U.O.P.W.A. They pointed out (in bold type) that Local 30, U.O.P.W.A., had become a "weapon . . . in the hands of the paid organizers of the U.O.P.W.A., WHO ARE NOT AND NEVER WERE INSURANCE MEN." They wrote that the local had a "mortal organizational weakness — its complete domination and control by the U.O.P.W.A. over its policies, its management and its finances." According to these agents, Prudential offered its employees "precisely nothing" in "Part I," as the contract was called. Furthermore, the union used the Local's money to carry on a campaign for the national contract in direct violation of the instructions of the Local's membership. And they observed that while the contract promised a $2.50 weekly increase, Prudential agents ultimately received only $1.50.

The dissident group did not excuse the U.O.P.W.A. officials for their failure to work with the New York Insurance Department either. A wage increase required the prior approval of this agency, a technicality they accused the union leaders of deliberately failing to comply with. U.O.P.W.A. officials simply agreed to Prudential's demands, they wrote, first for the state-wide agreement and then for the national contract. The writers of the letter even questioned the use of the Honest Ballot Association, for they alleged that "there was no deadline for voting, no open count of votes, no check of bona fide union members in the count."[36]

The letter left a good deal unsaid. The New York agents were disillusioned over "Part I," but this was merely the last of a long list of grievances the agents endured as union members. For example, David Fay, a former executive board member of Local 30, U.O.P.W.A., expressed the general climate of opinion in a letter he wrote to Matthew Hogan, the A.F. of L. Council organizer in Ohio. Fay wrote:

> Pru men in New York City are stunned from the shock of the
> so-called contract . . . [which] puts them back where they were
> in the old days of pressures and speed-ups. Their financial

[36]"An Open Letter to the Industrial Insurance Agents of Greater New York," from The American Federation of Industrial and Ordinary Insurance Agents of Greater New York, A.F. of L., n.d.

condition is worse than ever despite the $1.50 blackmail. Debits are small, women are being put on the job . . . . Worse than that all the men have lost hope. We are indeed paying dearly for our mistake in ever tying up with the abominable outfit calling itself U.O.P.W.A. We can forgive them for selling the agents to Pru body and soul for two years in return for dues deduction . . . . But we cannot forgive them for robbing them of hope and of their faith in Trade Unionism.[37]

The U.O.P.W.A.'s leadership did not take this and other accusations quietly; they chose to publicize the reasons for the union's defeat in Ohio. Lewis Merrill, the president of the organization, summed up for his membership a series of arguments purporting to offer the definitive explanation. He acknowledged his union's failure to explain the meaning of "Part I" to the Ohio agents, and to show them it was a good agreement for war time conditions. He went on to write:

The A.F. of L. and particularly the Independent, neither of which has been able independently to duplicate these benefits for the agents in any area or in any major company, rushed into Ohio, attacked the U.O.P.W.A. contract and offered agents promissory notes of unlimited demands which these organizations have no way of paying for. The A.F. of L., for example, put forward demands for a $60.00 weekly increase. A number of Ohio agents, uninitiated in the realities of bargaining, fell for this appeal.[38]

Then Merrill got to the heart of the matter when he wrote:

The union failed to prepare the agents for the only kind of campaign A.F. of L. and the Independent could carry on: a campaign not FOR agents, or FOR any progress, but AGAINST THE U.O.P.W.A. on the basis of slander, anti-Semitism, the red bogeyman, in fact, the whole bag of tricks.[39]

Merrill could well afford to be frank. His union had a thirty-one state contract with Prudential, an agreement with Hancock and was negotiating with Metropolitan. His appraisal of the Ohio election at first seems unusual; he should have ignored his rivals' criticism.

[37]Letter from David Fay to Matthew Hogan, July 7, 1943.

[38]*Office and Professional News,* November, 1943, p. 6.

[39]*Ibid.*

The activity of former U.O.P.W.A. agents hurt his cause, to be sure, yet this could be attributed to thwarted ambition. Upon further consideration, however, Merrill's remarks fit into a pattern of words and deeds that he and others were practicing from the beginning of the union's existence.

What these were and how they affected the membership of the U.O.P.W.A. will have to wait for the next chapter. Because it is important at this time to treat of the compensation aspects of U.O.P.W.A. insurance contracts, this question will now be developed as if the U.O.P.W.A. were a haven of bliss for union-minded debit agents.

THE COMPENSATION ISSUE

In October 1941 the U.O.P.W.A. signed an agreement with the John Hancock Mutual Life Insurance Company, calling it "the first nationally negotiated contract with a major company." As a result of the contract the union became bargaining representative for one thousand Hancock agents in New York and five hundred debit men in Boston. By the end of 1942, the union's contract with the company covered 2,500 agents in five states and seventeen cities.[40] The organizational and bargaining history of the union with Hancock between the years 1941 and 1945 approximates its experience with Prudential: haggling for certification among the labor boards, charges and countercharges by its competitors, certain contractual gains — all of which have been detailed in these pages.

While the U.O.P.W.A. was unable to sign anything even slightly resembling a national contract with the Metropolitan Life Insurance Company, the union relentlessly pursued its objective of achieving labor board victories with the company. In 1942, for example, the union again won an election in Greater New York by a vote of 1,182 to 778.[41] During the next three years, the U.O.P.W.A. was certified in the states of New Jersey, Pennsylvania, Illinois, Massachusetts, Missouri, Michigan, Connecticut and Rhode Island, thus adding six thousand additional Metropolitan agents to its Greater New York membership. The only state the union lost in this string of victories was California where in March 1944 the U.O.P.W.A.

[40]*Ibid.*, October 15, 1942, p. 1.

[41]*Metropolitan Life Ins. Co.*, 5 S.L.R.B. 458 (1942).

was defeated by a vote of 349 to 217.[42] In these elections there was the usual scramble for position on the ballot by the A.F. of L. insurance locals, and in Wisconsin, the U.O.P.W.A.'s nemesis, the independent International Union of Life Insurance Agents, captured the Metropolitan agents.[43]

It was necessary for the U.O.P.W.A. to negotiate separate contracts with Metropolitan in each of the states in which it won certification, because the company demanded this arrangement. And, to complicate matters still further, bargaining sessions with the company, as well as those with Prudential and Hancock, were enacted against the backdrop of labor-management relations conducted during war time.

The "no-strike pledge" was one of organized labor's enduring contributions to the war effort. Disputes arose that had to be referred to the National War Labor Board, however, and the insurance unions applied to the Board for a redress of grievances as frequently as did other organizations of comparable size. The very complicated compensation feature of the insurance unions' contracts is a case in point and, since New York regulated industrial insurance in the United States, the War Labor Board was not equipped to grant union demands without first seeking a ruling and, eventually, an adjudication from the state. In consummating agreements both company and union were forced to postpone any definite contractual obligations concerning compensation, although the unions argued that the companies were capable of granting salary increases. The companies just as strongly pleaded inability to adjust agent earnings because of the New York Insurance Law.

The experience of the unions in dealing with compensation questions was, with small variation, similar in all of the "Big Three" companies. Since the stature of the U.O.P.W.A.'s Local 30 was enhanced by the very reason that it was in New York City, it is the development of this large affiliate's bargaining efforts with Metropolitan, under the auspices of the War Labor Board, that brings the dilemma of agent compensation into focus.

On June 11, 1942, the U.O.P.W.A. won an election in Metropolitan's Greater New York agency offices. The Labor Board then

[42]*Office and Professional News,* November, 1943, p. 1; & January, p. 3; February, p. 5; March, p. 5; April, p. 3; and August, p. 3 (1944).

[43]*Prudential Ins. Co.,* 43 N.L.R.B. 962 (1942).

certified the union as bargaining representative for the company's debit agents in the area. Neither company nor union could arrive at a satisfactory compromise in the negotiations and, so, the union had the case certified before the War Labor Board on October 24, 1942. Through the pressure of the Board, company and union reached agreement on all points, except the compensation issue, and on May 7, 1943, the participants signed a contract for Metropolitan agents in Greater New York.

The contract provided for recognition of seniority in promotions, an arbitration and grievance clause, union security in the form of dues deduction, and the stipulation that both labor and management abide by the decision of the War Labor Board on the question of increased compensation. Concerning the latter item, the union wanted an average weekly increase of $7.00, while the company pleaded inability to pay under the New York Law.

The compensation issue remained unresolved for the next sixteen months. Both union and company used all the forces at their command to obtain a settlement from the Board. U.O.P.W.A. officials, for example, sent a delegation of Local 30 agents and their wives to Washington in late November 1943 to urge quick action on the case. While meeting with members of the Board the New Yorkers made such remarks as: "We can't get by with $3.00 shoes; we're on our feet all day pounding the debit and we need the best." One agent said: "We don't work in overalls either. Suits wear out awful fast these days." And an agent's wife testified: "I never see my husband. He has to eat out all the time if he expects to cover all his calls. He should be paid for expenses incurred." The delegation returned to New York assured that the "factual presentation of their case would be completed by the first week in December."[44]

The Board instructed a regional panel in New York City to hear the compensation case, and this group recommended that the company pay a $2.85 weekly increase to the agents and a back pay settlement of approximately $250.00 per agent, retroactive to October 24, 1942, the date on which the case was certified to the Board. Metropolitan appealed the decision to New York's Regional War Labor Board on the grounds that it was illegal in New York State to grant both the increase and the retroactive pay. The com-

[44]*Office and Professional News,* July 1, 1942, p. 1; & June, p. 1; October, p. 2; & December, p. 3, (1943).

pany further contested the increase in compensation, in view of the "Little Steel Formula." A company spokesman asserted that Metropolitan agents averaged $57.90 during the first quarter of 1943, and he said that this was 15.6 per cent above the last quarter of 1942. The company official based his estimates on the fact that the nationwide increase in income, caused by wartime production, had also raised the sales of insurance.

The New York Regional War Labor Board then heard the case and upheld the findings of the panel.[45] Both company and union thereupon sent officials to protest the decision, the union, interestingly enough, claiming that the award was not sufficient. Metropolitan simply restated the arguments previously cited.

After both sides presented their briefs to the National Board, the U.O.P.W.A.'s Local 30 proposed a compromise: if the company would pay the $2.85 weekly increase, it could hold in escrow the retroactive pay under the joint trusteeship of the Manufacturer's Trust Co., Cecil J. North, a vice president of Metropolitan, and Leon W. Berney, director of the union's insurance division. According to a union official, the company at first rejected the proposal, alleging that sections 213 and 213A of the New York Insurance Law forbade the payment of retroactive pay. He also quoted Metropolitan as saying that if this phase of the dispute could be resolved the company might consent to pay the $2.85 increase, "or any other sum ordered by the Board in the future."

The union took up this question with the New York Insurance Department and, according to the union's evaluation of the meeting, the State Superintendent found nothing in the law to prevent the awarding of the back pay.[46]

Meanwhile, the War Labor Board was doing some investigating of its own and, after examining the evidence, referred the entire compensation issue to a special subcommittee which held hearings on April 5, 1944. At length, the full Board handed down its decision. It upheld the recommendation of the Regional War Labor Board. The national Board also lumped together the cases involving Metropolitan agents in New Jersey, Massachusetts, Pennsylvania, Michi-

[45]*Metropolitan Life Ins. Co.*, Reg. W.L.B., case no. 11-D-11, (2733-D), (1943).

[46]U.O.P.W.A., C.I.O., *Convention Proceedings* (Philadelphia, Pa., 1944), pp. 57, 92-93.

gan, Connecticut and Illinois, since U.O.P.W.A. locals in these states had also petitioned the board for a decision on the compensation issue by the time the New York case was certified to the Board. The Board further decreed that if neither company nor union could agree on its recommendation they should hire an arbitrator.[47]

In explaining the Board''s decision the U.O.P.W.A. president, Lewis Merrill, asserted:

> It provides there shall be a test case in the courts as to whether there is anything in the law of New York which prevents payment of back pay.... In the meanwhile, Metropolitan will deposit about seven or eight hundred thousand dollars under the joint trusteeship of North and Berney.[48]

The National War Labor Board's decision proved invaluable from the union's viewpoint. In the first place, the Board sustained its ruling in a case involving Metropolitan with two A.F. of L. insurance locals.[49] Furthermore, both Prudential and Hancock abided by the ruling, paying their agents wage increases, although the former company had no retroactive pay dispute with which to contend.[50]

Metropolitan followed the Board's decision on the wage increase and paid the sum required by the Board. However, the company appealed the Board's decision on the retroactive pay issue to the United State Federal Court, Southern District.[51] It would take another year before the court would hear the case, and then Metropolitan would reject its decision. By the time the company was ready to free the funds, the U.O.P.W.A. was no longer in existence.

In relating this series of compensation cases it is apparent that insurance labor unions wielded considerable influence. Whether the companies would have petitioned the New York Insurance Department for a compensation increase in the absence of a labor organization is debatable. That the U.O.P.W.A. and the A.F. of L. Insurance

[47]*Metropolitan Life Ins. Co.*, N.W.L.B., case no. 2773-CS-B, 111-6463-D, (1944).

[48]U.O.P.W.A., C.I.O., *Convention Proceedings* (Philadelphia, Pa., 1944), pp. 139-40.

[49]*Metropolitan Life Ins. Co.*, N.W.L.B., case no. 111-14499-J.B., (1945).

[50]*Office and Professional News*, March, 1943, p. 3.

[51]*Insurance Career*, May, 1948, p. 8.

Council sought a ruling from the War Labor Board is a matter of record, and their work constitutes one of their major accomplishments during the war years.

At its 1944 convention, the U.O.P.W.A. was able to report some additional gains in the white collar field. Since the previous convention the union had signed over seventy new contracts making a grand total of over four hundred agreements with such widely divergent firms as Paramount Pictures, United Artists, Curtiss Wright in Buffalo and the Title Guarantee and Trust Co. Prudential agents in Kansas organized a group of clerical workers in the Cudahy plant in Wichita; there the office employees chose the U.O.P.W.A. by a vote of fifty-six to one. At the convention a union official also spoke of a membership figure in the insurance division in the vicinity of 50,000. He asserted that the union's rate of growth was greatest among midwestern insurance agents.[52]

Notable among the insurance division's accomplishments was its organization of the office workers in The Maccabees, a fraternal organization in Detroit. The employees voted for the union in February 1942 and in May of that year signed a contract providing for a union shop, a pension plan and an adjustment in minimum salaries from $75.00 to $85.00 per month. In the fall of 1943, the union negotiated a new contract with the company by which the workers were to receive an increase in monthly salaries, plus a salary scale with job classification. Both of these clauses were contingent upon War Labor Board approval.[53]

In the state of Massachusetts the U.O.P.W.A. won a back pay case pertaining to four thousand agents of the "Big Three." A Commonwealth court determined that the Metropolitan, the Prudential and the John Hancock owed these agents over one million dollars in pay, retroactive to July 1938, the time the state's lapse bill went into effect. The union estimated that each agent would receive an average of $250.00 as a result of the decision.[54]

OTHER SUCCESSES

[52]U.O.P.W.A., C.I.O., *Convention Proceedings* (Philadelphia, Pa., 1944), p. 60.

[53]*Office and Professional News,* April 1, p. 3 & June 1, p. 1, (1942); and October, 1943, p. 3.

[54]*Ibid.,* February 15, 1942, p. 8.

The U.O.P.W.A. was also successful in organizing Negro insurance companies. For example, in April 1942 Local 22 in Philadelphia organized a majority of the forty agents employed by the Provident Home Industrial Mutual Life Insurance Company, and in February 1944 an independent group of agents working in the Southern Aid Society, a company employing over one hundred debit men, voted to affiliate with the U.O.P.W.A. A union official made it known that typists "with seventeen years experience [were] earning $14.00 per week and that agents averaged $25.00 per week" in the latter company.[55]

In January 1943, the Office Workers' evened the score with the A.F. of L. by signing a contract for one hundred thirty-five agents employed by the Colonial Life Insurance Company in New Jersey. Just two years prior to this event the A.F. of L. Council had won an election involving the company's agency force in Greater New York.[56]

The U.O.P.W.A. authorized one strike during the war. On February 16, 1942, one hundred agents of Local 30, New York, struck the Unity Life and Accident Company for a period of four weeks. The dispute was settled through the intervention of the New York Insurance Department.[57]

In spite of these successes the U.O.P.W.A. was in trouble, as events in Ohio proved. There was something basically wrong with the organization, and the union's catch-all type structure contributed to the problem. It is this internal weakness that must now be considered.

[55]*Ibid.*, May 15, p. 3 & August, p. 3 (1943); March, p. 5 & June, p. 2, (1944).

[56]*The New York Times*, January 2, 1941, p. 10; & *Office and Professional News*, February, 1943, p. 2.

[57]*Office and Professional News*, March 15, 1942, p. 2.

CHAPTER 3

CERTAIN AGENTS LAPSE THEIR POLICIES IN
A POOR-RISK ORGANIZATION

As a labor organization, the United Office and Professional Workers of America, C.I.O., failed both its members and the American labor movement. The union was never a large one; at most it possessed fifty thousand members and even this figure is disputed. Because of its diminutive size certain writers, such as Jack Barbash and Herbert Harris, discount its importance.[1] But criticism on the basis of numerical strength alone misses the point. The U.O.P.W.A. offered a haven for that segment of white collar and professional employees who believed in trade unionism and who thought that organization offered a status unattainable in the non-union, traditionally prestige jobs of banking, insurance and the like. Furthermore, the union was the first labor organization ever to achieve bargaining recognition from the large insurance companies and other white collar industries.

Yet, the United Office and Professional Workers of America passed up a once-in-a-lifetime opportunity, and that for one simple reason: the union's leadership was a tool of the Communist party. Such a statement necessarily requires proof.

How It All Began

The United Office and Professional Workers of America, C.I.O., was in reality an amalgamation of several left-wing organizations. One of these groups was composed of members of the Rank-and-File Movement, a combination of social workers who banded together during the Great Depression. When the U.O.P.W.A. was founded, members of the Movement went into the Office Workers'

---

[1]Barbash brings this out when he writes that the U.O.P.W.A. was "largely shadow and no substance," in his *The Practice of Unionism* (New York: Harper & Bros., 1956), p. 350; and Harris is even more pointed: he calls the union an organization that is "more nominal than real in [its] existence," *American Labor* (New Haven: Yale University Press, 1938), p. 412.

social service unions.[2] The Rank-and-File Movement in turn was an
outgrowth of the American Association of Social Workers which was
established in 1921.[3] Another group making up the Movement was
the New York Association of Federation Workers, and this latter
society was composed of agencies supported by the Federation of
Jewish Philanthropies.[4]

According to Jacob Fisher, the historian of the Movement, the
Rank-and-File proposed a "return to social work of the concern
with larger social issues of the progressive era in American life."[5]
Among the larger social issues advocated by the Movement were a
proposed fund for the defence of Tom Mooney and the Scottsboro
boys, a protest to the German ambassador over Nazi excesses and
free milk distribution to the unemployed. In themselves, these proposals lack significance. Another writer, Vera Shlakman, pointed
out that the Rank-and-File Movement "challenged the assumption
of the identity of interest between the executive and the practitioner."[6] She went on to observe that "the executive was moved by
necessity with administrative costs," whereas the practitioner felt
divorced from this consideration and moved toward the labor movement.

A second group that produced the U.O.P.W.A., C.I.O., was said
to be made up of an alliance of socialists and communists who, in
the Spring of 1936, planned "joint fraction work" in the trade
unions. Daniel Bell writes that Rose Wortis and Jack Stachel,
representing the communists, and Frank Trager and Herbert Zam,
representing the socialists, founded an organization that entered the

[2]Nathan Glazer, *The Social Basis of American Communism* (New York:
Harcourt, Brace & World, 1961), pp. 142-43. The writer is indebted to Mr.
Glazer for his cross reference citations to the subsequently quoted works of
Jacob Fisher and Vera Shlakman.

[3]Vera Shlakman, *Science and Society*, "White collar unions and professional organizations," Summer, 1950, vol. XIV, no. 3, p. 220.

[4]Glazer, *loc. cit.*

[5]Jacob Fisher, *Rank and File Movement in Social Work*, 1931-1936 (New
York: New York School of Social Work, 1936), p. 4.

[6]Shlakman, *loc. cit.*

United Office and Professional Workers of America.[7]

Finally, the U.O.P.W.A. consisted of the Office Workers Union, an organization that had been affiliated to the Trade Union Unity League and that had operated as a dual union. It was the membership of this group that had attempted to bore into the A.F. of L.'s Bookkeepers' Local 12646 in New York City and that had ultimately been expelled.[8] When the House Un-American Activities Committee was investigating Communism, one observer suggested that the U.O.P.W.A. "has as its basic background" the Office Workers Union of the Trade Union Unity League.[9]

Of the individuals who made up the leadership of the United Office and Professional Workers, Lewis Merrill is one of the few persons whose history is in any way documented. A Canadian by birth, he joined the Bookkeepers, Stenographers and Accountants' Union, Local 12646, in 1930. He was only twenty years old at the time, and in 1931 he went to work as an office employee for Local 281, Sheet Metal Workers' Union, in New York City.[10] John P. Frey, the president of Local 281 would later accuse Merrill of being a Communist. He said that as a delegate to the A.F. of L. conventions Merrill had "associated with and voted with known communists."[11] Whether Frey was correct or not about Merrill, the *Daily Worker* eulogized him for contributing to the Party's successful "boring" into the A.F. of L. with the words:

Within the A.F. of L. he [Merrill] led the fight to permit the

[7]Daniel Bell, "The Background and Development of Marxian Socialism in the United States," *Socialism and American Life,* ed. by Donald Drew Egbert and Stow Persons (Princeton: Princeton University Press, 1952), vol. 1, p. 382. The writer has discovered no reference other than Bell's in this regard.

[8]The Office Workers' Union went into the A.F. of L. sometime prior to May 17, 1935, the date on which the Trade Union Unity League was disbanded. Labor Research Associates, *Labor Fact Book,* III (New York: International Publishers, 1936), p. 100.

[9]U.S. Congress, House, Special Committee on Un-American Activities, *Investigation of Un-American Propaganda Activities in the United States,* 75th Cong., 3d Sess., 1938, vol. 1, p. 100.

[10]*The Ledger,* November, 1935, p. 8.

[11]U.S. Cong., *Investig. of Un-American Propaganda Activities,* 75th Cong., 3d Sess., 1938, vol. 1, p. 100.

Office Workers' Union of the T.U.U.L. to become a part of the A.F. of L. and won it.[12]

Sam Baron is another person who questioned Merrill's background. Baron was Merrill's immediate predecessor as president of the B.S. & A.U., Local 12646, and he described the situation in the Local at the time of his return to the union from the 1935 A.F. of L. convention. He said that he was informed by the "Communist faction of the union that they would not permit certain members of the union to run for office because they disagreed with their politics." Baron rejected the proposal. He told the "Communist faction" that at the convention he had fought for the right of Communists to remain inside the trade union movement and that the proposed action would make the Local appear ridiculous. According to Baron, the group then played its ace. He related the following incident:

> Merrill . . . a communist, came to me with a proposition: the communists would support me for president of the Union if I would not fight in the battle that was to occur in the Union between them and the elements they couldn't take. I threw Merrill out of my office.[13]

Merrill defeated Baron at the next election in October 1936.[14]

Baron also mentioned that Norma Aaronson, a leader of the B.S.&A.U., Local 12646, was a Communist and a prime mover of dual unionism. Baron described the dual union as the group that flourished independently "until they decided to bore into the A.F. of L. . . . When the dual union was liquidated, she [Norma Aaronson] came into B.S.&A.U."[15] He said that she had also offered the left wing's support in the next election if he remained neutral.

[12]*Daily Worker,* October 4, 1942, p. 5. Quoted in: U.S. Cong., House, Special Committee on Un-American Activities, *Report on C.I.O. Political Action Committee,* 78th Cong., 2d Sess., 1944, p. 127.

[13]U.S. Cong., *Investig. of Un-American Propaganda Activities,* 75th Cong., 3d Sess., 1938, vol. 4, pp. 2529 & 2531. Baron admitted to the Committee that he was a Socialist, an alternate delegate of the executive committee of the Socialist Party of America, and a candidate for the House from Kings County, N.Y., on the Socialist Party ticket.

[14]*The Ledger,* November, 1936, p. 7.

[15]U.S. Cong., *Investig. of Un-American Propaganda Activities,* 75th Cong., 3d Sess., 1938, vol. 4, pp. 2530 & 2670.

Baron also cited as "known communists" Morris Yanoff and Peter K. Hawley, both of whom were members of the B.S.&A.U., Local 12646, and later prominent in United Office and Professional Workers' circles.[16] Yanoff was an organizer for the Bookkeepers' union and was elected eighth vice president of the U.O.P.W.A. at its founding convention. Hawley was treasurer of the Bookkeepers' union when Merrill defeated Baron, and it was said of him that he "served as a member of the union executive board longer than anyone else."[17]

This then was the situation at the time the C.I.O. granted an international charter to the United Office and Professional Workers of America: two identifiable groups, the social service workers and the office workers of the defunct Trade Union Unity League — the latter firmly implanted in the Bookkeepers union — merged and elected Lewis Merrill president of the new union. These were joined by one hundred and fifty insurance agents from Metropolitan, Prudential and John Hancock offices in New York City, by commercial artists, etc.

The conduct of the founding convention in 1937 was not so sanguine as previously indicated. Speakers derided the A.F. of L. for its fifteen-year record of refusing "to establish an international union of white collar workers . . .[and for] exacting heavy per capita taxes from federal locals and offering no assistance." Merrill spoke about the "hindrance and obstruction" of the Federation, and he cited an example of this when he said:

> It recently reached a climax with the revocation of the charter of the Chicago local [stenographers'] and the withdrawal from the A.F. of L. by the New York and Philadelphia locals.[18]

He stated that this condition "clearly demonstrated the impossibility of further progress with the A.F. of L." To those present who thought further progress possible, Len DeCaux, the C.I.O. news editor, was later quoted as recommending the avoidance of "sectionalism and factionalism which held back organization, and which was one of the sicknesses of the A.F. of L."[19] One observer described how "sectionalism and factionalism" were eschewed; he said:

[16]*Ibid.*, p. 2670.
[17]*The Ledger*, January, 1936, p. 12; & June, 1937, p. 2.
[18]*Ibid.*, June 1937, p. 1.
[19]*Ibid.*

The Stalinists made it plain that they intended to achieve unity, but their idea of unity was to systematically expel anyone who disagreed with them.[20] Another delegate remarked that Merrill conducted the convention by asking for comment on "canned proposals." Those who objected to them he "caustically rebuked."[21]

According to the union newspaper, much of the delegates' time was taken up with listening to and adopting resolutions which, in the writer's estimation, had a "party-line" flavor: they sent greetings to Tom Mooney, petitioned for the release of Hapgood Powers and pleaded for the "restoration of civil liberties in Maine." The delegates applauded messages of congratulations from Harry Bridges, the Aluminum Workers of America, and the Philadelphia Newspaper Guild.

The delegates to the convention voted on a dues scale of $.55 to $1.50, the latter for the insurance agents, and adopted a temporary constitution. They elected Merrill president of the Union and Eugene Turner its secretary treasurer.[22] Louis Vannett, a member of the Bookkeepers' Local from Philadelphia, became first vice president.[23] The delegates also chose Leo Cohen of the Social Service Union as third vice president and Morris Yanoff of the Office Workers' as eighth vice president.[24]

The names of the other members of the executive board sound like trains in the night, because none of them appear at the second convention. Whether these persons merely served a useful purpose, that is, whether their presence on the board facilitated the writing of the constitution, is a matter of conjecture.

[20]U.S. Cong., *Investig. of Un-American Propaganda Activities,* 75th Cong., 3d Sess., vol. 1, p. 258.

[21]*Ibid.*

[22]*The Ledger,* June, 1937, p. 2. Turner's name disappeared from the record in 1940.

[23]*Ibid.* Vannett retained this job until the 1940 convention, when he became a member of the union's executive board. He called a strike against the Sun Life Ins. Co. in Philadelphia in 1942 and was expelled from the union for failure "to promote the war effort." U.O.P.W.A., C.I.O., *Convention Proceedings* (Albany, N.Y., 1942), pp. 14-16.

[24]*The Ledger,* June, 1937, p. 2. After 1942 Cohen is no longer mentioned.

When the delegates returned to their locals, they were not universally acclaimed. Jerome King, an expelled officer of the National Maritime Union, told of the sharp struggle that took place within the United Office and Professional Workers' between the "communists and those who were fighting to throw off the Stalinist yoke of oppression that was being placed around their necks." King wrote that there were charges of "bosses' stooges, labor spies, Trotskyite and all the rest" made by the competing factions. He also observed that the intra-union strife was highlighted by threats of returning to the A.F. of L. and that a non-Communist element in a San Francisco local did in fact gain control and seek re-affiliation with the Federation.[25]

Jockeying for position within the locals persisted throughout the first year of the U.O.P.W.A.'s existence and continued through the second convention in May 1938. On the very first day of that meeting President Merrill attempted to placate certain of the delegates by observing:

> We can have instead of a centralized, authoritive organization, an international union exercising those powers loaned it from time to time by local unions and exercising power of co-ordination, of information and occasionally of initiation. I don't think that kind of an international can win out.

Then he said a startling thing:

> We are ready to go back to the A.F. of L. any time that the interests of our membership are guaranteed, the continuation of the principles guiding the activities of the C.I.O. are preserved, the ability of these principles to secure scope for their operation is made possible.[26]

[25]Jerry King, et al, *We Accuse (From the Record): A Factual History of the Seamans' Labor Movement* (New York: P. O. Box 63, 1940), p. 90. King also reported that the U.O.P.W.A. Bookkeepers' were employed in the chief Eastern seaboard locals of the N.M.U. in the summer of 1937. He asserted that the right-wing N.M.U. members literally "chased all the office workers out" of the Maritime Union's headquarters in New York. He also related that Catherine Lewis controlled the U.O.P.W.A. office staff in the Mine Workers Union, and that her father warned the national C.I.O.'s regional directors about hiring them. John L. Lewis had heard that the U.O.P.W.A. was supplying "confidential facts" on union business to Communist officials, *Ibid.*, pp. 91 & 93.

[26]U.O.P.W.A., C.I.O., *Convention Proceedings* (Washington, D.C., 1938), pp. 5 & 13.

At this point it was hard for many of the delegates to know what Merrill had on his mind.

The delegates received the "call" to the 1938 convention on the basis of Article III of the temporary constitution. It read as follows:

> Each local union shall be entitled to one vote for every fifty (50) members. . . . The maximum number of delegates from any local union shall not be larger than ten.[27]

Though the second part of the article appears innocent enough, it was used to gain control of the organization, as will be shown. During the 1938 convention the union's leadership presented the document they had been commissioned to write. Sumner Slichter includes an analysis of the U.O.P.W.A.'s constitution in his study of the subject, and his comparisons prove helpful in any evaluation of the union's organizational structure. There appear to be three provisions in the union's constitution that are pertinent and that show the extent of the national union's control. In the first place, the U.O.P.W.A.'s constitution contained a provision whereby the president had the power to "discipline or support local officers without appeal." Secondly, the union's executive board was empowered to "remove an international officer without appeal." And thirdly, the union required approval of strikes by the national "in nearly all cases."[28] Slichter's study illustrates that only two C.I.O. unions granted their president the power Merrill received under the first point. His work further reveals that five C.I.O. unions had constitutional provisions similar to the second and that only two C.I.O. unions included a clause in their constitutions analogous to the third.[29] Each of these provisions the United Office and Professional Workers' officers made use of as time went on.

The delegates to the 1938 convention unanimously re-elected Lewis Merrill as president. During the course of the proceedings he said that the total membership of the union was 45,000, which, he added, "represented an increase of 36,000 since the May, 1937, Convention." He also mentioned that the union had 20,000 members

[27]Convention Call, press release.

[28]Sumner Slichter, *The Challenge of Industrial Relations: Trade Unions, Management, and the Public Interest* (Ithaca: Cornell University Press, 1947), p. 187.

[29]*Ibid.*, pp. 181, 187 & 189.

in the insurance division alone.[30] These figures were doctored, however. According to one union critic, Merrill "failed to note that the treasurer's report showed only a paid membership of 16,000."[31] Sometime later the U.O.P.W.A.'s leaders corrected the discrepancy; they said that in 1938 the union had 13,000 dues paying members, almost five thousand of whom were enrolled in the insurance division.[32]

The delegates selected Leon W. Berney, the director of the insurance division, as second vice president, and they also chose five other members of the division for the nine-man vice presidential roster. It seems likely that some of the latter fought the Merrill wing of the union during the next two years, for at the 1940 convention the union delegates, contrary to the wishes of the majority leadership, voted in an executive board strong enough to check the power of the dominant group.[33]

Merrill must have recognized that his activity after the 1938 convention could only enkindle the flames of opposition. Benjamin Stolberg, for example, described how Merrill convoked meetings of U.O.P.W.A. locals "for some non-union purpose, such as peace and democracy," and illustrated just what this entailed. He wrote:

> The meeting is packed with non-union Communist party members and sympathizers — housewives, real-estate agents, dentists, college kids. Then some crucial union business is introduced and the meeting 'endorses' the administration viva voce.[34]

Between the 1938 and 1940 conventions two events occurred which all but destroyed the organization and which prompted Merrill to remark that the union "had to undergo many trials." He went on to say:

> There were efforts on the part of the I.L.G.W.U. to split Local 16 before its re-entrance into the A.F. of L. . . . . Then we saw

[30]U.O.P.W.A., C.I.O., *Convention Proceedings* (Washington, D.C., 1938), pp. 7 & 16.

[31]U.S. Cong., *Investig. of Un-American Propaganda Activities*, 75th Cong., 3d Sess., 1938, vol. 1, p. 259.

[32]U.O.P.W.A., C.I.O., *Convention Proceedings* (Chicago, Ill., 1940), p. 22.

[33]*Ibid.*, p. 50.

[34]Benjamin Stolberg, "Communism in American Unions," *Saturday Evening Post*, September 5, 1939, p. 55.

> Local 30, Industrial Insurance Agents, riven from end to end
> with factionalism, organized around the most irrelevant ques-
> tions. The Secretary of the A.F. of L. took occasion in March,
> 1939, to announce to the press that some twelve locals of the
> U.O.P.W.A. had applied for A.F. of L. charters. This was all
> based on lies . . . . Local 30 is now more united in its member-
> ship and leadership than at any time in the past.[35]

The New York Times covered the Garment Workers' dispute
with Local 16 and the facts appear to be as follows. Members of
Local 16, U.O.P.W.A., had obtained employment at I.L.G.W.U.
headquarters in New York City and started to cause friction among
the Garment Workers' staff. In retaliation the right-wing I.L.G.
W.U. leaders cultivated those persons in the Office Workers' Local
16 who they knew were dissatisfied with the union's national leadership. On March 20, 1939, a rump group of the Local passed a
resolution, accusing the U.O.P.W.A. of Communist domination and
calling their Local "a sorry failure as a trade union." Peter Hawley,
the Local's president and a vice president of the U.O.P.W.A., denied
the charge and stated that the Garment Workers were causing the
unrest in an attempt to bring more members back into the A.F. of
L. David Dubinsky, president of the I.L.G.W.U., refused to honor
Hawley's request that the Garment Workers stop the revolt. At a
special meeting of Local 16 close to five hundred of the rank and
file voted to quit the U.O.P.W.A. and to seek affiliation with the
A.F. of L.'s Office Workers' Council. Only twenty-five of those
present cast a vote of confidence in Local 16 and the U.O.P.W.A.
leadership.[36]

This was only the beginning. On March 27 Frank Weikel, the
president of the Office Workers' International Council, A.F. of L.,
announced that his organization had received "inquiries" from
U.O.P.W.A. locals in twelve cities, all of them large and all of them
containing the bulk of the union's clerical membership.[37]

[35]U.O.P.W.A., C.I.O., *Convention Proceedings* (Chicago, Ill., 1940),
p. 111.

[36]*The New York Times,* March 21, 1939, p. 1.

[37]*Ibid.,* March 28, 1939, p. 14. The cities are: Buffalo, Bridgeport, New
Haven, Newark, Philadelphia, Pittsburgh, Boston, Baltimore, Cleveland, Los
Angeles, Chicago, and St. Louis.

The dissension in these locals paled in comparison to what occurred in the union's insurance local in New York City, however. Merrill had described the "factionalism" in Local 30 as "organized around the most irrelevant questions." Such was not the case.

THE TEMPORARY NATIONAL ECONOMIC
COMMITTEE INVESTIGATES INSURANCE

On January 19, 1939, Merrill addressed the Public Affairs Committee of Philadelphia and explained that his organization had persuaded the Temporary National Economic Committee to include in its hearings on the insurance industry an inquiry into the personnel practices of the Metropolitan Life, the Prudential and the John Hancock companies.[38] Merrill failed to mention that the executive board of Local 30 urged him to consider the significance of placing insurance agents before the T.N.E.C. They stated that the union was foolhardy in believing that companies, which did not even recognize the organization's existence, would refrain from retaliating against those debit agents who testified about company practices.[39] Merrill disagreed. He also persuaded a large number of the Local's membership to disregard the warning of their executive board.

Led to believe that they would be quizzed about their everyday experience, one hundred Metropolitan agents appeared before the Committee in February 1939. They were misinformed, as the Committee counsel expressed no interest in the matter. Instead, he noted the prescriptions of the New York Insurance Law regarding the election of members to a mutual insurance company's board of directors, and he went on to describe the Law. He said that the New York Law required that the companies hold elections every two years and that they submit the names of nominees and the exact date of the election to the policyholders at a specific time; that the Law further obliged the companies to offer an opposition slate of candidates; and that the Law specified that policyholders could vote for new board members either in person, by proxy or by mail.

[38]U.O.P.W.A., C.I.O., *Convention Proceedings* (Chicago, Ill., 1940), p. 18.

[39]Letter to Lewis Merrill, president of U.O.P.W.A., from the Executive Board of Local 30, U.O.P.W.A., April 4, 1939. (*Mimeographed*).

Members of the T.N.E.C. then depicted the manner in which Metropolitan (the company had twenty-nine million policyholders in 1939) had conducted its previous election. Since it was an obvious impossibility for the firm to communicate by mail with the twenty-nine million policyholders, Metropolitan developed a system whereby its agents attached a notification of the election to a policy at the time of the premium payment. This occurred during the last quarter period before the election took place. The company had also instituted the practice of sending about one million ballots to its district office managers, who in turn distributed them in groups of about forty or fifty each to every agent. The manager instructed the agents to return the ballots, signed, within a period of from seven to ten days.

After this recitation a Committee member asked the Metropolitan agents one question: how they obtained the signatures of the policyholders on the ballots they returned to the district office? To a man, thirteen of the agents testified that it was their custom to forge the policyholders' signatures on the ballots. Each said that the practice was a common one and that it was undertaken with the full knowledge of the assistant manager and even, in some instances, of the manager himself. The deception was a long standing one, in vogue in fact when they first joined the company. When the Committee counsel asked each man why he engaged in the practice, the agent pleaded pressure.

One man asserted that it was understood that if the ballots were not signed and delivered on a specific date, the agents "couldn't get their pay." The others declared that this was not their experience. They did testify, however, that the signing was done in the open, or in the company washrooms, and that they joked about exchanging pens, the manner of copying policyholders' names, etc. One agent disclosed that his debit was non-English speaking and consequently he "had to sign" for the policyholder. Others mentioned that the policyholders in general showed a lack of interest in the election.

Leroy A. Lincoln, the president of the Metropolitan, was present during the testimony and repeatedly interrupted the men, protesting his ignorance of the practice and the innocence of the company. At one point he said: "I insist on the right to say that I have never heard of such a practice, and, of course, don't countenance it in any way, shape, form or manner."

When the two-day session ended the T.N.E.C. Counsel excused the remaining debit agents, explaining that further evidence of the practice could only be cumulative. He stated that the testimony was introduced "to show that the practice was widespread." To add a fitting close to the agents' confession the vice-chairman of the Committee asserted that the Congressmen "quickly recognized that none of these ballots signed by the agents affected the outcome of the elections."[40]

The "outcome" of the agents' testimony was never in doubt. Two weeks after the conclusion of the hearings the Metropolitan discharged the thirteen men and had their New York licenses revoked. The leaders of the United Office and Professional Workers of America then began to beat their breasts. They said that T.N.E.C. chairman, William O. Douglas, had assured them that no reprisals would occur. It was discovered too late that no law existed to protect the men, they said. Freeing themselves from all responsibility the union officers said:

> Regardless of its legal inability, the government, in the eyes of all decent citizens, cannot be absolved for the fate of the thirteen . . . . These men have performed a distinct service to the nation. It is a matter of regret that telling the truth . . . should require courage, but it did . . . and was forthcoming.[41]

The union officials then organized a policyholders' rally to gain moral and monetary support for the dismissed agents. And Leon Berney argued before a New York legislative committee investigating insurance for the abolition of the proxy system of voting.

Meanwhile, Local 30, U.O.P.W.A., was in a shambles. It became public knowledge on March 27, 1939, that several members of the Local's executive board had accused the union of betraying them and had sought affiliation with the A.F. of L. insurance local in New York.[42] These men denounced the union for putting the Metropolitan agents before T.N.E.C. in direct violation of their recommendation. Merrill countered the defection by proclaiming a state

[40]U.S. Cong., *T.N.E.C. Hearings,* Part 4, "Life Insurance," pp. 1294-313; 1346, 1362, 1409-410.

[41]U.O.P.W.A., C.I.O., *Convention Proceedings* (Chicago, Ill., 1940), p. 20.

[42]*The New York Times,* March 4, 1939, p. 19 & March 28, 1939, p. 14.

of emergency and suspended the entire executive board of the Local. The members of the board immediately repudiated the suspension, informing Merrill that no such emergency existed.

On April 4, 1939, eight of the Local's executive board members addressed an open letter to Merrill in which they proclaimed that "the Local had become a shell of its former self" under his direction. They charged Merrill with the loss of "more than three thousand members" and at length faced up to an issue that had been smoldering for some time. The letter reads in part:

> In your mad endeavor to gain control of our Local Union you have foisted upon us so-called organizers who were incompetent, arrogant, lacking in experience and who knew of only one loyalty, subservience to the Communist Party.[43]

The board members charged that Merrill had insulted officers and members of the Local during conferences, had usurped the rights that belonged to an autonomous local and had used the Local's treasury in a questionable manner. The men wrote that instead of assisting the Local at a time when it was attempting to organize insurance agents, the U.O.P.W.A. made the Local pay thousands of dollars into the national union office. The letter continued:

> When we finally could no longer pay, instead of the International giving us a helping hand, you under duress demanded and got demand notes from our Local Union. We maintain that such an act as this has never occurred in the history of the entire trade union movement and that its ethics are so questionable that it has no place in a bona fide trade union.[44]

The writers of the letter concluded with the hope that Merrill would see the error of his ways and that "he would withdraw the heavy destructive hand" he had placed upon Local 30. The tragedy of the episode lies in the fact that many insurance men lost faith in the labor movement.[45] The executive board of Local 30 accused Merrill of driving "3,000 members" out of the union, and the

---

[43]Letter to Lewis Merrill from Executive Bd. of Local 30, April 4, 1939.

[44]*Ibid.*

[45]Letter to Matthew Hogan, A.F. of L. organizer, from David Fay, July 10, 1943. Fay was former executive board member of Local 30.

U.O.P.W.A. leaders corroborated this figure by listing the Local's size as "800 members" in 1940.[46]

Merrill was no doubt shaken by the events in Local 30. Yet, he and his insurance division had a splendid rallying cry. The year 1939 might have been a time of trial, but it was also a year of accomplishment. The Court of Appeals of the State of New York declared insurance agents "employes" under the meaning of the state's labor act, and the union had been certified as a bargaining agent by the New York Labor Board. The union assured its diminished membership that it had played a major role in achieving these victories. Merrill and the insurance division made good use of them.

The brave "thirteen" had meanwhile written to President Roosevelt to ask his assistance, and the U.O.P.W.A. officers had duly publicized the letter.[47] And the union leaders could dream of the future day when the whole T.N.E.C. affair would enshrine them in a pantheon of "insurance agents' heroes."

THE RECORD SPEAKS FOR ITSELF

Dreams are short lived, however, and there were too many agents (and office workers) in and out of the U.O.P.W.A. whose memories were long and who did not hesitate to furnish information to various organizations interested in Communist infiltration. For example, on January 3, 1940, the Dies Committee singled out the United Office and Professional Workers of America as one of the "10 or 12 C.I.O. unions whose leadership is more than tinged with Communism."[48] Merrill reacted to the Committee's accusation by asserting that it offered "not one scrap of evidence to support this malicious allegation."[49]

Yet, even at that early date, the Committee had compiled sufficient evidence to make the charge stick. The union had entered upon what national C.I.O. would later call the 'Six Periods,' or changes of viewpoint corresponding to the policy of the Communist

[46]U.O.P.W.A., C.I.O., *Convention Proceedings* (Albany, N.Y., 1942), p. 218.

[47]*Ibid.*, Chicago, Ill., 1940, pp. 20-21.

[48]*The New York Times,* January 4, 1940, p. 1.

[49]*Ibid.*

Party for the United States.[50] While C.I.O.'s evaluation of the U.O.P.W.A. need not be examined here, it is necessary to consider the union's record, from other public sources, to show that the Dies Committee was not, in Merrill's phrase, "supporting a malicious allegation."

In the summer of 1941, for example, *Office and Professional News,* the union's official organ, carried the following comment:

> We see no justification for involving the United States in the international scramble for power and territory . . . . Our policy of national defense is trying to send the United States into war.[51]

And at the union's 1940 convention the delegates approved the C.I.O.'s position on peace and passed a resolution stating that the U.O.P.W.A. was "unalterably opposed to any involvement of the United States in the European War."[52] In November of 1940, the union's newspaper endorsed neither Roosevelt nor Wilkie; the editor accused Roosevelt of deserting "in recent years his program of progressive social and labor organization."[53] While many non-Communists espoused the same or similar sentiments, the record shows that the official union pronouncements on war and peace followed closely the official doctrine of the Communist Party.

This position caused Merrill some anxious moments at the 1940 convention of the C.I.O. When asked to answer specific questions about his union's Communist leanings, he said that the "U.O.P. W.A. would not tolerate the administration of the national or the local organizations by any clique."[54]

[50]*Official Reports of the Expulsion of Communist Dominated Organizations From the C.I.O.,* "United Office and Professional Workers of America," Washington, D.C., 1954, pp. 57 ff.

[51]*Office and Professional News,* July-August, 1940, p. 8.

[52]U.O.P.W.A., C.I.O., *Convention Proceedings* (Chicago, Ill., 1940), p. 90. The C.I.O. was itself having trouble with the Communists at this time and during subsequent years. cf. Max M. Kampelman, *The Communist Party vs. the C.I.O.: a Study in Power Politics,* (New York: Praeger, 1957), pp. 3-60.

[53]*Office and Professional News,* October, 1940, p. 4.

[54]*Ibid.,* November-December, 1940, p. 5. Although Merrill made his remarks at the C.I.O. convention, it is of interest that the U.O.P.W.A. newspaper reprinted part of the text. It seems fair to conclude that the leftists had not completely taken over the union at this time. It also seems correct to assert that Merrill was never completely taken in by the Communists, a point that will be made later in this work.

His words appear ambiguous, and his organization's future course did nothing to allay the suspicions of its critics. For example, published accounts indicate that in the summer of 1941, after Germany invaded the Soviet Union, the U.O.P.W.A. leadership made an immediate about-face in its estimation of American foreign policy. Merrill wrote a letter to his brother unionist, Rockwell Kent, the artist, expressing his profound sympathy for the Russian people. He went on to write: "I think the Soviet Union will prove a reliable ally and that American promises of aid should be promptly fulfilled."[55] Finally, in November 1941, Merrill laid down the challenge: "I stand for an immediate declaration of war against Germany and the opening of the Second Front."[56]

Merrill and the leadership of the United Office and Professional Workers played no variation of this theme until D-Day. For example, the August 1942 issue of the union newspaper carried the refrain: "Open that Second Front Now. *Now.* Why the fight for the Second Front is Labor's Front Now." The union continued to hammer away at the theme and culminated its efforts in the September 1942 issue of its newspaper by putting the question: "When will the Second Front be opened? This is the life and death question for all the United Nations."[57]

The union held a convention in September 1942 in Albany, New York, at which time the delegates were called upon to "Win the peoples' war." Hearing that American labor had sent greetings to Soviet and British labor, the convention assembled was asked to "guarantee to the people of India, Puerto Rico and other colonial peoples . . . their emancipation." Furthermore, the delegates were admonished that "the magnificent resistance of the Soviet Union had made possible the complete triumph of the United Nations."[58]

But the most "complete triumph of the United Nations" could occur only if the United States opened the "Second Front." The lyrics changed as time went on, but the theme remained the same.

[55]*Office and Professional News*, August, 1941, p. 6.

[56]*Ibid.*, November, 1941, p. 5.

[57]*Ibid.*, August, p. 1 & September 15, p. 4, (1942).

[58]U.O.P.W.A., C.I.O., *Convention Proceedings* (Albany, N.Y., 1942), p. 9.

For example, the left-wing members of the U.O.P.W.A.'s Local 16 dramatized the urgency of the Second Front in the words:

> Delay is perilous. The very victories which have created opportunities are being snatched back because we have not yet taken the offensive in Europe. Already this has cost us Kharkov . . . [and] permitted Hitler to transfer 15 divisions from Western Europe.[59]

In October 1943 the union newspaper reported a speech Merrill delivered before another U.O.P.W.A. affiliate, Local 19. He posed an interesting question and offered an equally interesting answer:

> Why do Churchill and Roosevelt, who are undoubtedly sincerely trying to conduct the war as a peoples' war, still delay the Second Front? They don't see it as a means of helping the Soviet Union, but regard the Second Front as correct strategy to insure our victory. [It becomes] more apparent every day as to why there is a delay in opening the Second Front . . . because we have not fully accepted or understood the possibility of partnership with the Soviet Union . . . . [We have] failed to grasp the might of Russia's fighting power.[60]

This same issue carried the headline: "Your War, Your Wages and the Second Front!" And in the same issue again, Merrill made reference to the presence of Russian warships in New York harbor during the Civil War which, he wrote, "meant the difference between defeat and victory for the United States." He discussed in his column, "In My Opinion," the supposed Anglo-American distrust of the Soviet Union and offered the following advice:

> We need a strong Soviet Union. If the Soviet Union is our friend we want her strong; if we want a stable world, a world without war, one vital to the national interests of the United States, then we want those powers strong whose national interests also need a stable world — a world without war. The Soviet Union is that kind of country.[61]

In response to his critics, he mentioned further that he had "no objection to being known as a friend of the Soviet Union, but it is not from such a spirit that I urge a firm cementing of U.S. relations. This friendship is for our own good."[62]

[59]*Office and Professional News,* April, 1943, p. 2.
[60]*Ibid.,* October, 1943, p. 4.
[61]*Ibid.,* September, 1943, p. 8.
[62]*Ibid.,* February, 1944, p. 1.

When the suspicion between the Western allies and Russia was alleviated at Tehran, the U.O.P.W.A. leadership was ecstatic, and the union newspaper reported that Merrill, who had recently testified before a Senate subcommittee on white collar employees' salaries, told the Senators: "Hitch Salaries to the Tehran Goal." Later in 1943 he wrote: "Our personal future and the future of our country for decades to come will be shaped by what is done to fulfill the Tehran decision." And in his column, he explained his ideology; he wrote:

> I am not a Communist . . . but one has a right in the United States of America to be anything from a theosophist to a Catholic, from a Townsendite to a Republican — or anything else he cares to invent. We don't judge people by labels. We're too practical for that. We judge them by what they do in fact.[63]

Naturally, his philosophy did not extend to membership in the Nazi party. He went on to assure his readers that Roosevelt was not a Communist "but worked with one at Tehran . . . for world peace." He concluded his profession of faith by observing:

> If we fail to acknowledge that American rights include the rights of being a Communist, we play into the hands of our native fascists, the quintessence of American reaction.[64]

In his keynote address to the U.O.P.W.A.'s 1944 convention Merrill grew eloquent. He said: "Any day now we will read of the launching of a simultaneous offensive that will destroy the Fascist beast."[65] And Merrill went on to re-election. The delegates also re-elected John Stanley in absentia to the post of secretary treasurer. Stanley had succeeded to the position in 1940 and at the time of the 1944 convention was in the armed forces.

REACTION SETS IN

It was a well known fact, in and out of labor circles, that the officials of the United Office and Professional Workers of America were promoting Communist ideology. Legally nothing could be done about it. If the national and state labor boards certified the

[63]*Ibid.*, January, p. 1 & June, p. 12, (1944).

[64]*Ibid.*, June, 1944, p. 12.

[65]U.O.P.W.A., C.I.O., *Convention Proceedings* (Philadelphia, Pa., 1944), p. 10.

union's insurance locals, for example, the companies had no choice but to bargain, although these same companies set up monumental road blocks to the bargaining process. To many, the conflict simply remained nothing more than a sparring match between a later day David and Goliath.

But the question remained: did the companies initially reject labor unionism because of the Communist issue? Certain published sources indicate that Communism was a primary reason for the companies' intransigence. For instance, O. W. G. Marquard, president of the Workingmen's Cooperative Association, told a union member that he would never recognize a "Communist organization."[66] And in 1938, when Local 30, U.O.P.W.A., was trying to win the certification election at Metropolitan, one manager was quoted as telling an agent: "If you want a promotion, you'll never get it while you're in that red union."[67]

The position of the Industrial and Ordinary Insurance Agents Council, vis-à-vis the question of Communist control, is difficult to evaluate. The A.F. of L. had had its fill of the office workers' during the 1920's and 1930's. It was pressured by events to grant federal local charters to groups of insurance men who exploited the Communist issue in competing with C.I.O.'s United Office and Professional Workers union. How far the A.F. of L. carried the crusade is a matter of conjecture, especially when the Federation's locals had internal problems of their own to contend with. George Russ, president of the Industrial and Ordinary Insurance Agents' Council, A.F. of L., stated bluntly that the organization did not have a "whole lot of money . . . . For every dollar we give an organizer the A.F. of L. also puts one up."[68] So, the Agents' Council was as much concerned with its own stability as it was with the U.O.P.W.A.'s alleged Communist domination. It was neither the A.F. of L. nor the companies, however, that played any great role in exposing and ultimately defeating the U.O.P.W.A. leadership. Rather, there were rumblings of dissatisfaction within the union's insurance division. In Philadelphia, for example, an insurance local erupted over the Red

[66]*Workingmens' Cooperative Assoc.*, 1 S.L.R.B. 60 (1938).

[67]*U.O.P.W.A. News*, March, 1939, p. 3.

[68]I.O.I.A.C., A.F. of L., *Report of the National 1945 Conference* (Washington, D.C., 1945), pp. 96, 98, 128-29, 138-40, 141, & 153.

issue.[69] But there was an even more dramatic house cleaning in Boston. On January 19, 1943, the U.O.P.W.A. leadership of Local 41 "voted unanimously to put on trial ten Hancock agents who disrupted the union and for attempting to establish an independent union." The group called itself the National Industrial Insurance Agents' Union and defeated the U.O.P.W.A. local in a Hancock election by a vote of 232 to 189. It was only after this election that Hancock decided to negotiate with the Boston area agents, and the U.O.P.W.A., after all its efforts at winning a contract from the company, was in no mood to be superseded by a rebellious local of its former agents. James Durkin, who had been put in charge of the election campaign and of the "trial" that followed, asserted that the independent was "company backed and supported." He attempted to justify his remarks by stating that the U.O.P.W.A. lost, either because many of the agents who voted were new to the business or had always opposed the union. His words are revealing:

> The independent won by about 100 votes from former members of Local 41. These votes came from two groups: a small group of splitters and disrupters, enemies of the U.O.P.W.A. win the war program, who have a long record of trying to obstruct union progress. The other group is made up of those who have been misled by promises and the propaganda of the disrupters.[70]

The union's newspaper took note of the fact that the National Industrial Insurance Agents' Union, A.F. of L., had called the C.I.O. "red," and that Ralph Dowling, an officer of the Boston Independent, was heard to say: "A vote for the C.I.O. is a vote for Loyalist Spain. Don't vote C.I.O."

During the same year, the U.O.P.W.A. lost an election in the Boston offices of the Metropolitan Life Insurance Company, an especially bitter defeat because the union lost by one vote. In his comments on the defeat, Lewis Merrill wrote:

> If U.O.P.W.A. had not been bedeviled with a running fight with company-aided, anti-war elements they would have won. But that is just the point. These are the very places we *must* win if we are to do our job for our country. It is a fact that it was this *kind* of operation that made us lose that proves our

[69]Supra, footnote no. 23.

[70]*Office and Professional News,* February, p. 2 & April, p. 3, (1943).

fundamental policy . . . should never have been departed from.[71]

The reaction to the U.O.P.W.A. leadership by the New York agents was somewhat different. In 1940, Local 30 had a membership of 880, and by 1942 the membership had increased to approximately two thousand. Former agent members of the Local were active among these men, portraying the union in the worst possible light. But their efforts were hampered by the spirit of the war and they had little money to spend on organizational activity.[72]

[71]*Ibid.,* November, 1943, p. 6.

[72]I.O.I.A.C., A.F. of L., *Report of* 1945 *Conference,* p. 266.

CHAPTER 4

WHEN IS A VICTORY NOT A VICTORY?

While officials of the United Office and Professional Workers of America were facing internal and external challenges caused by the Communist and other issues, the leaders of the union's insurance division were moving ahead on economic and legal fronts. It is possible that their ideology determined their approach to economic and legal problems, although such a conclusion is difficult to prove. On the basis of the record, the U.O.P.W.A. leadership accomplished a good deal in the areas of agent compensation, union security and judicial decree, all of which were beneficial to the debit men.

It is important, of course, to consider the Office Workers' achievement within its proper context. The Industrial and Ordinary Insurance Agents Council, A.F. of L., as well as the independent International Union of Life Insurance Agents, were at work simultaneously on the same or similar goals. It must also be noted that the U.O.P.W.A. quite often hitched its wagon to the star of a legislative body or private group that was totally unconnected with organized labor, or at least to the aims of the union. The end product of this manifold activity was satisfying to the union's leaders, regardless of the means whereby a particular goal was achieved.

This chapter, then, will deal in part with the economic, legislative and judicial gains the United Office and Professional Workers' won, or shared with other organizations. The record is impressive. In their own way, the leaders of the union fought tirelessly for America's debit insurance agents and other white collar employees. They did not achieve all they wanted, yet they accomplished a good deal.

That they ultimately failed to sustain this effort is due as much to their lack of vision in the adaptability of American capitalism as to their miscalculation of the American workers' reaction to change. This was indeed unfortunate, for the leaders of the U.O.P.W.A. could, in all justice, pronounce their work successful; a small union had ventured into areas where there was no precedent and quite often came out with rewards that would have been unthinkable a few years before.

72

Yet most of these same leaders persevered to the end in a single-minded purpose, a goal that denied the union the degree of respectability it required to sell itself and to survive. This chapter will, therefore, conclude with a description of the rumblings on the "right" that will ultimately spell the doom of the United Office and Professional Workers of America.

During the middle 1940's, the union devised a number of assaults on the strongholds of the insurance industry. Among items considered negotiable, the union leaders wanted an improved grievance procedure with all the companies under contract. The union's president, Lewis Merrill, defined a grievance "as anything that bothers the agents."[1] His clinical approach was scarcely appreciated by industry management, and nothing was achieved in this regard. But the union did obtain lesser results in the grievance clause of its contracts. For example, it achieved an especially rewarding concession from Metropolitan; the company agreed to extend the conference period from seven to fourteen days and to permit the aggrieved party the use of an arbitrator.[2]

The union shop was another provision sought by the U.O.P.W.A. It never scored any success with either Prudential or Metropolitan in this demand, but the union did acquire a partial victory in Hancock.[3] Prior to this event, the union sustained a crushing blow to its Hancock membership in the Boston area, a point already mentioned. Because of the Communist issue, many of the agents separated from the U.O.P.W.A.'s local and formed an independent association, the National Insurance Agents' Union. In 1943 the group won a Massachusetts' Labor Board election, and shortly thereafter the agents affiliated to the A.F. of L. local in the city.[4]

[1] *Office and Professional News*, December, 1945, p. 3.

[2] *Insurance Career*, May, 1946, p. 17.

[3] Strange to say, the Metropolitan negotiated a maintenance-of-membership clause with the A.F. of L. insurance local in Maryland. The company insisted, however, that "failure to preserve good standing membership" be the subject of arbitration. cf. *Agreement between the Metropolitan Life Ins. Co. and the American Federation of Industrial and Ordinary Agents' Union*, #23322, affiliated with the A.F. of L., March 17, 1944.

[4] *John Hancock Mutual Life Ins. Co.*, Commonwealth of Mass., Before the Labor Relations Commission, Case no. CR 698; & *Hancock*, 57 N.L.R.B. 700 (1944).

The U.O.P.W.A. leaders could not tolerate the defection. They planned to regain the Boston Hancock membership by obtaining a state-wide election in Massachusetts. If the union could win the election, they reasoned, the Boston agents would have to capitulate.

However, the Industrial and Ordinary Insurance Agents' Council, A.F. of L., sought to increase its Hancock membership and petitioned the New York Board for a state-wide election among Hancock agents in New York State. While the Board heard the case, union and company officials instructed the American Arbitration Association to poll the agents. The Association conducted the survey, and the U.O.P.W.A. leaders took heart. Over three thousand men manifested the desire to remain within the union, and only nine hundred agents voted against labor representation.[5]

The A.F. of L. Insurance Council promptly filed an unfair labor practice charge against Hancock for its use of the American Arbitration Association. The Board denied the charge but asserted that in the future such an action "could be considered an unfair labor practice." The New York Board also refused the Council's request for a state-wide election; the union was unable to show a "substantial interest" in the state's Hancock agents.[6]

On the basis of the results of the American Arbitration Association's poll, Hancock negotiated a national contract with the U.O.P.W.A. The contract provided for a modified form of the union shop which granted any agent who was unwilling to join the union the right to have his initiation fees and monthly dues sent to "any national charity selected in the sole discretion of the Company."[7]

[5] *Office and Professional News,* March, 1945, p. 1.

[6] *John Hancock Mutual Life Ins. Co.,* 8 S.L.R.B. 24 (1945). In commenting on the situation, a New York City A.F. of L. insurance agent asserted: "A year ago, our union had a chance to capture or to organize most of these men . . . and they were willing to come along with us. But we didn't have enough backing." cf. *National* 1945 *Conference,* I.O.I.A.C., A.F. of L., p. 261.

[7] *Agreement between the John Hancock Mutual Life Ins. Co. and the United Office and Professional Workers of America, C.I.O.,* March, 1945, art. 3. The union also had various forms of union shop agreements with such firms as the Golden Eagle, Kenton and Campbell Associates and the Boston Mutual Life Ins. Co. cf. *Insurance Career,* May, 1946, p. 5.

As for the Boston Hancock agents, the U.O.P.W.A. defeated the A.F. of L. Insurance Council in an election conducted by the Massachusetts Labor Board in April 1945. These men therefore came under the modified form of union shop agreement.

Negotiating with Metropolitan

While the U.O.P.W.A. signed an agreement with the Metropolitan Life Insurance Company for its Greater New York members in the spring of 1942, the union did not achieve a multi-state contract with the company until 1945. Early in that year, contract negotiations for a "nation-wide" settlement with company officials broke down, and the Metropolitan subsequently sent a letter to its agents in the eight states in which the union had won certification elections.[8] According to a union news item, the company wanted to know whether the debit men desired an automatic deduction of dues. When the agents replied in the affirmative, the company signed an agreement with the union. Extremely simple in content, the pact contained two main provisions: a grievance clause and dues deduction.[9]

The new contract contained an unusual feature. Each time it was re-opened or came up for renewal the company demanded that the union bargain on a state by state basis. This undoubtedly caused union officials an enormous amount of work, particularly since the organization's major contracts with insurance companies all expired around the same time.

Once the union had signed with Metropolitan, it added the company's agencies in Ohio and Indiana to its membership roster. The U.O.P.W.A. also attempted to enroll company agents in California, Kentucky, Colorado, Florida, Washington and Upstate New York, but in none of these areas did the debit agents want union representation. In commenting on the loss of these states, Leon W. Berney, director of the union's insurance division, made the following observation:

These recent events prove that basically the non-union agents are convinced at this time, at least, when favorable economic

[8]By 1945, U.O.P.W.A. represented the Metropolitan agents in Greater New York, New Jersey, Pennsylvania, Massachusetts, Connecticut, Michigan, Rhode Island and Missouri.

[9]*Office and Professional News*, April, 1945, p. 1.

conditions are providing high salaries, that the companies can be relied upon to provide them with a high standard of living and security. But this is unrealistic.[10]

In spite of these lost elections, the union leaders could take encouragement from one development: Canadian locals began to seek reaffiliation. In June 1944 the union granted a charter to a group of agents in Vancouver, British Columbia, and in the following January, the agents won elections in Metropolitan and Prudential district offices in that city. By 1946, the union had locals in such cities as Toronto, Montreal, Quebec and Winnipeg. Moreover, at the time of its 1948 convention, all of the Prudential agents in the Province of Quebec were represented by the union.[11]

AN ADDITIONAL NOTE ON COMPENSATION

In January 1945 the United Office and Professional Workers' petitioned the National War Labor Board to grant the Hancock agents an immediate $5.00 weekly increase, part of which was to consist of a higher commission on monthly intermediate insurance. The union argued that the adjustment was necessary to bring Hancock agents' salaries into line with those paid by Prudential and Metropolitan, and that such an increase accorded with the "Little Steel Formula." On August 7 a Board panel granted the debit men an increase of only seventy-seven cents per week, which, in addition to the forty-eight cents it had previously granted, brought the weekly gain up to $1.25.

The union protested the award but had no choice in the matter. The $1.25 was to remain in effect, the decision read, until such time as New York amended its Insurance Law to provide a six and one-half per cent commission on monthly intermediate insurance. It should be noted that at the time the law allowed a commission of four and one-half per cent on this type of policy.

The panel further demanded that the company institute a back pay settlement, retroactive to January 1, 1945, the date on which the union had petitioned for the increase. Hancock abided by the Board's decision and granted the increase and the back pay.[12]

[10]*Ibid.*, August, 1948, pp. 1-2; & May, 1946, pp. 2 & 8.

[11]U.O.P.W.A., C.I.O., *Convention Proceedings* (Brooklyn, N.Y., 1948), p. 30. The union had dropped the Canadian affiliates in 1940.

[12]*John Hancock Mutual Life Ins. Co.*, National War Labor Board, No. 111-13503-D.

Metropolitan's acceptance of a War Labor Board decree was another matter altogether. In a case dating back to 1942, the Board had ordered the company to increase its agents' salaries, and the company so acted. Moreover, the Board required that the company grant its agents a back pay claim. This Metropolitan refused to do, and the case dragged through the courts. The dispute reached its final stage, or so the U.O.P.W.A. leaders believed, in December 1945, when both company and union presented briefs before the U.S. Federal Court, Southern District, New York.

Company counsel argued inability to pay because of the restrictions of the New York Law. The U.O.P.W.A.'s attorney questioned the power of the New York Insurance Department in the light of the recent United States Supreme Court decision in the *South-Eastern Underwriters'* case. He also reminded Metropolitan that Hancock had initially refused to award its agents a back pay settlement and had so acted out of fear of the New York Insurance Department.

In rebuttal, Metropolitan's counsel contended that the high court's decision in *South-Eastern Underwriters'* preserved for the states the right to continue to regulate the insurance industry. He pointed to the recently enacted *McCarran Act* as verification of his opinion and, more importantly, as vindication of his company's decision.[13]

On June 3, 1946, the court decided the case in favor of the U.O.P.W.A. and ordered the company to grant the retroactive pay.[14] However, the company refused and persisted in its refusal right up to the time of the union's expulsion from the C.I.O.[15]

[13]*Office and Professional News,* January, 1946, p. 3.

[14]*Ibid.,* August, 1946, p. 2.

[15]Not content with the court's decision, the Metropolitan instituted proceedings in the New York courts. Finally, on February 24, 1950, the Appellate Division of the New York Supreme Court upheld the state Supreme Court's decision in ruling against Metropolitan. cf. *The Metropolitan Life Ins. Co. v. James Durkin,* 276 App. Div. 394. The company appealed this decision to the state's highest tribunal and was again told, on July 11, 1950, to award the retroactive pay. cf. *The Metropolitan Life Ins. Co. v. James Durkin,* 301 N.Y. 376. Further appeal was necessary to determine the length of time the dispute covered, and the Court of Appeals of the State of New York clarified the issue. The court decided that Metropolitan would have to pay its agents for a period covering October 24, 1942, to September 18, 1944. The court also ruled that Metropolitan would have to pay withholding taxes on the award. On this basis the sum increased from about $800,000.00 to over $1,000,000.00.

Metropolitan's contention that the states should regulate insurance poses a question that had long puzzled legal experts. It has already been noted that New York, for all practical purposes, controlled the selling of industrial life insurance in the United States. Because of the Armstrong Investigation and frequent checks on the industry, New York had come to occupy a place of eminence in the field. The State's Insurance Department handed down regulations that were respected by the other states, although at times they were not fully appreciated.[16]

Since New York had such a large market, and since "foreign" companies like Prudential and Hancock wanted to preserve their operation in this market, the state required that they conform their selling in every state to New York Law. When the sales of Metropolitan Life, a New York based firm, are added to those of Prudential and Hancock, it can be seen that the power of control of New York is enormous.

Yet, it may be asked why one state should possess an abundance of power in one area of business, and why the federal government should regulate industry of an interstate nature in all others. Granted that the national government began to regulate interstate business only in 1937, why should the U.S. Supreme Court have chosen to overlook the insurance industry?

These and other questions vexed the minds of the legal experts. More importantly, they bothered the leaders of the small insurance unions, and they wanted answers.

Is Insurance Interstate Commerce?

The Court of Appeals of the State of New York ruled that agents were 'employes' in a case involving Local 30, U.O.P.W.A., and the Metropolitan Life Insurance Company. The court handed down its decision on the basis of the "due process" clause of the state's constitution. While granting the absence of a "commerce clause" in New York's constitution, the court decreed that "due process for us

16cf. U.S. Cong., *T.N.E.C. Hearings,* Part 12. As a case in point, high officials of the Metropolitan and Prudential objected to New York's prohibition on the sale of industrial endowment policies in the state. However, both firms, along with John Hancock, abided by the decision of the New York Insurance Department, pp. 5892 & 5903. Originally this prohibition extended to the other states as well. Because of complaints the provision was amended to apply to New York exclusively.

is the same due process to which the Federal Congress is subject when it exercises its commerce clause."[17] Since the decision was applicable only to New York, companies not operating in the state were able to refuse recognition to insurance unions on the grounds that insurance was not interstate commerce.

This point was made perfectly clear in a number of cases involving insurance firms and insurance unions. For example, in 1939 an A.F. of L. insurance local argued before the N.L.R.B. that a dispute existed between its members and the Washington branch of the Sun Life Insurance Company of America. The company pleaded that it was not engaged in interstate commerce and was therefore outside the jurisdiction of the Board. The Board disagreed and found that a question of commerce had arisen. Its decision reads in part:

> The operation of the company has a close, intimate and substantial relation to trade, traffic and commerce within the District of Columbia and tends to lead to labor disputes burdening and obstructing commerce and the free flow of commerce.[18]

The Board ordered an election. The A.F. of L. local won, but the company refused to recognize the union, insisting that it was not engaged in interstate commerce.

Identical cases arose involving the A.F. of L. Insurance Council, with the Home Beneficial Association of Richmond, Virginia, and the Equitable Life Insurance Co. in Washington. In each of these instances the companies were found to be engaged in interstate commerce by the Board, and each firm protested that it was not.[19] Since the interstate issue was still open, the Board's scope of operations was necessarily limited.

In denying the N.L.R.B.'s jurisdiction insurance firms had a precedent. In 1869, the Supreme Court of the United States in *Paul v. Virginia* declared that insurance companies did not engage in interstate commerce. Samuel Paul, an agent for several New York groups, sold insurance in Virginia without first purchasing a license, an action that violated the state statute which regulated 'foreign'

[17]*The Metropolitan Life Ins. Co.,* 280 N.Y. 194 (1939).

[18]*Sun Life Insurance Co.,* 15 N.L.R.B. 817 (1939).

[19]*Home Beneficial Association,* 17 N.L.R.B. 37 (1940); & *Equitable Life Ins. Co.,* 21 N.L.R.B. 37 (1940).

insurance companies. He was fined $50.00 in a circuit court of the Commonwealth. The case was reviewed by the United States Supreme Court.

Paul maintained that the Virginia licensing law was invalid by reason of its "discriminating provisions between her corporations and the corporations of other States," and that in this instance the Virginia law was in conflict with the "commerce clause" of the federal Constitution. However, the court upheld the Virginia statute and unanimously agreed that the law did not offend the commerce clause, because "issuing a policy of insurance is not a transaction of commerce."[20]

In a series of cases spanning the next seventy-five years, the Supreme Court upheld the 1869 decision; these involved the supervision and control of companies, the regulation of insurance rates and the compensation of insurance agents.[21]

On June 5, 1944, the high court seemingly reversed its long-standing rule on insurance companies. The majority of the court decreed that insurance firms are subject to the jurisdiction of the National Labor Relations Board and that companies conducting interstate business are liable to anti-trust prosecution. Interestingly enough, the insurance unions were not directly involved in either of the court's decisions. For in the ruling pertaining to the N.L.R.B., it was the Office Employees International Council, A.F. of L., that was directly responsible for having the case heard by the court.[22] In 1942, members of the Council struck the Chicago offices of the National Polish Alliance of the United States of North America, and the National Labor Board intervened. The Board eventually settled

[20]*Paul V. Virginia,* 8 Wall. 168 (1869).

[21]cf. *LaTourette v. McMaster,* 248 U.S. 465 (1919); *Stipcich v. Metropolitan Life Ins. Co.,* 277 U.S. 311, 320 (1928). These are cases exemplifying the "relations generally of those engaged in the insurance business." cf. also, *German Alliance Ins. Co. v. Lewis,* 233 U.S. 389 (1914), which is an example of the fact that insurance is subject to "supervision and control." cf. also, *O'Gorman & Young v. Hartford Fire Insurance Co.,* 282 U.S. 251 (1931). All of these cases are cited in Edward S. Corwin, (ed.), *The Constitution of the United States (Annotated)* (Washington: U.S. Government Printing Office, 1953), p. 1021.

[22]*Polish National Alliance of the United States of North America,* 42 N.L.R.B. 1375 (1942).

the dispute by ordering the company, a fraternal organization, to re-instate certain of the workers it had discharged, to cease discouraging membership in the Council and to bargain with its office workers. The firm rehired the discharged employees and ceased to discourage membership in the union, but it refused to bargain on the grounds that it was not a business engaged in interstate commerce. The N.L.R.B., therefore, appealed the case to the Supreme Court, which ruled in favor of the Board.[23]

In the second instance, *United States v. South-Eastern Underwriters' Association,* the Supreme Court by a four to three decision ruled that insurance companies were subject to the anti-trust laws of the United States. Writing the majority opinion, Justice Hugo Black asserted that insurance is a business in which there is a "continuous and indivisible stream of intercourse among the states composed of collections of premiums, payments of policy obligations . . . " and the like. Justice Black went on to write that since insurance is interstate commerce in every sense of the term, it must fall under the "commerce clause" of the Constitution. He concluded by saying: "We cannot make an exception of the business of insurance."[24]

Neither decision positively ruled on the question of interstate commerce. In *Polish National Alliance* the court determined that the insurance industry was subject to the N.L.R.B., and in *South-Eastern Underwriters'* the court asserted that insurance companies were liable to prosecution under the anti-trust laws of the country. It has been observed that Justice Black's understanding of the commerce clause is one which "does not of itself appropriate anything exclusively to the national government — except possibly the duty to see to it that state laws do not discriminate against interstate commerce."[25]

The *South-Eastern Underwriters'* decision in particular led to

[23]*Polish National Alliance* v. *N.L.R.B.,* 322 U.S. 643 (1944).

[24]*United States* v. *South-Eastern Underwriters' Assn.,* 322 U.S. 533 (1944). The defendant association and its membership of nearly three hundred private stock fire insurance companies and twenty-seven individuals were indicted for alleged violation of the Sherman Anti-Trust Act.

[25]Alpheus T. Mason and William M. Beaney, *American Constitutional Law: Introductory Essays and Selected Cases,* (Englewood Cliffs: Prentice-Hall, 1954), p. 189.

much misinterpretation. In an effort to clarify the issue the United States Congress in 1945 passed into law the *McCarran Act,* which permitted the states the right to continue regulating insurance companies. The Act reads in part:

> The Congress hereby declares that the continued regulation and taxation by the several states of the business of insurance is in the public interest, and that silence on the part of the Congress shall not be construed to impose any barrier to the regulation or taxation of such business by the several states.[26]

But the federal congress did not surrender its authority completely. By adding a three year moratorium to the implementation of the Act, the congress specified that if after this period of time the states did not comply with the provisions of the Act then the Sherman Act would be effectuated where needed.[27] Congress intended that the Supreme Court's decision in *South-Eastern Underwriters'* be brought to bear on the insurance companies.

In 1946, the Supreme Court declared on the constitutionality of the *McCarran Act* in a case involving the Prudential Insurance Company of America. The court upheld the Act, and its decision reads in part:

> Congress' purpose was broadly to give support to the existing and future State systems for regulating and taxing the business of insurance. This was done in two ways. One was by removing obstructions which might be thought to flow from its own power, whether dormant or exercised, except as otherwise provided in the Act itself or in future legislation. The other was by declaring expressly and affirmatively that continued State regulation and taxation of this business was in the public interest and that the business and all who engage in it 'shall be subject to' the laws of the several States in these respects.[28]

The *McCarran Act* has served as a guidepost for the insurance industry. Since its enactment and subsequent court ruling, the companies have remained under the jurisdiction of the individual states

[26]U.S. 59 *Stat.* 33 (1945).

[27]*Ibid.*

[28]*Prudential Life Ins. Co.* v. *Benjamin,* 328 U.S. 408 66 S. Ct. 1142, 90 L. Ed. (1946). The state of South Carolina imposed a three per cent tax on a 'foreign' insurance company, while permitting local companies to remain tax free.

in which they operate. However, the insurance industry is still subject to the Supreme Court's decisions in the *Polish National Alliance* and *South-Eastern Underwriters'* cases.

In practice, two of the "Big Three" firms, Prudential and John Hancock, were using the services of the N.L.R.B. prior to the 1944 decisions of the Supreme Court.

As time went on the insurance labor organizations referred to both decisions in attempting to bring about improvements they considered necessary for the well-being of the agents. Yet, it is difficult to assess the full weight of these decisions with regard to labor union activity. When labor lawyers attempted to plead a case before a legislative body, they never failed to include a reference to *South-Eastern Underwriters'*, particularly. If the reference convinced the legislators, its use might be held beneficial to the agents. Like the federal interpretation itself, the labor union's success in using the Supreme Court decision remains cloudy.

Organized labor had other issues to contend with, and it is these that must now be developed.

POSTWAR ECONOMICS

Like many persons, in and out of the trade union movement, the officials of the United Office and Professional Workers of America forecast an economic depression of gigantic proportions at the end of World War II. With special emphasis on the insurance industry, a spokesman for the union's insurance division predicted that insurance sales would decline sharply in the years ahead. He put it this way:

> I am sure you are as aware as we are of the dangers of a large volume of lapses, and the decrease in the number of prospects for new insurance, that may result from the dislocation and loss of jobs, resulting from the cutback and the slowness of reconversion of war industry to peace time production.[29]

To remedy the anticipated downward cycle he advocated a novel approach. He proposed that welfare agencies include the payment of insurance premiums in their welfare budgets.

Lewis Merrill addressed himself to a more readily attainable goal. He told a group of delegates to an insurance division conference that the U.O.P.W.A. must achieve an increase in monthly commission

[29]*Office and Professional News,* July, 1945, p. 3.

rates for its agent members, for they would be, Merrill believed, among the prime losers in the forthcoming economic depression. He admitted that such a contractual gain had to be realized in the absence of the National War Labor Board and that the union faced opposition from the companies and from a too rigorous interpretation of the New York Insurance Law.[30]

It has already been mentioned that New York increased the commission on monthly intermediate insurance in 1946.[31] Since it was by selling this type of insurance that U.O.P.W.A. officials hoped to get the agents through the postwar depression, a more detailed account of the union's efforts at increasing the commission seems in order.

In 1939, New York had amended its Insurance Law, thereby granting the companies permission to pay a renewal commission, or collection fee, of four and one-half per cent on monthly intermediate insurance. Between 1940 and 1945 the leadership of the U.O.P.W.A. had attempted to influence New York's lawmakers to amend the law a second time; they proposed that the commission be increased to six and one-half per cent. Every effort ended in failure.[32]

When the Second World War ended, the union's leaders redoubled their efforts and they found an unexpected ally. The Prudential supported the increased commission. A union newspaper report quoted Valentine Howell, a vice president and actuary of the company, as saying:

> Our agents believe that the 4 and one-half per cent collection commission for monthly policies is out of line as compared with the 12 per cent commission on weekly policies. Their natural reaction is to sell weekly policies, where, in fact, the insured would be better off with monthly policies.[33]

The union leaders soon began to use Howell's statement as an endorsement; they also said that Hancock, a one-time opponent of the increase, was in favor of the higher commission rate.

[30]*Ibid.*, December, 1945, p. 3.

[31]"Monthly intermediate insurance" is a form of life insurance, written by an industrial agent who collects monthly premiums at the home of the insured. It is issued in amounts of less than $1,000.00.

[32]*Insurance Career,* January, 1946, p. 14.

[33]*Ibid.,* February, 1946, p. 4.

In January 1946 Senator William F. Condon and Assemblyman Robert F. Crews introduced into the New York State Legislature a bill that would increase the commission on monthly intermediate insurance to six and one-half per cent. Again, it is impossible to know how much influence the U.O.P.W.A. leaders had on the New York legislators. But the bill was introduced, and that was all they cared about.

The lines of battle on the amendment became clearly identifiable. On one side, the U.O.P.W.A., along with the A.F. of L. Insurance Council, Prudential, Hancock and the New York Councils of the C.I.O. and the A.F. of L., favored passage of the bill. In opposition were the New York Insurance Department and the Metropolitan Life Insurance Company. According to one union source, the U.O.P.W.A. had an edge over the Metropolitan, for the union leaders were able to anticipate the company's defense. They had obtained "a secretly prepared Metropolitan memorandum against the bill and rebutted everything" before the apparently speechless attorneys of the company.[34] For its part, the New York Insurance Department rejected the amendment on grounds that are rather complicated and that go beyond the scope of this work.

The Condon-Crews' bill was enacted and signed on April 6, 1946, and the pertinent section of the amendment reads as follows:

> Renewal commissions, or collection fees, after the first of the year, may be paid for the duration of such policies to the collection agent in an amount not exceeding 6 and one-half per cent of the renewal premiums.[35]

To the depression-minded U.O.P.W.A. officials this was a victory of great significance. Even though the "Big Three" companies did non grant their agents the full commission, union leaders emphasized their role in securing the amendment to the New York Law.

In line with the increased commission on monthly intermediate, the union officials proposed still another plan. They called it "Depression Insurance." Toward the end of 1946, James Durkin, a member of the union's executive board, developed the idea of a $50.00 minimum guarantee for service of the weekly debit and a

[34]*Ibid.*, April, 1946, p. 2; & *Office and Professional News*, April, 1946, p. 2.

[35]*Laws* of the State of New York. Passed at the 169th Sess. of the Legisl., Insurance Law, para. 213, subdiv. 13, amended, Chapter 555, pp. 1196-197.

$10.00 across the board increase. Looking for something more suitable than the term, "Depression Insurance," Durkin coined the phrase "50 and 10."[36]

Although Durkin and other officials of the union acknowledged that the agents were averaging more than $50.00 per week, they said that the uncertain state of the nation's economy suggested the guaranteed minimum wage. They also proposed the $10.00 increase because of what they called the widening gap between the average earnings of the agents and the cost of maintaining a decent standard of living. On March 14, 1947, the U.O.P.W.A. delivered an ultimatum to the "Big Three" companies: either they grant the "50 and 10" or the agents would go out on strike.[37]

The insurance companies were ready to call the union's bluff, however. In the first place, the union could not support a strike against any of the large companies. Secondly, and more importantly, industry management knew that the U.O.P.W.A. was passing through an administrative crisis. Although he was still president of the union, Lewis Merrill had been strangely quiet for the past several months. The union's ultimatum might very well have been an attempt to allay the agents' suspicion. The U.O.P.W.A. continued to press its slogan, but to no avail. Office managers did not even notice those agents who were wearing "50 and 10" buttons. Upon questioning his manager, one Prudential agent was told that the only way the men could obtain a remedy was to improve their production.

John Hancock made a token effort to placate the union. In August 1947 union officials conferred with company management. Leon W. Berney, director of the union's insurance division, told Hancock representatives that the "cost of operating a debit and doing business had practically doubled in the last twelve months." In reply a Hancock vice president, Olin Anderson, was quoted as saying that his company planned to adjust the first year commission. According to Berney, Hancock's revaluation of the commission would bring a "net increase of from $20.00 to $60.00 per year per agent." The union accepted the company's offer, but made it clear

[36]*Office and Professional News,* February, 1947, p. 3.

[37]*The New York Times,* March 15, 1947, p. 8.

that the proposal had nothing to do with "50 and 10"[38]

Meanwhile, the U.O.P.W.A. had authorized numerous strike votes, a tactic that proved embarrassing to the union's leaders. They did not want to admit publicly that the companies would never grant the "50 and 10," nor did they want the agents to think that the union was losing its militant spirit. Accordingly, the leadership chose to ignore the strike authorizations, although they continued to preach the merits of "50 and 10."

A RESOLUTE "SMALLER" COMPANY

While U.O.P.W.A. officialdom tried to convince the insurance agents of the wisdom of its postwar economic policy, the union was undergoing a radical change. The New York agents who had defected to the A.F. of L. over the T.N.E.C. affair and who were partially responsible for the union's defeat in the Prudential election in Ohio were using their influence to convince the loyal insurance agents of the union's left-wing domination. A charge of Communist infiltration during the war could be readily denied, but, when the conflict ended and the union adopted the anti-American line of the Soviet Union, the charge became much more serious and was not so easily dismissed. Besides, the sudden disappearance of Lewis Merrill, the union's president, caused many of the agents to wonder about the internal state of their organization. Merrill's leave taking will not be chronicled here, but his absence from the union during the postwar period only intensified the struggle that would culminate in the union's downfall.

One of the most dramatic chapters in the history of the U.O.P.W.A. arose out of a dispute with a smaller firm, the Monumental Life Insurance Company.[39] When the battle was fought, the union was entering the last phase of its existence. Throughout the struggle Monumental's management adopted an unsophisticated approach

[38]*Office and Professional News,* September, 1947, p. 8. In fact, both Hancock and Prudential revised the commission upward by about one per cent. cf. U.O.P.W.A., C.I.O., *Convention Proceedings* (Brooklyn, N.Y., 1948), p. 13.

[39]The company was incorporated under the laws of Maryland in 1858 as the Mutual Life Insurance Co. of Baltimore. Prior to 1938 the Monumental had operated on a mutual basis. At that time it acquired capital stock. In July 1935 the company changed its name to its present designation. cf. Moody's, *op. cit.,* 1958, p. 35.

to the insurance labor-management relationship, a field in which precedent, if nothing else, urged a degree of tact that was lacking in company officials. Monumental Life was not dealing with a fledgling labor organization, and its officials should have known that certain practices would never be upheld by the National Labor Relations Board. But the U.O.P.W.A. leadership in turn developed an unwise policy toward Monumental management. A more enlightened group would have realized that a bad internal situation made its organization open to attack. The union officials were not enlightened, however, and they chose to treat the company's managers with an attitude bordering on contempt.

When the conflict occurred, Monumental Life had a certain amount of experience with labor unions. A number of the company's debit agents were initially organized by the A.F. of L. in the early 1940's; a federation local won a Labor Board case against the company in 1943, but this victory seems to have failed to produce any lasting effect on Monumental's agency force as a whole.[40]

In December 1944 the United Office and Professional Workers of America entered upon the scene with plans to organize Monumental debit men in Ohio and Missouri.[41] Julius Walther, an agent the company had dismissed for union activity, conducted the first phase of the Ohio campaign. On January 15, 1945, the regional office of the N.L.R.B. in Cleveland heard hearings on a U.O.P.W.A. petition for an election among the company's Ohio agents, with the result that the Board ordered the company to reinstate Walther and the company complied.

On February 17 the Board conducted further hearings, and Walther, the only Monumental agent present, asserted that the company's Cleveland manager had said that Monumental wanted nothing to do with the U.O.P.W.A. Walther quoted the manager as saying: "As far as the union is concerned, I can find enough on practically any man in the office to get rid of him." Walther also stated that the same manager had told him that he was "just hanging on by his shoe strings." Present at the hearings was the Cleveland office manager, and he denied that he had made any of the allega-

---

[40]*Monumental Life Ins. Co.*, 67 N.L.R.B. 244 (1946). The Board found the company engaging in the usual "commerce," and it ordered the management to reinstate two agents it had dismissed for union activity.

[41]*Office and Professional News*, March, 1945, p. 8.

tions. However, on March 10, 1945, Monumental again dismissed Julius Walther.

The next day the company's Youngstown manager read the agents a lengthy report from the home office in Baltimore. In substance the document purported to prove that Leon W. Berney, the director of U.O.P.W.A.'s insurance division, had told Monumental's president, Leo P. Rock, that the union's sole concern was "in collecting dues and not . . . with the Walther discharge case." When asked about the letter, Berney swore that his primary interest was mutual agreement and harmony and that "he did not wish to get side tracked in the Walther case at that time."

The U.O.P.W.A. filed an unfair labor practice charge because of the Walther dismissal. The dispute did not last too long because, in late March, both company and union reached an agreement in which both determined to discuss the possibility of a nation-wide election. The union dropped the charge against the company.

Negotiations soon proved useless, however, as the company instituted a program that caused the union grave concern. Acting independently, Monumental management granted, on April 19, the "highly controversial" concessions which the union had originally requested.[42] The union's leadership reinstituted the unfair labor practice charge and furnished the Board and the company's agents with proofs that Monumental officers had acted in a high-handed manner. The Board found the union's arguments convincing and ordered that an election take place on August 2, 1945.

Pre-election activity was feverish. The company sponsored three luncheons for the agents in Cleveland, Akron and Columbus. Leo P. Rock, the company's president, addressed the first gathering at Columbus and, among other points, he directed the agents to consider the type of men they wanted to represent them. He asked: "Who is Lewis Merrill? Who is Leonard [sic] Berney? And who is Julius Walther?" The N.L.R.B. record shows that on the following day Rock spoke to the Cleveland men and urged them not to vote for the U.O.P.W.A. on election day. He also pointed out that Merrill had put a "picket line around the White House before

[42]*Monumental Life Ins. Co.*, 67 N.L.R.B. 244 (1946). The "highly controversial" concessions included such points as the elimination of the morning office call and the company-determined distribution of industrial allotments and quotas. The U.O.P.W.A. expressed concern because of the unilateral nature of the concessions.

Russia's entry into the war with Germany, and after Russia's entry, advocated the United States' entry into the war."[43] He repeated his allegation that Berney told him that the company's agents in Missouri, where the U.O.P.W.A. had recently won a labor board election, were "earning enough money for their needs and the U.O.P.W.A. was interested in a contract covering them so as to be able to share in their earnings.[44]

The election was held and the union lost, by a vote of seventy-eight to fifty-five. On August 9, the union filed an objection with the Labor Board, alleging "interference and other unfair labor practices by company officials prior to the election." The Board's regional director agreed and proposed that the election be set aside. The full Board concurred and ordered a new election.[45]

Meanwhile, the United Office and Professional Workers stepped up its activity among the Monumental agents in Ohio and, by a happy coincidence, held its sixth annual convention in Cleveland in February 1946. At that time, James Durkin, a member of the union's executive board, spoke out strongly against the company and its president, Leo P. Rock. He said in part:

> The president of that company, who, with some naivete, does not realize what it means to tangle with the organized agents, as represented by the U.O.P.W.A., has engaged in the most slanderous activities, the cheapest kind of pettifogging, misrepresentation and slander to destroy our union. I want to say from this convention to Mr. Leo Rock, the president of Monumental: Rock, with our present strength we are calling you and we are going out to organize Monumental in the rest of the states, and that is going to be done, and if you don't go along,

[43]*Ibid.* Rock later confessed that he gained this information from the *New York Daily Mirror,* a tabloid, he said, "that was not his paper."

[44]*Ibid.*

[45]*Monumental Life Ins. Co.,* 69 N.L.R.B. 247 (1947). The Board reached its decision on the basis of the *May* case (*Matter of May Department Stores,* 61 N.L.R.B. 25), in which the Board had held that the issuing of a waiver in an unfair labor practice case did not imply that the union granted to the company the right to engage in prejudicial utterances. One member of the Board disagreed in the citing of the *May* case because, he wrote, it constituted a violation of free speech and the First Amendment. cf. also *Colonial Life Ins. Co.,* 72 N.L.R.B. no. 102.

it is going to put you right out of the game.[46]

This kind of talk became more common as Durkin ultimately rose to the office of president of the organization. His speech probably convinced a sufficient number of Monumental agents and, to Durkin's way of thinking, served a useful purpose in the days prior to the second Monumental election which the N.L.R.B. had scheduled for October 26, 1946.

Throughout the month of September the company's Cleveland agents staged demonstrations and, on one day, all but two of them carried picket signs around the company's office for one hour. In this manifestation of solidarity they had the assistance of many of the city's "Big Three" insurance men. At another time, Monumental debit men refused to report to work until late in the morning.

Election day arrived, and the union polled the majority of votes in the company's Ohio offices. The union promptly asked Monumental management to combine contract negotiations for the agents in Ohio and Missouri where talks were already in progress. And to underline the victory, a U.O.P.W.A. spokesman said the company's agents in Pittsburgh, Chicago and Detroit had requested to join the union.

However, the union's leaders did not count on Monumental's resolve. Company officials refused to consolidate negotiations for its agents in Ohio and Missouri, and when the union proposed its program of "50 and 10," the union shop and improved retirement and disability payments, the company's denial was perfunctory. In the face of the company's obduracy, agents in St. Louis reported late for work, and the Cleveland group voted in late January 1947 to strike the company. A union newspaper reporter tersely described the mounting tension; he wrote:

> Monumental seems to be looking for trouble and is likely to get it, if it doesn't come across with the negotiation demands of some 275 agents in Ohio and Missouri, whom the union represents.[47]

Company and union met in February 1947. Talks proved unproductive, although Monumental offered a salary increase averag-

[46]U.O.P.W.A., C.I.O., *Convention Proceedings* (Cleveland, O., 1946), p. 198.

[47]*Office and Professional News*, February, 1947, p. 3.

ing $2.50 per agent per week. The union rejected the proposal on the grounds that "it didn't even scratch the surface of the company's $2 million in assets." Meanwhile, the company fired an agent in St. Louis. It also seriously offended union sensitivities: it sent into the Missouri state bargaining session "minor officials who could do nothing but promise to tell the company about it."[48]

Since the dispute was becoming too big for Julius Walther to handle, the U.O.P.W.A. replaced him with three of its top organizers in the Midwest region. These were Anne Berenholz, Morris Yanoff and Jerome Shore, all of them old hands at carrying out national office policy. James Durkin undertook overall direction of the campaign and set March 17 as the deadline for company acceptance of the union's demands. As the conflict deepened Durkin and his lieutenants set up a strike fund, asking all of the union's locals around the country to support the Monumental agents.

On March 16, both sides refused to budge from their former positions and, on the following day, three hundred and fifty Monumental agents in Missouri, Ohio and the city of Detroit went out on strike.[49] Pickets were thrown around the company's offices in these areas, and many agents bore placards that read: "50 and 10 for all insurance men."[50] Company officials instituted complaints about the strikers, asserting that they threatened with violence those agents who reported for work. As if to lend support to this accusation, the union newspaper later described how striking agents followed strikebreakers to their homes and publicized their names. In Detroit agents pursued one non-striking agent in a sound truck.

According to a union report, the strike was ninety per cent effective. Many policyholders refused to pay their premiums to non-striking agents. Members of the steel, auto, electrical and other C.I.O. unions, as well as members of the A.F. of L., walked the picket line with the striking agents. Several of the company's agents in the Chicago area joined in the strike, although the union had not organized that city. A union spokesman related that the company had appealed to its policyholders through newspaper ads to pay their premiums by mail.[51]

[48]*Ibid.*, March, 1947, p. 1.

[49]*The New York Times,* March 18, 1947, p. 28. The company's Detroit agents had been previously organized.

[50]*Office and Professional News,* April, 1947, p. 1.

[51]*Ibid.*, May, 1947, p. 2.

Monumental officials questioned the union's optimistic accounts of the strike's effectiveness. On March 19, two days after the strike began, they issued a statement in which they showed that only ten of the company's twenty-five offices in the two states and Detroit were effected, and that these were operating at better than fifty per cent efficiency.[52]

On March 31, the U.O.P.W.A. officials called a meeting in Cleveland of all the agents' representatives participating in the walkout. Also attending were agents from the company's offices in Pennsylvania and Illinois. At this one-day session the union's officials decided to institute a complicated legal maneuver: they wired the insurance commissioners of the areas affected by the strike and of the state of Maryland (the home base of Monumental), requesting them to investigate the company's use of policyholders' funds to fight the union. James Durkin, who was chairman of the meeting, proposed still another inquiry. Recalling that the Temporary National Economic Committee had uncovered information pointing to stock manipulation at the time Monumental dropped its mutualization, he demanded that the case be reopened and investigated.[53] Neither of these proposals was carried out.

On April 9, Leo P. Rock, president of Monumental, attempted to coax the men back to work and "settle the dispute later." When this failed, he sent telegrams to each of the striking agents, asking them to return to their jobs. He also instructed the company's assistant managers to visit the homes of each of the agents to enlist their support. None of these plans succeeded. Finally, Monumental obtained an injunction which entitled it to impound the debit books of the striking agents. The men refused to surrender them.[54]

By April 11 the company was ready to capitulate, or so the U.O.P.W.A. reported. The strike ended on April 12, and a contract was eventually drawn up for the company's agents in Ohio, Missouri and Detroit.[55] The union leadership referred to the contract as a

[52]*The New York Times*, March 20, 1947, p. 21.

[53]*Office and Professional News*, April, 1947, p. 1. For Durkin's reference, cf. *T.N.E.C.*, "Investigation into Life Ins.," Part 12, p. 5620.

[54]*Office and Professional News*, May, 1947, p. 1.

[55]U.O.P.W.A., C.I.O., *Convention Proceedings* (Brooklyn, N.Y., 1948), p. 13. Michigan agents were included in the agreement without a labor board election.

"smashing victory" for the agents, and their phrase is accurate. The new agreement provided for a complete union shop, a compensation increase averaging $6.00 per week — the company had originally offered $2.50 — and one week of back pay for each week of the walkout. The company also granted what the union described as a "first" in the insurance industry; it agreed to "split" or reduce debits and to make the reduction of the debit the subject of arbitration. The U.O.P.W.A. regarded the debit splitting as an "important safeguard against depression." Although the union did not obtain its projected program of "50 and 10," the leadership regarded the $6.00 weekly increase as a "tremendous step toward [that] goal . . . in all the companies."[56]

Characteristically, a union officer implied that the Monumental settlement was a gain for the proletariat; he said:

> Here an arrogant management sought to reimpose the dictatorship of management on the agents.[57]

But the desired outcome of the "smashing victory" was not in the cards. What turned out to be U.O.P.W.A.'s last activity among Monumental agents ended in failure. Only two months after the union had negotiated the contract with the company, it lost a Labor Board election among the company's Chicago agents. This was a bitter defeat for the union, because the A.F. of L. Insurance Council, now interested in the company, came within one vote of causing a three-way tie. The results of the balloting showed that neither organization achieved a victory, for twenty-eight agents voted for no union, twenty-seven for U.O.P.W.A. and twenty-six for the A.F. of L.[58]

Both unions immediately petitioned the Board for a new election. The Board denied the U.O.P.W.A.'s request in words that will become familiar as this story progresses. The Board's decision simply read that a "representation petition filed by a union which has failed to comply with the affidavit and filing requirements of the amended National Labor Relations Act is dismissed."[59]

[56]*Office and Professional News,* May, 1947, p. 1.

[57]U.O.P.W.A., C.I.O., *Convention Proceedings* (Brooklyn, N.Y., 1948), p. 13.

[58]*Office and Professional News,* July, 1947, p. 8.

[59]*Monumental Life Ins. Co.,* 75 N.L.R.B. no. 93 (1948). The Board did grant to the A.F. of L., a complying union, the right to preserve its petition.

During this time the leaders of the United Office and Professional Workers of America were delving deeply into the no man's land of noncompliance with the loyalty oath of the Taft-Hartley Law. Stiff-necked to the last, these men and women assured their membership that such a policy would in no way deter the union from its role as the nation's number one white collar organization. To prove their point they engaged in other strikes, notably against *Parents' Magazine,* the Brooklyn Y.M.C.A. and Federal Telephone and Radio.[60]

Their forecast was inaccurate. They did not reckon with the opposition within the union fold and from the national C.I.O. Furthermore, the U.O.P.W.A. depended upon the insurance division for its strength. If the insurance agents defected, the union was doomed. That is exactly what happened.

[60]*Office and Professional News,* April, 1947, p. 1. All told, over two thousand U.O.P.W.A. members were on strike at this time.

CHAPTER 5

THE AGENTS TEST THE PECULIAR TWIST THEORY

Throughout its short history the United Office and Professional Workers of America, C.I.O., adhered to the Communist Party line.[1] During World War II, with its spirit of "getting the job done" and of indulgence toward the Soviet Union, it was neither easy nor generous to label the union's policy as anti-American. However, when the war ended and the United States government framed a foreign policy designed to thwart the ambition of Russia, the ruling body of the U.O.P.W.A. denied the value of the American commitment and chose rather to promote the goals of the Kremlin. Yet, even then it was at times difficult to distinguish between the program of the union's official clique and that of the anti-Communist, for both frequently sought programs that appeared identical.

Uncovering sufficient proof of the left-wing domination of a labor organization required time and patience. At war's end the C.I.O. was not in a position to draw up a list of charges against a union such as the U.O.P.W.A., because the national union itself was not free from Communist infiltration. The C.I.O. had, therefore, to pursue a two-fold operation. In the first place, it had to set its own house in order, and secondly, it had simultaneously to interest sufficient numbers of U.O.P.W.A. rank and file to vote their leaders out of office. The record shows that this was an extremely complicated process and that the second of its double-pronged attack was never achieved.

It took several years for the C.I.O. to publish an account of its findings against the U.O.P.W.A., and, at the time of its appearance, the union was no longer in existence. The account of the indictment which the C.I.O. put under the heading of *Official Reports* contains much useful information. Among other things, the C.I.O. accused the U.O.P.W.A. of promoting programs "with a peculiar twist." To cite but one example, the *Official Reports* illustrated the difference between the union's espousal of the immediate postwar demobilization of America's armed forces and that of the rest of the country. The document put it this way:

[1]The writer does not contend that all of the union's officers were party faithful; the Communist element, however, was strong enough to control the organization.

An editorial in the September 1945 issue of its [U.O.P.W.A.'s]
newspaper declared that the problem of getting the boys back
home was the same problem as the problem of securing a
decent postwar world, and that problem, in turn, depended
upon the maintenance of unity among the Big Three.[2]

In itself the quote has the benefit of hindsight. But it was on the
basis of this and other arguments that can be best described as
cumulative that the C.I.O. was able to formulate its "peculiar twist"
theory. It is this accumulation of evidence that must now be
examined.

The *Proceedings* of the U.O.P.W.A.'s 1946 convention show that
the union was indeed promoting programs "with a peculiar twist."
On that occasion the union's leaders prevailed upon the delegates
to subscribe to eleven resolutions, ranking first in the order of convention business and all of them critical of American foreign policy.
The audience heard American Big Business described as "fascist"
and applauded various speakers who sought to equate legitimate
foreign business ventures with a new form of imperialism. The
American presence in China, Indonesia, Greece, her policy toward
Palestine, Spain, Argentina and India, her "violations" of the
Tehran and Potsdam agreements, all indicated that the American
government betrayed the American citizen who, above all, sought
Big Three Unity. At this convention the delegates voted to vest
control of atomic discoveries in the United Nations. They also approved the formation of a third political party in the United States
if these goals were not met.[3]

It should be pointed out that, prior to the convention, the leaders
of the U.O.P.W.A. had invited the Federation of Architects, Engineers and Technicians, C.I.O., to merge with the union. Composed of about five thousand members, the organization was led by
Lewis Alan Berne and has been called Communist-dominated.[4] The
merger proposal was consummated at the convention.

THE RESIGNATION OF LEWIS MERRILL

[2]*Official Reports of the Expulsion of Communist Dominated Organizations
from the C.I.O.*, "United Office and Professional Workers of America,"
Washington, D.C., 1954, p. 64.

[3]U.O.P.W.A., C.I.O., *Convention Proceedings* (Cleveland, O., 1946),
pp. 5-6.

[4]Kampelman, *loc. cit.*, p. 45.

While Lewis Merrill continued to act as spokesman for the Office Workers' anti-government policies, he was apparently having second thoughts about the union's future. His attitudes show up for the first time in the November 1946 issue of *Office and Professional News,* the union's official publication. Addressing himself to the question: "Are Communists a menace in the trade unions?" he assured his readers of his loyalty to the C.I.O., an organization which he described as a "patriotic force that has sought to serve the entire nation." He went on to evaluate the wave of anti-Communism enveloping the United States:

> The real reason against Communists is that they are the carriers of unpopular ideas, the main one being that people should **own and operate the plants and** factories and other means of production. Naturally, those who own the plants and factories and other means of production, and the newspapers and radio as well, don't like such ideas propagated. They like it less and less when the Soviet Union, which does operate on this principle, grows stronger and stronger.[5]

Although this quote might indicate nothing more than Merrill's economic philosophy and his naïveté about the Soviet Union, it could just as well mark the beginning of Merrill's disillusionment with the ruling faction of the U.O.P.W.A. His statement seems to have gotten him into trouble at the C.I.O. convention in November 1946. When the national union met the previous year Merrill was a member of the resolutions committee, but in 1946 his name appears in the *Proceedings* as a delegate only.[6] It was at this convention that Merrill allegedly made contact with the "right-wing," because sometime after the convention concluded he met with Philip Murray and the president of the Westinghouse Salaried Employees' Union in Pittsburgh. The purpose of this and subsequent meetings was to explore the possibility of uniting the forces of the Westing-

[5]*Office and Professional News,* November, 1946, p. 8. Perhaps Merrill began to fear for his personal safety. His article was occasioned by a remark attributed to a labor-management consultant who said: "When they [the Communists] stand up and you see the white of their eyes—shoot!" Merrill replied: "When they invite Communists to stand up and be shot, I imagine it's me they are talking about. Naturally, I don't like the idea."

[6]C.I.O., *Convention Proceedings* (Chicago, Ill., 1946), p. 19. This observation is based on the assumption that the leftists in C.I.O. appointed several of their number to the various convention committees.

house group to those of the U.O.P.W.A.'s insurance local in Pittsburgh, and thus to have a base upon which to secure the votes for a drastic change in the union's leadership. Merrill is also supposed to have approached members of the New York insurance local and asked for support, but it was not forthcoming.[7]

In December 1946, Merrill precipitated a crisis. Max Kampelman writes that Merrill resigned as "contributing editor of the *New Masses* and as a trustee of the pro-Communist Jefferson School of Social Science." The same author also refers to the adoption of a new policy, through Merrill's insistence, by the U.O.P.W.A.'s executive board wherein the national union stated its opposition to interference by any outside organization, including the Communists. Merrill's action took the left-wing by surprise, for, according to Kampelman, the *Daily Worker* editorialized that Merrill's new program "gladdened the hearts of the red baiters." The publication's editor further suggested that the U.O.P.W.A.'s position "went far to the right of the C.I.O. convention statement."[8]

Merrill's status in the union remained unclear for the next several months. His name received scant notice during the time of the U.O.P.W.A.'s strike against the Monumental Life Insurance Company. In January 1947 he journeyed to Boston, ostensibly to induct new officers into the union's insurance local in that city. When he completed the task, he tried to convince the agents to pass a resolution against those insurance companies which, he said, had used the tactic of red baiting to "split and divert agents in the past from their fight for pay gains." These companies employed this same approach, Merrill said, in their opposition to the union's recently stated bargaining proposal of "50 and 10."

The first concrete indication that Merrill was through as the U.O.P.W.A.'s president occurred in May 1947, when the union newspaper, *Office and Professional News,* failed to carry his regular column. Then the July 1947 issue announced that he had resigned

[7]Interview with Charles Heisel, vice president of the Insurance Workers International Union, August 5, 1959. At the time under consideration Heisel was president of the U.O.P.W.A.'s insurance local in Pittsburgh, a member of the national union's executive board and the director of the union's Pittsburgh region.

[8]Kampelman, *loc. cit.,* p. 99. The *Daily Worker is,* of course, referring to C.I.O.'s famous "compromise resolution" at the 1946 convention.

for reasons of health. In a letter dated June 5, 1947, Merrill informed the union's executive board that his physician had ordered a period of complete rest and the discontinuance of all union activity. He wrote to the board that he was "sure the labor movement will triumph over its current difficulties." As a token of gratitude the members of the board immediately established a fund for Merrill's medical expenses. This totalled $5,000.00, and the members contributed.[9] Merrill's name and influence thereafter faded from view, to be resurrected once or twice by persons who chose to recall his name at the 1948 U.O.P.W.A. convention.

It is difficult to evaluate Merrill's leadership as president of the union. In these pages he has been shown as a man who followed a policy that the national C.I.O. would later call Communist inspired. Yet on his own admission he was not a Communist. At the 1948 C.I.O. convention Allan Haywood pointed out that neither Prudential nor Hancock would negotiate with the U.O.P.W.A. unless a representative of the C.I.O. participated in the bargaining sessions.[10] This is undoubtedly true. Moreover, Haywood and others of his critics would naturally fail to credit Merrill with anything worthwhile. However, it was due to his dogged perseverance that insurance negotiations were made to work. If the story of Merrill's contact with Philip Murray is true, and the writer has no reason to question it, it is a pity that he was unable to convince the great numbers of New York agents that he could eliminate the union's leadership. With New York in his grasp he might have saved the U.O.P.W.A.

The Administration of James Durkin

James Durkin was chosen by the union's executive board to succeed Merrill in the latter part of June 1947. At the time of his selection, he was thirty-five years old. His biographer notes that he was born in New York City, attended Blessed Sacrament School in Brooklyn and received his secondary education in Jamaica, N.Y. After a year at the College of the City of New York, Durkin obtained employment with the Equitable Life Assurance Society in 1931 and remained with the company until he helped to found the U.O.P. W.A. in 1937. Subsequently, he served as a national representative

[9] *Office and Professional News*, February, 1947, p. 4 & July, 1947, p. 2.

[10] C.I.O., *Convention Proceedings* (Portland, Ore., 1948), p. 340.

of the union in Boston, assisting in the organization of Hancock and Boston Mutual agents and of the social service workers. He labored as an organizer for the union's New York City insurance local, and he spent several years in administrative posts in upstate New York. One of his chief contributions was the formulation of the U.O.P. W.A.'s bargaining demand for "50 and 10."[11]

Varied sources show that when Durkin became president of the union, he had compiled a record of Communist activity. In 1946, he signed a petition to have the Communist Party candidates in New York State listed on the state's election ballot. He was a director of the *Far East Spotlight*, a journal cited by the Joint Fact-Finding Committee to the 1948 Regular California Legislature as a Communist front organization.[12] According to testimony presented before the Senate Judiciary Subcommittee, Durkin was active in the Jefferson School. He also served as chairman of the Greater Boston Communist Party Labor Committee, contributed $50.00 to the Communist Party in Buffalo, and, between 1943 and 1945, was active in the Communist Political Association.[13]

In one of his first public statements, Durkin outlined his union's future course of action. He said in part:

> I will not be a party to any witch-hunting or conspiracy by employers or government agencies, which would disenfranchise any section of our membership or divide our people by subjection to fascist-like controls which follow the path of Hitler Germany.[14]

Soon after his election, Durkin had the opportunity to lead the union's Financial Employees' Guild in a strike against the Brooklyn Trust Company. The dispute occasioned an outburst of vituperation, involving the U.O.P.W.A. with the Association of Catholic Trade Unionists. Through the pages of its newspaper, *The Labor Leader*,

[11]*Office and Professional News,* July, 1947, p. 1.

[12]*Communist Party Independent Nominating Petition. Would YOU Sign This? Officers of the U.O.P.W.A. Did!* Prudential Press, November, 1948, no. 36725.

[13]U.S., Congress, Senate, Subcommittee of the Committee on the Judiciary, *Hearings, Investigation of the Administration of the Internal Security Act,* "On Subversive Control of the Distributive, Processing and Office Workers of America," 1st and 2nd Sess., 1951-1952, p. 5.

[14]*Office and Professional News,* July, 1947, pp. 1-2.

the A.C.T.U. told the story of the strike and wrote that the bank employees were "guinea pigs in a C.P. trade union experiment." The article referred to the dismissal of three bank employees — the cause of the strike — as "alleged" dismissals and observed that the strike was "designed to promote the idea of class war." Durkin accused the A.C.T.U. leadership of siding with the Brooklyn Trust management. He also offered the Catholic group the following piece of advice:

> I am aware and proud of the numerous fine contributions that Catholics have made in the labor movement and in the U.O.P.W.A., along with men and women of all creeds. I am loathe to conclude that the article is an indication that you have finally come to the course of out-right strike-breaking. I cannot believe that represents good Catholicism or good trade unionism.[15]

The union lost the strike, and readers of *The Commonweal,* a Catholic weekly, discovered something about Durkin. A member of A.C.T.U. made the following observation in the publication: "If there was any question of Merrill's loyalty to the Communist Party, there is certainly no question about Durkin's."[16]

Undeterred by the Brooklyn Trust fiasco, Durkin appeared at the 1947 C.I.O. convention and condemned the Taft-Hartley Law. It should be noted that Durkin's appraisal of the Act was not unusual; Philip Murray had already called it the "first step in the direction of fascism." What was peculiar about Durkin's remarks was his willingness to put the life of his organization in jeopardy. He said that his union was refusing to sign the Law's anti-Communist affidavit and explained his position in these words:

> U.O.P.W.A. will not sign because we believe that to try to do so would leave nothing but greater disaster for the workers involved, and would disarm them from the necessity of making an all-out fight against this legislation. We do not think that our action is going to engender difficulties for us. It may momentarily.[17]

15*Ibid.,* August, 1947, p. 7.

16John Broderick, "What color's that white collar, Mr. Durkin?" *Commonweal,* XLVI (August 22, 1947), p. 447.

17C.I.O., *Convention Proceedings* (Boston, Mass., 1947), p. 171.

Durkin left the convention and, according to Max Kampelman, met with a group of Communist Party members and left-wing C.I.O. leaders in New York City. Those present were told to disregard "everything that happened" at the convention and that the Party had decided to endorse the candidacy of Henry A. Wallace whose announcement was momentarily expected.[18]

The meeting was top secret. If the insurance agents had known of Durkin's presence, it seems likely that they would have left the union sooner than they did. The record shows that only one local president challenged Durkin's remarks to the C.I.O. convention. In Providence, Rhode Island, Max Shine cut off dues payments to the national union, arguing that the deduction could not legally be sent to a noncomplying union.[19] He was expelled by the executive board, but his reaction to Durkin was only the beginning. Defection was in the air at the U.O.P.W.A.'s 1948 convention in Brooklyn.

THE 1948 CONVENTION OF THE UNITED OFFICE AND PROFESSIONAL WORKERS OF AMERICA

The seventh convention of the U.O.P.W.A. convened on Monday, March 1, 1948, at the Hotel St. George in Brooklyn, N.Y. For the first time in the union's history there arose organized opposition of any substance. Composed of a group of insurance men from Massachusetts, Missouri and Pennsylvania, the right-wing group rejected the U.O.P.W.A.'s official position on the Taft-Hartley Law. They also decried the union's condemnation of American foreign policy and its recent proposal to endorse the candidacy of Henry A. Wallace.[20] These men arrived in Brooklyn heartened by the anti-U.O.P.W.A. publicity in the New York press. Three days prior to the opening of the convention, Nelson Frank of the *New York World Telegram* rebuked the union for its Communist domination and stated that Lewis Merrill had been expelled as union president because he was not a Communist.[21] On the evening before the

---

[18]Kampelman, *loc. cit.*, p. 144.

[19]*Insurance Career*, April, 1948, p. 11. The newspaper refers to the decision of a Rhode Island Supreme Court justice who declared Shine's action unconstitutional.

[20]*C.I.O. News*, March 8, 1948, p. 8.

[21]U.O.P.W.A., C.I.O., *Convention Proceedings* (Brooklyn, N.Y., 1948), p. 38.

convention opened the agents called a press conference, and, through their spokesman, Leo Wallace, president of the Lynn, Mass., insurance local, expressed the belief that the policies of the U.O.P.W.A. were akin to those of the United Electrical Workers, the Furriers, the Farm Equipment Workers and other left-wing C.I.O. unions. Wallace promised that the right-wing agents would overthrow the U.O.P.W.A. officers "no matter how long it takes."[22]

When the convention officially opened, James Durkin exercised considerable caution during his welcoming speech. He was aware of the press conference, and he led into his topic by observing that the union had prospered in spite of its refusal to take the loyalty oath. The union, he noted, had contracts with Metropolitan, Prudential and John Hancock as well as agreements with Wayne Pump in Fort Wayne, C.B.S. Radio, the screen offices in New York City, Shell Oil, Union News of New England and New Jersey, the Arthur Murray Dance Studios, Cutter Laboratory, the Fort Wayne offices of International Harvester, Federal Telephone and Radio in New York and New Jersey, and the Trust Company of New Jersey.[23]

After saying this much, he began to shift his emphasis and spoke out against the opposition. Glancing at a copy of *The New York Times,* he took sharp aim at those agents who had criticized the U.O.P.W.A. to New York newspaper reporters. He said:

> Chief among the weapons used to sow intimidation and division among labor's ranks is the hysteria against progressives and Communists that is flowing from the N.A.M., and the halls of government, and filling the columns of our newspapers.[24]

Durkin then yielded the platform to an insurance agent, a member of Local 30, N.Y., who introduced a resolution condemning those debit men who had participated in the meeting with the press. A

[22]*C.I.O. News,* March 8, 1948, p. 8.

[23]U.O.P.W.A., C.I.O., *Convention Proceedings* (Brooklyn, N.Y., 1948), pp. 10-11. To complete the list, the U.O.P.W.A. had contracts with the Trust Co. of N.Y., the National Savings Bank of Albany, N.Y., The Title Guarantee and Trust Co., N.Y., the Merchants Bank of New York, the Retail Credit Bureau of Boston, I. Miller, Remington Rand, Mackay Cables, Western Union and about twenty-two of the so-called "smaller" insurance companies. Several of these agreements had accrued to the U.O.P.W.A. at the time of the merger with the Technicians' Union.

[24]*Ibid.,* p. 19.

delegate arose to challenge the resolution, but Durkin ruled him out of order. Berney, whose division was under fire, asked for permission to speak; his words were caustic. "It is a type of pigeon for me," he said, "whether the person doing it is good or bad." And he made his meaning crystal clear when he observed that "Westbrook Pegler is second-rate, compared to Nelson Frank." Durkin then presented the resolution to the delegates who quickly approved the condemnation of the rebellious insurance agents. Durkin pledged that from thenceforth press conferences were to be limited "to contact with the press through union channels."

On the second day of the conclave the U.O.P.W.A. leadership pulled the rug from under the opposition. Henry A. Wallace was on hand to deliver his speech, but, before he began, the chairman of the credentials' committee proposed a preliminary plan for voting at the convention. The strategy involved a modification of the union's constitution. Stating that locals had been forewarned in late 1946, he asked the delegates to rewrite the document to read as follows: "In order to vote all other obligations due to International Union are [to be] paid up one (1) month prior to the month of the International Convention."[25] The opposition raised such a storm of protest that voting on the amendment was postponed.

James Durkin finally introduced Henry A. Wallace amidst a roar of cheers from the convention delegates. When quiet was restored, Wallace attempted to expose the two American political parties as reactionary forces and pledged himself to lead the United States into a new future through his Progressive Party.

During the afternoon session, Leon W. Berney spoke and, taking up Durkin's theme of the previous day, explained that the insurance agents were in an excellent bargaining position in spite of the union's refusal to sign the Taft-Hartley affidavit. When Berney completed his observations, a delegate from New York City, no doubt mindful of the remark of Brigadier General McAuliffe to the Germans at Bastogne, issued the following challenge:

> To you, Leroy Lincoln and Carroll Shanks, nuts. Nuts to you, Mr. Taft. Nuts to you, Mr. Hartley. Nuts to all betrayers of the common man, be they in Wall Street, Washington, on our doorstep or among management.[26]

[25]U.O.P.W.A. Constitution, as amended, 1948, Art. III, Sect. 5.

[26]U.O.P.W.A., C.I.O., Convention Proceedings (Brooklyn, N.Y., 1948), p. 99. Lincoln and Shanks were presidents of the Metropolitan and Prudential respectively.

This outcry amused the grim-faced officers of the U.O.P.W.A. They were so delighted in fact that they reintroduced the preliminary credentials' committee report on voting, and the delegates approved the amending of the constitution.

The remainder of the day was devoted to a resolution condemning discrimination in all of its forms. Particular emphasis was placed upon the discriminatory practices of the "Big Three" insurance companies: the delegates condemned the firms for their alleged refusal to write new business on Negro and Puerto Rican lives and for reducing commission rates to agents who wrote policies on Negroes living outside New York State. The delegates resolved to condemn Metropolitan Life "for fostering Jim Crowism" in the company's housing developments in New York City. There was nothing wrong with the resolution if the conditions described were true. But union leaders decided to expand the resolution on discrimination into a general criticism of American foreign policy. The delegates dutifully condemned the United States' government.

The next day Durkin's followers brought up the question of compliance with the Taft-Hartley Law. One delegate explained that the union's locals were against the law in general, and that twenty-eight of them favored a policy of noncompliance. It was also stated that seven of the locals disapproved the action of the national officers; four of these were insurance locals.[27] The chairman of the resolutions' committee then asserted that members of his committee had voted in favor of noncompliance by a vote of eighteen to one. He asked the convention delegates to act in a similar manner.

Before the vote was taken, Durkin called on various union delegations to speak on the question. Eight persons accepted his invitation, and only two, the representatives of the insurance agents, expressed disagreement with official union policy. One speaker, Albert Forscher, president of the Philadelphia local, entered the motion that the union's leaders be required to take the loyalty oath, because of what he termed "public aversion to the Communist Party."

Leo Wallace, the leader of the opposition group, then pointed out that the N.L.R.B. would not accept election petitions from a noncomplying union, and he said that the Board could refuse the organization a place on the ballot should an election occur in a

[27] *Ibid.*, pp. 25-35, 105-124.

company under contract. He concluded his remarks with an appeal on behalf of those insurance debit agents who had accumulated seniority in their companies:

> We know that if we go back and have to tell them that it is not going to be complied with, as they desire, that is going to leave a serious concern in the minds of those men who have twenty-five or thirty years of service with these companies. If they are called to go on strike, the company may, under certain circumstances, refuse to rehire them, and fire them and they will have lost all they have put in there in their lifetime.[28]

When Wallace concluded his speech, Durkin recognized Leon Berney. In response to Wallace's appeal, Berney simply insisted that compliance did not prevent strikes. Assuming the role of the professor, he instructed the delegates in the meaning of patriotism, asserting that the American Republic faced dangers unparalleled in its history. He termed the Taft-Hartley Law "foreign, un-American, anti-American."

Durkin closed debate and called for a show of hands on the Forscher amendment. This was defeated by a "standing vote." Then he submitted the resolution on noncompliance and, although the "ayes" had it, he permitted a roll call. The results of the balloting indicated that the resolution won by a vote of more than ten to one.

The leaders of the United Office and Professional Workers of America could feel well satisfied. They obtained victory on the constitutional amendment and went on record as opposing the Taft-Hartley non-Communist affidavit. They wanted more and were waiting for the right opportunity to propose it.

During the course of the speech-making Frank Fay, a Boston insurance agent, proposed that the delegates condemn the actions of the Soviet Union in Eastern Europe. Durkin listened patiently and exploded:

> And I say to the President of the United States, and to the F.B.I. and Tom Clark and J. Edgar Hoover — it is on the record, you don't have to look for it. As time passes, and the American people move, it is what we and the people stand for that will come out on top, and you and the things that you stand for will be relegated to oblivion.[29]

28*Ibid.*, p. 139.

29*Ibid.*, p. 159.

After this outburst, the delegates took up the question of endorsing the candidacy of Henry A. Wallace. Durkin told the convention that "all twenty-one members of the resolutions' committee unanimously supported" Wallace and asked the delegates to act in like manner. At one point, an insurance delegate interrupted the proceedings by saying that the union should condemn the third party as the C.I.O. executive board had done and that the national officers were worthy of contempt for their endorsement of Wallace. Another man observed:

> In 1940, I heard Roosevelt called a fascist warmonger by the very same people who, in 1944, called him "Our Beloved President." I don't know what they would call Roosevelt, if he were alive today. Perhaps it is a good thing for Mr. Roosevelt that he died when he did.[30]

A Boston insurance delegate reported that his local union membership, in the presence of James Durkin, had refused to endorse any candidate until such time as the union members had the opportunity to study the platforms of the various candidates. He read his local's resolution:

> Resolved: That the national officers shall refrain from an action that would commit the union or its membership toward encouraging or promoting the candidacy of Henry A. Wallace.[31]

The delegate requested a roll call vote on the resolution, and Durkin informed him that his motion was out of order. Suspecting that the insurance agents' opposition was critical, the union president began to hedge; he explained that the resolution did not constitute a formal endorsement of Wallace. Durkin said of the resolution that it reaffirmed the right of each member and each local to support whatever party they thought best represented the interests of the U.O.P.W.A. membership. He said that the majority of the delegates considered Wallace the most qualified. He went on to say that a vote on the resolution did not constitute a formal endorsement of the candidate; rather it was a manifestation of sympathy for Wallace and the "third party movement." He called

[30]*Ibid.*, p. 184.

[31]*Ibid.*, p. 185.

for a vote, and, as expected, the delegates "manifested their sympathy" for Wallace by an overwheming majority.[32]

The final day of the meeting dawned on a gathering of angry, deeply disappointed and defeated men. Having resisted every type of blandishment from the A.F. of L. Insurance Council, the agents discovered that the U.O.P.W.A. was now, more than ever before, under the control of the leftists. Speculation on the cause of defeat was useless. If only they had been able to gain the support of the New York agents, they might have preserved the union. Yet, every resolution, every policy approved by the convention simply increased Communist domination of their union and employer opposition to it.

Attributing motives to the New York agents was too facile a solution. The right-wing opposition was told by the New Yorkers that a housecleaning of the U.O.P.W.A. could be accomplished only by remaining inside the union. The others disagreed, believing such a notion impractical. The events of the past few days indicated that changing the union's leadership was a task far more difficult than any of them had imagined.

For those agents of the right-wing who had stayed in Brooklyn for the final day of the convention, the outcome was predictable. But it required the vision of men far more sagacious than they to forecast just how far the union's leaders would go. All of the agents admitted that the U.O.P.W.A. was walking a tight rope when it instituted the program of "50 and 10." Yet they granted that such a bargaining proposal might succeed if the agents remained united. Since unity had become impossible such a demand was no longer negotiable. The U.O.P.W.A. officials thought otherwise. On this last day of the convention they insisted that the sum be raised to "65 and 15." The delegates approved, and members of the right-wing group of insurance agents were aghast.

During the morning session the union's leaders ran true to form. Their handpicked delegates denounced the United States government for all manner of evil doing. They said that the so-called "Hollywood Ten" had been deprived of civil liberties. They denounced as egregious violations of the Federal Constitution deportation charges against John Santos. And they also wrote their own

[32]*Ibid.*, p. 189. The result of the voting is as follows: on a per cent basis, 67.7 per cent favored the candidacy of Wallace, 13.1 per cent voted against him, and 18.2 per cent of the delegates abstained.

version of the Marshall Plan. Durkin had previously proposed that the United States make an outright grant of some twenty billions of dollars to the United Nations. The world organization in turn would then dispense economic assistance to those nations most in need.[33]

The afternoon was given over to the election of officers. None of the right-wing agents had even bothered to offer a slate of opposing candidates. Consequently, Durkin, John Stanley, Leon Berney, Bernard Mooney, Joseph Levy, Lewis Alan Berne, Morris Yanoff and Aaron Schneider were re-elected without opposition.[34] As the curtain of the final act was descending on the slick production staged by a little group of office workers, someone in the hall began to sing: "Solidarity Forever." It can only be surmised whether the right-wing insurance debit men were present to hear the refrain.

That night the delegates were treated to a banquet. The U.O.P. W.A. officers had invited twenty-eight persons prominent in political and labor circles in New York. Nineteen of these personalities were members of left-wing C.I.O. organizations. After dessert was served, the delegates witnessed scenes from the then current Broadway production: "The Cradle Will Rock."[35]

There could be no more fitting description of the next episode in U.O.P.W.A.'s history.

THE RIGHT-WING AGENTS STAGE A PRODUCTION OF THEIR OWN

Leo Wallace, the leader of the anti-Communist opposition, returned to his Lynn, Massachusetts, local determined to expose the union's left-wing domination. According to a U.O.P.W.A. publica-

[33]Durkin's program contained a gimmick. The U.N. was to let out contracts to American business which, in turn, was to pay to the organization in the form of a tax any excess profits realized in the course of oversea's investment. cf. Letter of James Durkin, January 27, 1948, paraphrased in "Resolutions Submitted to 1948 U.O.P.W.A. Convention." p. 74.

[34]With the exception of Berney and Mooney, all of these persons were accused of having Communist associations. cf. *Communist Party Independent Nominating Petition* . . . Prudential Press, November, 1948, no. 36725.

[35]U.O.P.W.A.-C.I.O., Seventh Constitutional Convention, *Banquet,* Hotel St. George, March 4, 1948. The guests were members of the United Public Workers, the Mine, Mill and Smelter, Transport Workers, United Electrical Workers, Packinghouse Workers, American Communications Assoc., the New York Newspaper Guild and the Furriers.

tion, Wallace refused to permit discussion of the convention's decisions at the meeting of the local. He is quoted as saying that the convention delegates had been "stupified by drink" and did not know what they were voting for.[36] Another union source accused Wallace of collecting the new dues authorization forms — on the basis of a convention decision — from the agents of the Haverhill, Salem and Lynn locals but of failing to deliver them to the national office. Furthermore, and this was the last straw, he was in contact with the C.I.O.'s United Paperworkers Union, seeking its assistance in establishing a temporary home for the right-wing insurance agents. Shortly after this contact, the Paperworkers began to raid the Lynn insurance local.[37] The union's official organ, *Insurance Career,* also carried the report that Wallace corresponded with "trusted" officers of the St. Louis insurance local. He allegedly told them of his work with the Paperworkers Union and asked them to influence the Missouri agents.[38]

The New England leadership of the United Office and Professional Workers of America became alarmed at these developments and instituted a series of moves designed to defeat both Wallace and the Paperworkers. Playing on the agents' fear of loss of union representation, the New England officials asserted that secession would be "mass suicide" and that the companies "would love to see this happen."[39] They explained that the 31-state Prudential contract was due to expire on October 1, 1948, and had only a few months to run. They said that the thought of negotiating with the company without the advantage of numbers, and without the U.O.P.W.A., was frightening. Attempting, therefore, to nip Wallace's movement in the bud, the region's leaders held a meeting of the loyal agents in Lawrence, Mass., on June 3. At that time, they prevailed upon the agents to expel Wallace, to suspend the Lynn local and to demand that Philip Murray stop the Paperworkers.[40]

[36]*Insurance Career,* May, 1948, p. 10.

[37]*Lynn No. Shore Agents Expel Wallace! Protest Paperworkers' Raiding to Murray.* 6/15/48.

[38]*Insurance Career,* June, 1948, p. 6.

[39]*New England U.O.P.W.A. News,* n.d.

[40]Lynn No. Shore Agents, *loc. cit.* The Paperworkers insisted that only thirteen U.O.P.W.A. members attended this meeting. cf. *Leaders' Bulletin,* U.O.P.W.A., C.I.O., July 1, 1948, p. 2.

Along with this action the New England leaders were able to convince agents in the region's largest locals, Boston, Springfield, Lynn and Providence, that they should remain loyal to the national union.[41] But they failed to stem the tide in other sections of the area. The president of the Portland insurance local joined the plotters and went over to the Paperworkers in June.[42] And in Connecticut, Robert Jordan, the leader of the New Britain group, fanned the flames of unrest not only among agents of his own local but among insurance men in New Haven, Hartford, Bridgeport, Stamford and Waterbury as well.[43]

Calling the Connecticut locals "autocratically ruled," the U.O.P.W.A. national officials suspended them *en masse*.[44] However, the first group that fell under the ax of the U.O.P.W.A.'s "cleanup campaign" was the St. Louis Local. Early in May 1948 the union's executive board met in Philadelphia to discuss the secession movement, the activity of the Paperworkers and, in particular, the failure of the St. Louis affiliate to return the new forms for dues deduction. Trying to make an example of the St. Louis agents, they suspended the membership and the Local's leaders, calling the latter "company stooges."[45]

The U.O.P.W.A. was more cautious in its handling of the Paperworkers Union. The first contact Durkin had with the organization occurred on May 25, 1948, or so the record shows. When he asked Harry Sayre, the union's president, to stop the raiding, Sayre told him that he was unable to do so.[46]

[41]*New England U.O.P.W.A. News,* n.d.

[42]*Leaders' Bulletin, loc. cit.*

[43]*Insurance Career,* June, 1948, p. 6. Jordan was a participant in the Providence secession with Max Shine after the 1947 C.I.O. convention.

[44]*Leaders' Bulletin,* p. 3. There were about eight hundred agents in these local unions.

[45]Heisel, Interview. Heisel suggested that the board's action was a "created issue," for most of the Local's officers would have given the cards to any member of the executive board other than the leaders of U.O.P.W.A.'s midwest region. Heisel also insisted that he was the only member of the board to vote against the suspension of the St. Louis Local.

[46]*Insurance Career,* June, 1948, p. 18.

113

Sometime in May, Charles Heisel, president of the U.O.P.W.A. insurance local in Pittsburgh, was approached by members of the Paperworkers Union. They informed him that a meeting was to take place in Washington on May 30 and requested his presence. Heisel attended and on that day left the U.O.P.W.A. He also accepted the Paperworkers' plan for establishing a semi-autonomous division of insurance agents within the structure of the union. Heisel's defection was a bitter pill for the U.O.P.W.A.'s leadership, for he was not only the president of a local numbering some nine hundred members, but he was also a member of the union's executive board and director of the Western Pennsylvania-West Virginia region.

Upon his return to Pittsburgh Heisel met with several members of his insurance local. They decided to hold a secret meeting on June 27, at which time they would seek the Pittsburgh agents' permission to take the local into the Paperworkers Union.

Word of the meeting leaked out, however. Leon W. Berney and Joseph Levy, a U.O.P.W.A. executive board member from Philadelphia, publicized the scheme and ordered a convocation of the Pittsburgh agents for June 30. Just why they gave Heisel a three-day grace period is unknown. When Berney's meeting was held, he told the agents that their local would have to be completely reorganized. The insurance men agreed and voted to replace Heisel with Ignatius Brennan, the vice president of the local.[47]

Meanwhile, Heisel had gone to Philadelphia to recruit for the United Paperworkers Union. Prior to his arrival in the city, the U.O.P.W.A. received a vote of confidence from its insurance Local there. Albert Forscher, the local's president had prevailed upon the 1,600 members to remain within the national union. Forscher, it seems, was one of those agents who believed that the leftist leadership of the U.O.P.W.A. could be overcome by remaining within the union.

The loyalty of the Philadelphia agents gave the union's officers a breather, but not for long. The Paperworkers simply continued raiding the insurance locals. When questioned about this by Philip Murray, Harry Sayre denied that his union's activity could be classified as raiding. He made the point that the insurance agents were convinced that the U.O.P.W.A. was not adhering to the national policies of the C.I.O. and that the agents were threatening

47Heisel, Interview, & *Leaders' Bulletin*, pp. 3-4.

to leave the parent body if they could not obtain a charter from another C.I.O. union. John Stanley, secretary-treasurer of the U.O.P.W.A., ridiculed Sayre's position, denying that the majority of the agents had any such intent. James Durkin even tried to convince himself and his union membership that only six hundred agents, at most, would join the Paperworkers.[48] But Durkin was frightened. He announced that he had asked Murray for a meeting in the shortest possible time. Murray passed the ball to Allan Haywood, the founder and honorary chairman of the Paperworkers' Organizing Committee, who, together with Sayre, met with Durkin and Leon W. Berney on June 12 and 13.[49] Nothing tangible was accomplished at the meeting, and the Paperworkers continued to sign up the insurance men.[50]

The New York agents continued to remain an anomaly. As the largest insurance local in the U.O.P.W.A., the majority of its agents voted to remain loyal to the national officers. In only two instances did any of the local's members decide to rebel against the national leadership. In one case, a Prudential agent, Oscar Schaeffer, ran against the local union president on the Communist issue. He was defeated and led a group of Prudential agents into the A.F. of L. Insurance Council. In the other case, a group of Prudential debit men simply left the labor movement.[51]

By August 2, 1948, then, the U.O.P.W.A. was still in control of the big insurance locals in New York, Philadelphia, Boston, Los Angeles and Detroit and had reorganized the locals in Pittsburgh and Lynn, Massachusetts. For all practical purposes, the U.O.P.W.A. had to write off the locals in Connecticut and St. Louis, and to suffer loss of face in the defections of Leo Wallace and Charles Heisel. August 2 stands as a halfway point in the union's struggle against its enemies, because it was on that date that the Paperworkers Union filed a petition for an election among the U.O.P.W.A.'s thirty-one state Prudential membership. Harry Sayre granted an interview to the press on that day and explained that the Paperworkers had complied with the Taft-Hartley Law while the

[48]*The New York Times,* June 3, 1948, p. 19.

[49]*Office and Professional News,* July, 1948, p. 1.

[50]*Leaders' Bulletin,* p. 5.

[51]*Insurance Career,* May, 1948, p. 10.

U.O.P.W.A. had not. For this reason, his union had to file with the N.L.R.B., or the C.I.O. would run the risk of losing the insurance men. He further observed that the C.I.O. did not condone the Paperworkers' activities, but that there was no other course of action open to his union. He concluded his remarks by saying:

> Ours is no selfish motive. We are not attempting to amalgamate the insurance men with the Paperworkers, but we are establishing a separate, semi-autonomous division with the ultimate purpose in mind of setting up an organization of, by and for insurance agents.[52]

Leon Berney naturally questioned Sayre's sincerity. He attacked both the Paperworkers and the A.F. of L. Insurance Council, pledging that his union would "fight the encroachment and defeat it."[53] Prior to the Sayre announcement, the A.F. of L. had tried to gain favor among the U.O.P.W.A.'s Prudential membership in Pennsylvania. On July 19, 1948, Matthew Hogan, an A.F. of L. insurance organizer, wrote to John Murphy, the A.F. of L. director of organization, and explained that his group had sent almost twenty thousand pieces of literature to the Pennsylvania agents. He was not successful, for the U.O.P.W.A. insisted, and correctly, that the A.F. of L. had received no more than forty authorization cards.[54]

To impress the U.O.P.W.A. membership of the importance of remaining in the union, Berney and others distributed thousands of leaflets designed to convince the insurance agents of the correctness of the union's position on the Taft-Hartley Law. One leaflet purported to show that the union's policy of noncompliance was not a violation of the law and that compliance was, indeed, voluntary. Challenging the Paperworkers Union, the U.O.P.W.A. officers asserted that, even if the organization should produce enough signatures in a state like Pennsylvania, the National Labor Relations Board would refuse to "allow a state election to replace national units." The leaflet went on to prove that should the Board permit an election, months of delay would ensue, to the detriment of the Prudential agents.[55]

[52]*The New York Times,* August 3, 1948, p. 13.

[53]*Ibid.*

[54]*Career,* October, 1948, p. 1. The A.F. of L. represented the Prudential agents in Delaware, Maryland, Virginia, the District of Columbia and Toledo, Ohio.

[55]"Your Questions Answered," U.O.P.W.A., Local 10.

In New York, Local 96, U.O.P.W.A., compiled another flyer. It quoted the words of the Solicitor of the United States Department of Labor who allegedly maintained that noncompliance did not bar an employer from negotiating with a noncomplying union.[56]

But the most telling declaration came from the Cleveland offices of the national U.O.P.W.A. The contents of the message were apparently written by the insurance agents of the Ohio-Kentucky Region and were addressed to the Paperworkers of Sandusky. Entitled "Don't Scab on Us," the letter reads in part:

> Just when we were about to open negotiations with the Prudential the Paperworkers wrote to the Prudential not to bargain with us. Your national officers are spending about $12,000.00 per month to get insurance agents to leave U.O.P.W.A. . . . You are a sister C.I.O. union. Don't let your National leaders use your dues and your Union to help the Prudential bust us. As fellow workers, brothers, we ask your help.[57]

Before long the national U.O.P.W.A. officers began to understand that something more was required than written appeals to the loyalty of the agents. Because they were sure of the outcome of their plan, the leadership decided as early as July 1948 to canvass membership sentiment on the union's policy toward the Taft-Hartley Law. They set early September as the deadline for returns on the referendum.[58]

Meanwhile, a union newspaper reported that Prudential was getting into the act. During August, Orville Beal, a vice president of the company, wrote to Prudential agents and stated that the firm would not bargain with the U.O.P.W.A. because of its failure to comply with the Taft-Hartley Law. Annoyed at Beal's interference, Durkin and Berney petitioned the company's agents to outsmart Prudential management. Their power was still considerable, because on August 24 many of the company's agents were "unable to write business."[59] Both union leaders wanted more than this. On September 1, agents from New York, New Jersey and Pennsylvania gathered around the Prudential's home office in Newark and carried

[56]"Questions and Answers on the Taft-Hartley Law," Executive Board, Local 96, U.O.P.W.A., New York City.

[57]"To the Paperworkers of Sandusky: Don't Scab on Us," Insurance Guild of Ohio-Kentucky, U.O.P.W.A., Cleveland, n.d.

[58]*Office and Professional News*, August, 1948, p. 2.

[59]*Career*, October, 1948, p. 1.

placards protesting the company's proposed action. Prudential officials called the police. Durkin and Berney, who were on hand for the demonstration, outwitted the police and gained access to the company's executive offices. Espying several familiar faces, they proposed to offer a deal to the company. Would Prudential management negotiate, they asked, if the U.O.P.W.A. leadership signed the non-Communist affidavit? The company officers were in no mood to play games with Durkin and Berney, and they insisted that their conversation was in no way to be construed as negotiations. One member of Prudential management told Durkin and Berney that demonstrations, such as they had just witnessed, had to cease. He also told them that work stoppages, slow downs and failures to write business were in violation of the contract. And Joseph Ferris, director of industrial relations for the company, is quoted as telling Durkin and Berney that Prudential would never deal with a "trouble maker" like John Stanley. The company promised no deals, no negotiations, no meetings. The situation, in other words, had not changed.[60]

Durkin and Berney then tried another approach; they consulted with members of the Paperworkers' executive board. Through the good offices of Allan Haywood, a meeting was arranged in his Washington apartment. Durkin and Berney offered to sign a truce, the terms of which were known only to themselves. If the Paperworkers would withdraw, they said, the U.O.P.W.A. would reinstate, without reprisal, all of the participants in the secession movement. The delegates of the Paperworkers Union made no promises. Durkin and Berney returned to New York and explained the strategy to their fellow officers. Both men were harshly rebuked and were told in no uncertain terms not to act on their own initiative again. The union officials declared the proposal null and void.

While Durkin and Berney had attended their mission, the results of the referendum on compliance with the Taft-Hartley became known, and this perhaps influenced the inner circle of the U.O.P. W.A. leadership to treat the two men as they did. If the union's figures are accurate, an overwhelming majority of the Office Workers' membership voted in favor of the union's position: 36,297

60 *Ibid.*

said they believed in noncompliance and only 6,055 disapproved the national officers' policy.[61]

It can be imagined that the union's leaders asked Durkin and Berney what more proof they desired. And in response they might have said they wanted proof that the Paperworkers Union would cease raiding their membership. Moreover, with the membership expressing itself against compliance, Durkin and Berney knew that the Paperworkers would simply step up their activity. The situation became so sticky that Philip Murray and Allan Haywood were soon forced to intervene. As early as May 1948 Murray had been informed as to what was going on. But he delayed taking action, possibly on the assumption that the U.O.P.W.A. itself would ultimately resolve the problem by complying with the Taft-Hartley Law. At any rate, he called a meeting in an attempt to resolve the dilemma posed by the Paperworkers and the forthcoming expiration of the Prudential contract.

Acting in behalf of Murray, Haywood met with the officers of the U.O.P.W.A. in Pittsburgh on September 8 and sought to convince the union's leaders that compliance was of primary importance. They scoffed at the idea. To quote Haywood's own words: "After many insults, they turned me down."[62]

Murray then decided that he had to meet with the group. Accordingly, he convoked a gathering of the U.O.P.W.A. and of the Paperworkers on September 10. The sum and substance of the meeting was that Murray demanded that the Paperworkers get out of the insurance field. The union acquiesced on September 28.[63]

Murray promised the insurance men that the C.I.O. would establish a separate organization for them in the near future. But this was easier said than done. He needed someone he could trust to take over the organization of the agents, and he was not exactly sure who could handle the job. Murray's problem, however, found scant sympathy among the insurance men. They were satisfied with the Paperworkers, and they resented Murray's seeming capitulation to the U.O.P.W.A. As a result of this, many of the agents joined the

[61]*Ibid.*

[62]C.I.O., *Convention Proceedings* (Portland, Ore., 1948), p. 340.

[63]*A Statement to Members of U.O.P.W.A. from their Delegates to the C.I.O. Convention,* n.d.

A.F. of L.'s National Federation of Insurance Agents Council.[64]

Murray's squeamishness about one C.I.O. union raiding another caused a grave crisis for the insurance agents, particularly those employed by Prudential. When Murray told the Paperworkers to cease raiding the U.O.P.W.A. insurance membership, the contract with Prudential had less than a month to run. The company's management had already stated their position on the United Office and Professional Workers of America. What Prudential did was sure to be copied by the Metropolitan and John Hancock.

[64]Heisel, Interview.

CHAPTER 6

THE AGENTS PICK UP THE PIECES

THE PRUDENTIAL HEARINGS

On October 1, 1948, the United Office and Professional Workers' contract with the Prudential Insurance Company expired. Organized agents in Boston and Rochester, N.Y., refused to write new business on that date, and there were strike votes taken against the company in diverse parts of the United States.[1] According to *The New York Times,* Prudential management admitted that the union's suspected Communist domination was the primary cause for their failure to negotiate a new contract; and they also stated that the company would not bargain until the union's officers signed the non-Communist affidavit of the Taft-Hartley Law. Furthermore, and in a surprise move, the company petitioned the National Labor Relations Board to conduct a new certification election on a state by state basis in each of the thirty-one states affiliated with the U.O.P.W.A.[2]

Calling the Communist charge "tripe," the union's leadership convened a group of Prudential agents in New York City. At the meeting they restated their demands for "65 and 15," union security and improved working conditions, and they voted to strike the company if necessary. On being questioned about the union's proposals, the Prudential management stated they were interested in only one issue, the representation of their agents.[3]

Meanwhile, the National Federation of Insurance Agents Council, A.F. of L., announced that it had enrolled sixty per cent of the U.O.P.W.A.'s Prudential membership.[4] An officer of the Council said that his organization would not honor the U.O.P.W.A. picket lines if a walkout took place; and he went on to characterize the

[1]*Career,* November, 1948, p. 3.

[2]*The New York Times,* October 1, 1948, p. 3.

[3]*Ibid.,* October 4, 1948, p. 10.

[4]The A.F. of L. Insurance Council adopted this new title in 1947. When Charles Heisel approached George Russ, he said that between five and six thousand Prudential agents were prepared to enter the A.F. of L. with him. Heisel, Interview.

[5]*The New York Times,* October 1, 1948, p. 3.

strike vote as "nothing more than an attempt by a desperate minority to coerce the majority."[5] He also related that the Council had adopted Prudential's plan for a state by state certification election and had already applied for permission to be on the ballot in Georgia, Oklahoma, North Carolina, and Rhode Island.

The A.F. of L. was not singlehandedly going to rifle the U.O.P. W.A. thirty-one state contract, however. Because it possessed agreements with Prudential in the important states of Ohio, Wisconsin and Minnesota, the independent International Union of Life Insurance Agents began to play for even higher stakes than the A.F. of L. Council. At about the time that the latter union petitioned the Board, the former requested permission to be on the ballot in Iowa and the populous states of Indiana and Illinois.[6]

During the first week of October 1948 Leonard Boudin, the Office Workers' attorney, made a motion that the union be included in the N.L.R.B. hearings, even though it had not filed for the thirty-one state Prudential unit. The Board's hearings' officer denied the motion. Boudin, therefore, issued the prompt rejoinder that he would seek an injunction to restrain the Board from holding any election in which the U.O.P.W.A. was not on the ballot.

While Boudin was threatening the N.L.R.B., Prudential allegedly became more active in the contest. On October 5 Orville Beal, a company vice president, stated that he had written Prudential's 14,000 agents, proposing to show that both Durkin and Berney had told him that three of the union's national officers were Communists. Asked for a comment, Durkin called Beal's letter a "tissue of distortions and fabrications." He maintained that it was an attempt to hide the real issue in the dispute: the company wanted an agency force free from any union meddling and nothing less.

On October 7 the regional director of the Board postponed indefinitely Prudential's request for an election. However, he did agree to a consent election in those states in which both the National Federation of Insurance Agents Council and the independent had requested to be on the ballot.[7]

During the following weeks Philip Murray wrote to the president

[6]*The Prudential Ins. Co. of America,* 80 N.L.R.B. 1583 (1949). The A.F. of L. apparently was not certain of its strength among U.O.P.W.A.'s Prudential membership, its boast notwithstanding.

[7]*The New York Times,* October 7, 1948, p. 25, & October 8, 1948, p. 21.

of Prudential, urging him to bargain with the U.O.P.W.A.; the company denied the request. In addition to this, Murray met with representatives of those agents who had expressed the desire to leave the union and to obtain a separate charter from the C.I.O. With regard to this contact, Murray was later quoted as saying that the men were greatly concerned about the U.O.P.W.A. leadership and the "irresponsibility of Durkin."[8]

On November 7, 1948, this same leadership began to show some signs of enlightenment. Aware of the impossibility of dealing with Prudential and the N.L.R.B. while they remained outside the pale of the Taft-Hartley Law, they met in New York City and resolved to sign the non-Communist affidavit. However, their method of compliance involved a radical change in the union's constitution. Under the guidance of Leonard Boudin, the executive board abolished the office of vice president and retained only the offices of president and secretary-treasurer. According to this method, only two of the union's leaders would have to sign the loyalty oath. The board then told James Durkin to stay on as president. In place of Stanley who resigned out of great "affection" for the labor movement, it appointed Bernard J. Mooney the new secretary-treasurer.

To circumvent the Law still further the board created a new post, "director of organization," and three lesser directorships, all of which came under the control of the prime director. Stanley assumed the position, "director of organization," Leon W. Berney and Joseph Levy became "directors" of the insurance division, and Lewis Alan Berne acquired the title of "director of the technical division." Since the Law did not include a provision about a "director of organization," the union's executive board concluded that Stanley and the other directors would not be obliged to sign the anti-Communist affidavit. When this technicality was taken care of, the remainder of the board resigned.

As a final point of business the board selected Durkin, Mooney, Richard Lewis, Berne, George Hansen, Osborne Landix and Stanley

[8]*Career,* December, 1948, p. 13.

to represent the U.O.P.W.A. at the forthcoming C.I.O. convention.[9]

On November 17 Durkin announced that his union had filed for an election for the thirty-one state Prudential unit, and, shortly thereafter, the Board notified the union that it was in compliance with the Law. Durkin thereupon asked the Board to dismiss the A.F. of L. Insurance Council's petition. The latter called this move "arrogant and foolish," insisting that it represented the majority of the Prudential agents.[10]

The scheme of the national officers for complying with the Law did not placate several groups of insurance men. For example, on November 12 a number of dissidents met in Newark to condemn the plan, and in Pittsburgh the Rev. Charles Owen Rice reportedly circulated a pamphlet among the agents in which he explained the moral implications of membership in a Communist dominated union.[11]

Chronologically, the C.I.O. convention of 1948 occurred before the N.L.R.B. conducted the Prudential election. Therefore, the events of the C.I.O. gathering will be chronicled before the outcome of that election is stated.

The C.I.O. Convention of 1948

On the very first day of the meeting, Philip Murray departed from his prepared text and expressed the desire that the Executive Board direct its attention to the problem of jurisdiction among the C.I.O.'s

[9]*Ibid.* Lewis had been acting secretary-treasurer of the union during Stanley's absence; Hansen was associated with the insurance locals in New York and Chicago; and Landix was in charge of organizing Negro agents in the New Orleans area. Norma Aaronson, a member of the board and possibly the U.O.P.W.A.'s most influential member, abstained from voting for compliance. She said at the time: "When insurance men came to me in the early days and were part of the A.F. of L., nobody asked me my political beliefs."

[10]*The New York Times,* November 18, 1948, p. 17. Citing *Craddock-Terry Shoe Corporation,* 76 N.L.R.B. 842, Kampelman asserts that the Board allowed certain of the unions to evade Sec. 9 (h) by changing their constitutions. However, the Board put a stop to "the ruse" in a case involving Donald Henderson and the Food, Tobacco and Agricultural Workers, a union with which the U.O.P.W.A. would later merge. cf. Kampelman, *The Communist Party vs. the C.I.O.,* p. 264.

[11]19 *News,* U.O.P.W.A., January, 1949, p. 1.

smaller affiliates. He said he had in mind such unions as the United Office and Professional Workers of America. Without hesitation he termed the union a failure, pointing to its diminished membership, its lack of success in organizing its jurisdiction, etc. He then gave Durkin the opportunity to defend his organization.

Durkin tried to establish that his union had a membership of 70,000 and that the U.O.P.W.A. had, among other things, obtained wage increases of approximately $1.5 million dollars for the Metropolitan agents alone. He called Murray's statement a "stab in the back" and said that the U.O.P.W.A. had not received any financial assistance from the C.I.O. since 1940. He derided the "hypocrisy" of the Paperworkers and that of the national C.I.O. for its ambiguous stand in supporting both the Paperworkers and the U.O.P.W.A. at the same time. Durkin then went on to give an account of his stewardship. He insisted that he was following the wishes of his union when he refused to sign the loyalty oath, opposed the Marshall Plan, supported the candidacy of Henry Wallace and endorsed the World Federation of Free Trade Unions. He further remarked that an identical motive impelled him as president of the New York State C.I.O. Council. He concluded his statement by observing: "It cannot but appear that there is reprisal; there is vindictiveness; there is revenge against the U.O.P.W.A. because of its difference of policies."[12]

When Durkin completed his speech, Philip Murray arose and denied Durkin's charge that C.I.O. had not lent the Office Workers financial assistance. He said that the national union had extended more financial relief to the U.O.P.W.A. than to any other C.I.O. affiliate. He went on to describe the union as having gone "through the process of complete distintegration." Then he spoke about Durkin in words that are filled with pity:

> The trouble with Jim Durkin is this: he does not understand trade unions. It is going to be extremely difficult for him to understand it. He cannot channel his thinking along trade union lines. Why he engages himself in these falsehoods is beyond me. I suppose that is how he lives. He cannot help it. As we go down the road, we discover many elements of irresponsibility. These are accidents of birth or what have you. They are things that belong to the chemical content of the

[12]C.I.O., *Convention Proceedings* (Portland, Ore., 1948), p. 175.

human body. They are afflictions that pursue men. I am not going to assume responsibility for the shortcomings of men like Jimmy Durkin.[13]

Murray concluded on a note of frustration. He said: "There is nothing I can do that can be of assistance to Durkin."

Later on in the proceedings John Stanley accused the national C.I.O. of conspiring with the Paperworkers Union. In rebuttal, Joseph Curran, president of the National Maritime Union and a recent convert to rightwing unionism, reminded Stanley that the U.O.P.W.A. "was busy assisting one side" in a recent election in his organization and asked whether that action could be construed as raiding.

Allan Haywood, who had been honorary chairman of the Paperworkers Organizing Committee, explained that he and Murray knew that the Paperworkers were raiding the U.O.P.W.A. and that both of them had ordered the union to withdraw. He then went on to examine his own work for the U.O.P.W.A. Declaring that neither Prudential nor Hancock would have granted the union a contract during the early years of its existence unless he were present at negotiations, he described the C.I.O.'s more recent efforts in behalf of the union. He said that he had met repeatedly with the U.O.P.W.A. and that he had personally, at Durkin's and Stanley's urging, drafted a letter instructing all of the C.I.O.'s organizers to assist the union in its struggle with Prudential. He asked the delegates to consider his work as a manifestation of C.I.O.'s continuing assistance to the union.

When Haywood completed his remarks, Murray took up the theme of investigating some of the smaller unions. He asserted that most of the time of the convention had been squandered by "representatives of these little organizations who have done nothing to build their unions." He said that the "U.O.P.W.A. has expended thousands of dollars of this organization's money on the floor of this convention, and it has not done a single, solitary damned thing to build up its own union."

Then he explained the small unions' failure to build their memberships. He said:

I am not going to protect cliques, small cliques of men whose interests are promoted and propagated by the *Daily Worker*

[13]*Ibid.*

and the Communist Party, from small organizations, from little membership in big industries, where people are yearning for the opportunity to become members of unions.[14]

By the time the convention adjourned the C.I.O. had put the United Office and Professional Workers on notice. Either the union conform to C.I.O. policy, that is, make its contribution to the national union's treasury and build its membership, or risk expulsion.

THE PRUDENTIAL ELECTION

On December 7, 1948, the leaders of the U.O.P.W.A. announced a meeting of the union's executive board for the following month. The wording of the announcement is interesting and indicates that the Office Workers' leaders had not learned one thing from the recent C.I.O. convention.

U.O.P.W.A. has made a substantial contribution and has become an important factor in the life of America. As a result the corporations and their hirelings in politics, in the press and in the labor movement have attempted to terrorize us and make difficult our path. We are going forward. We will win.[15]

But the path to victory, which they desired to achieve "within the framework of the C.I.O.," would be far more difficult than they imagined.[16] In the first place the national C.I.O. delivered the union a body blow by proclaiming its intention of forming an insurance affiliate within the next several weeks. Then, leaders of both the National Maritime Union and the Transport Workers Union revealed that they were severing their relationship with the union

[14]*Ibid.,* p. 344. Concerning Murray's remarks about the small unions, Saposs writes: "The evidence and arguments of the C.I.O. that the Communist-dominated unions failed to pursue pure trade-union procedures are rather tenuous. It is at least partially true that the leadership of some of these unions, particularly those like FTA (Food, Tobacco, Agricultural and Allied Workers) and U.O.P.W.A., had ineffective leadership and devoted considerable time and money to Communist Party activity. *No other union efforts, however, were more successful in the field covered by these jurisdictions.*" (emphasis added) cf. David J. Saposs, *Communism in American Unions* (New York: McGraw-Hill, 1959), p. 184.

[15]*The New York Times,* December 28, 1948, p. 40.

[16]9 *News,* U.O.P.W.A., January, 1949, p. 1.

when their respective contracts expired.[17] Finally, both the A.F. of
L. Insurance Council and the independent made frequent use of
Philip Murray's anti-Durkin, anti-U.O.P.W.A. statements.[18]

Meanwhile, the N.L.R.B. handed down a decision on the Prudential election. The Board denied the company's allegation that
the U.O.P.W.A. was not a bona fide trade union. It therefore
ordered a secret ballot election for the thirty-one state unit. However, the Board interjected the ruling that the participation of any
union hinged upon local union subscription to the Taft-Hartley
Law. The majority of the Board directed this decision at the
U.O.P.W.A., which, at the time it decided to comply, forbade its
locals any involvement with the Board without its prior approval.[19]
The U.O.P.W.A. evidently relaxed the prohibition, because after
some delay, the Board set the election for March 18, 1949.

All of the participants engaged in a vigorous campaign. The National Federation of Insurance Agents Council, A.F. of L., and the
International Union of Life Insurance Agents, independent, distributed thousands of newsletters, and their organizers addressed
numerous gatherings of Prudential agents.[20] The company expressed its views of the situation, relying on the "free speech" section of the Taft-Hartley Law. A booklet entitled, *The Communist
Party Independent Nominating Petition. Would YOU Sign This?
Officers of the U.O.P.W.A. Did!* and bearing the imprint of the
Prudential Press, offered photostatic reproductive evidence that the
U.O.P.W.A. was Communist dominated, and that its principal
officers were either card carrying Communists, or had subscribed to

[17]*The New York Times*, December 28, 1949, p. 40. The *Times'* account
includes the report that the Industrial Union of Marine and Shipbuilding
Workers had granted charters to defecting locals of U.O.P.W.A. social service employees and that the Union News Co. and the major motion picture
studios in New York had challenged the union's right to represent their
employees.

[18]*19 News,* U.O.P.W.A., January 1949, p. 1.

[19]*The Prudential Ins. Co. of America,* 80 N.L.R.B. 1583 (1948), & *Ibid.,*
81 N.L.R.B. 295 (1949). In the latter case, Board chairman Paul Herzog
pointed out that Prudential had contended that the local union in fact
engaged in collective bargaining, whereas the union professed that such was
not the case. Herzog believed that further hearings would enable the Board
members to know just who was correct.

[20]*Our Voice,* November, 1963, p. 2.

Communist front organizations or causes over an extensive period of time. The booklet also contained a picture of union members marching in the May Day Parade in New York in 1948.[21] In addition to this, the company wrote a letter to its agents urging them to refrain from voting for the union, or so the latter stated. Referring to the letter as "Beal's last stand," the union denounced the company for interference.[22]

At length the date of the election arrived, and the U.O.P.W.A. received fewer votes than the A.F. of L. Council, although the latter organization did not obtain a majority. The Labor Board ordered a runoff election between the two unions and set July 8 as the date. The U.O.P.W.A. immediately instituted an unfair labor practice charge against Prudential and called the National Federation of Insurance Agents Council a company union. According to a U.O.P.W.A. newspaper account, the Board concurred in the charge of interference. Consequently, it required Prudential to post notices specifying that it favored neither union, and it also commanded the company to negotiate with the union if it won the election. Meanwhile, tension within the organization continued unabated. A group calling itself a Committee of Agents demanded that the U.O.P.W.A. release its insurance charter and allow the agents to affiliate to the C.I.O. on a "federal charter" basis. The Committee's appeal was such that on April 8, 1949, the U.O.P.W.A. national officers called a meeting of insurance men whose opposition to the Committee was well known. On the following day, they met with Irving Abramson, the legal adviser of the Committee, and urgently requested the withdrawal of the C.I.O.-backed organization. Abramson rejected the proposal, stating in clear-cut language that the C.I.O. would ultimately obtain the U.O.P.W.A. insurance charter. To show them that he was intent on his mission, his Committee circulated a petition among the U.O.P.W.A. insurance locals, urging the members to seek a separate charter from Murray.

The U.O.P.W.A. leaders camouflaged their anxiety by calling the Committee an "unauthorized rump gathering." The C.I.O. was not impressed. Instead, it increased its activity among the union's insurance membership. Ernest Pugh, the C.I.O. regional director,

[21]*The Communist Party Independent Nominating Petition . . .*, Prudential Press, November, 1948, #36725.

[22]*Career,* March 15, 1949, p. 1.

for example, tried to persuade agents of the Southern Aid Society to negotiate a new contract as a "Committee of Employees" rather than as members of the U.O.P.W.A.

Emboldened by the C.I.O.'s support, three members of the Committee delivered an ultimatum to the union's leaders: either the U.O.P.W.A. agree to a separate charter by 2 P.M., April 28, or they would call a meeting of dissident agents and publish the outcome in the press. This tactic backfired, however, and, on the day of the proposed exposure, loyal agents in New York and Philadelphia summoned their forces and enacted a resolution which read as follows:

> We propose to stick together in our union, the U.O.P.W.A. We urge prompt action by our National officers and our executive board against anyone who proposes to split our ranks with any effort to set up another union or seek another charter for insurance agents.[23]

During this time Durkin made one last effort to stop the C.I.O.'s interference and to enlist its support in the Prudential runoff election. Knowing the C.I.O.'s position on the Taft-Hartley Law, he tried to obtain a jointly worded draft against it. The C.I.O. made no guarantees. He thereupon accused the national union of attempting "to enchain members of the C.I.O. to the program of Truman."[24]

The runoff election finally occurred, and the National Federation of Insurance Agents Council, A.F. of L., defeated the U.O.P.W.A. by a vote of 7,405 to 4,789. Thus, the work of almost a decade came to an end. Union officials attributed the crushing defeat to men like Charles Heisel and Leo Wallace and to what they termed the "pro-employer atmosphere" of the campaign. Trying to brush aside his disappointment, James Durkin said: "A.F. of L. unity is unity with the company."[25]

At that stage of the game Durkin and his fellow officers would have settled for any kind of unity. And after the 1949 C.I.O. convention they would even have settled for a labor union.

THE C.I.O. CONVENTION OF 1949

Right-wing C.I.O. officials went into the 1949 convention with the

[23]*Ibid.*, May 1, 1949, p. 2.

[24]*Ibid.*, September, 1949, p. 3.

[25]*Ibid.*

votes to deliver a decisive defeat to the left-wing faction. They decided to amend the constitution so that 'Communists' and 'fascists' would never again occupy positions of power within the organization. The left-wing protested vigorously, John Stanley, a U.O.P. W.A. delegate, among them. He said:

> If we are to amend this constitution, we should amend it for the evils that are present in the labor movement today and which need extra attention; we should amend it to go forward and organize the unorganized.[26]

His plea went unheeded. By a two-thirds vote the delegates empowered the C.I.O. executive board to remove any officer or board member and expel any affiliate "the policies and activities of which are consistently directed toward the achievement of the programs or purposes of the Communist Party, any fascist organization, or other totalitarian movement."

At this same convention the C.I.O. voted to expel the United Electrical Workers and the Farm Equipment Workers' unions and to set up trial boards to judge nine individuals and ten unions on charges of having consistently followed the Communist Party line. Included among this group was James Durkin and the union of which he was president, the United Office and Professional Workers of America.[27]

C.I.O. Expels the United Office and Professional Workers of America

The C.I.O. made the U.O.P.W.A. eat crow. It appointed Emil Rieve, president of the Textile Workers Union, as chairman of the trial committee, and, as co-examiners, Joseph Beirne of the Communications Workers and, of all people, Harry Sayre, the president of the Paperworkers Union. Rieve informed Durkin that the board would hold an informal hearing in Washington on December 15, 1949, that the union was forbidden counsel and that only executive board members could testify.[28]

On November 26 Durkin sent identical replies to Rieve and

[26]*C.I.O. News,* November 14, 1949, p. 6.

[27]*C.I.O. Constitution,* as amended, Section VI, Art. 10, 1949, & *C.I.O. News,* November 7, 1949, p. 3.

[28]*Career,* December 1, 1949, p. 3.

Philip Murray. His main point was a clever one: the C.I.O. had exceeded its authority in convening the trial board because the U.O.P.W.A. had failed to vote for the modification of the C.I.O. constitution. However, if there had to be a hearing, Durkin wrote, he wanted an "open trial" in New York City. He further insisted on his union's right to counsel, to cross-examine hostile witnesses and to an unlimited number of union members to speak in behalf of the organization. Durkin treated the appointment of Rieve, Beirne and Sayre with contempt, and he accused the C.I.O. of interpreting "its constitution for narrow, political and partisan purposes." He concluded his lengthy report on the trial procedure with the recommendation that a board of prominent persons sit in judgment on his union. Among others, he suggested the Chief Justice of the United States, the former Secretary of Labor, Frances Perkins, and John L. Lewis.[29]

If nothing else, Durkin knew how to touch a raw nerve. Murray evaded the proposal about Lewis by relying that the "larger" C.I.O. unions had voted to amend the constitution. And he upheld the amendment, calling it "valid despite the fact that some unions or persons might have [been] opposed."[30]

Rieve answered Durkin's letter on December 9, 1949. He denied the request for the "open trial," and advised that only Durkin, Stanley, Berne, Mooney and Berney would be permitted to attend the Washington hearing. The union's attorney, Leonard Boudin, then got busy, and, on December 12, petitioned the Federal District Court in Philadelphia for an injunction against the C.I.O.[31] Boudin argued that the C.I.O.'s proceedings against the U.O.P.W.A. were in violation of the Federal Constitution and the Bill of Rights.

[29]*Ibid.*, Durkin wrote that Rieve's Textile Workers had raided U.O.P. W.A.'s jurisdiction in a Connecticut mill. He asserted that the record of Sayre's union was well enough known to disqualify him, and he said that Beirne knew nothing of the C.I.O. Constitution. Durkin reminded both Murray and Rieve that until Beirne's entrance into the national union, the Communications' Workers had been vilified by C.I.O. officials. Perhaps this observation prompted Murray to replace Beirne with Martin Wagner, president of the Gas, Coke and Chemical Workers. The C.I.O. explained that the trial's delay occasioned the Beirne replacement. cf. *Official Reports . . . C.I.O.*, "Expulsion of U.O.P.W.A.," p. 56.

[30]*C.I.O. News*, December 5, 1949, p. 3.

[31]*Career*, December 15, 1949, p. 1. Boudin named as defendents Emil Rieve who had lived in Philadelphia at one time and George Craig, the C.I.O. regional director in the city. The Public Workers joined the U.O.P. W.A. in bringing the suit.

Boudin's action caused the C.I.O. to postpone the hearings until December 19. Meanwhile, Arthur Goldberg, acting in behalf of the national union, questioned the jurisdiction of the Philadelphia court, asserting that neither the C.I.O. nor the U.O.P.W.A. had their headquarters in that city. He also denied that the C.I.O.'s expulsion procedure violated either the Constitution or other federal statutes. Philip Murray expressed himself again on the situation. He repeated the basic and only premise governing the C.I.O.'s punitive measure against the U.O.P.W.A. Calling the organization one of the "six left-wing unions" in the C.I.O., he explained that it was "no longer in good standing because [it] had fallen in arrears on per capita payments to C.I.O." Apparently irked by Boudin's effrontery in bringing suit against his union, Murray directed the national C.I.O. to file a countersuit against the U.O.P.W.A. in the U.S. District Court in Washington for $18,700.00, a sum the C.I.O. claimed it lent the Office Workers in the early years of its existence.

In the meantime, Judge J. Cullen Ganey of the Philadelphia court denied the U.O.P.W.A.'s request for the injunction on the grounds that his court had no jurisdiction. Free to act, the C.I.O. convened the trial board. The hearing was a short one. About forty members of the U.O.P.W.A. tried to gain entrance into the committee room, but this was denied them.[32] Stanley Ruttenberg, the C.I.O. assistant counsel, offered documentary evidence showing that the U.O.P.W.A. leadership had, from the beginning of the union's existence, followed the Communist Party line to the letter. A few years after the hearing, the C.I.O. summarized Ruttenberg's indictment in the form of an official report. The document contains the "Six Period" analysis of the various shifts undertaken by the Communist Party in the United States. All of those periods, the *Official Reports* concludes, were followed by the United Office and Professional Workers of America. One section of the Report deserves quoting, at least in part:

> Of great significance is one single fact. Never in the history of the U.O.P.W.A. had any policy ever been adopted which in any way runs counter to the policies of the Communist Party or to the interests of the Soviet Union as those interests are

[32]*C.I.O. News,* December 26, 1949, p. 12. Recalling the proceedings against the New York C.I.O. Council, Rieve said: "We want a hearing — not a riot!"

reflected in the program of the Communist Party. If the Communist Party program had been a consistent one, this absence of conflict might not be significant. But, in view of the fact that in a period of 10 years the Communist Party had taken almost every conceivable position on every issue of public importance in the United States, the absence of any conflict between the position of the party and the position of this union is of great significance. The constant parallel between the position of the Communist Party and the position of the U.O.P.W.A. cannot possibly be explained by coincidence. The reason it cannot be so explained is that the policies of the Communist Party, as we have stated, have undergone repeated violent shifts, shifts which are explainable only on the basis of the party's subservience to the interests of the Soviet Union. And the policies of the U.O.P.W.A. have, in each instance, exhibited the same fatal shift.[33]

The C.I.O. document lists the various phases of the union's official policy and attempts to show that it faithfully adhered to every twist and turn of the program the Party had dictated for the United States.

In summary form, the "Six Period" analysis can be stated as follows. During the 'first period,' the Soviet Union urged a system of collective security with the Western Powers against Nazi Germany. The 'second period' dates from September 1939; Russia and Germany signed the non-aggression pact, and Roosevelt became the "Fascist warmonger." Germany's invasion of the Soviet Union ushered in the 'third period.' During this time the American people were to render assistance to Russia and Britain. The 'fourth period' began with the Japanese attack on Pearl Harbor and found the Communist Party demanding an immediate opening of the Second Front in Europe. The 'fifth period' continued the theme of the Second Front and culminated in the Tehran Agreement. Finally, the 'sixth period' evolved slowly and ultimately consisted in the Party's attack on President Truman's domestic and foreign policies and on the C.I.O.

The *Official Reports* then goes on to detail how the U.O.P.W.A. leadership aided and abetted the Communist Party's policy for the United States by identifying itself completely with the 'six period'

[33]*Official Reports . . . C.I.O.*, "Expulsion of U.O.P.W.A.," pp. 61-2.

master program. Since much of the C.I.O.'s criticism appears in previous parts of this work, the writer considers it unnecessary to repeat these points. However, certain of the C.I.O.'s conclusions are pertinent and deserve consideration. For example, the national union found that the U.O.P.W.A. directed its policies "toward the achievement and the purposes of the Communist Party rather than the objectives set forth in the constitution of the C.I.O." The union found further that it was not charging the Office Workers Union for its failure to adopt C.I.O. policy. The basic charge, the C.I.O. asserted, "is much more fundamental . . . this union has not adopted its policies on the basis of the honest objectives of American industrial unionism . . . . The charge, in short, is disloyalty to American trade-unionism." The C.I.O. made much of the fact that it was not judging the U.O.P.W.A. on the basis of isolated instances of its conformity to Communist Party policy. Rather, the *Report* concluded, this union "by following the twists and turns, the zigs and zags, of the Communist Party line has prevented itself from genuinely representing the interests of the white-collar workers of America."[34] The *Report*, in fine, limited itself to an evaluation of the union relative to the labor unionism practiced in the United States.

When the hearing was over, James Durkin was quoted as calling the trial "rigged." To this observation he added: "In reality, C.I.O. policies represent the program of the reactionary employers and their political agents. C.I.O. leaders have taken over Hitler's big weapon — the crusade against Communism."[35] Some time later Boudin filed a second injunction petition against the C.I.O. in the Federal District Court in Washington. And on the same day, the U.O.P.W.A. issued an eight-point refutation of C.I.O.'s charges which began with the words: "We don't intend to defend ourselves, but we will give an account of ourselves." Writing for the union, James Durkin observed that his organization had resisted "the betrayal of C.I.O. by its current leadship." He went on to claim, among other things, that the C.I.O. had failed to organize the unorganized, had failed to repeal the Taft-Hartley Law and, because of its pro-Administration policy, was attempting to lead the world into another war.[36]

[34]*Ibid.*, pp. 57-65, & 67-69.

[35]*C.I.O. News*, December 26, 1949, p. 12.

[36]*Statement by U.O.P.W.A., C.I.O. to C.I.O.*, December 19, 1949.

Because of Boudin's appeal the C.I.O. took no further action at
that time. At length, on February 6, 1950, the federal judge dismissed the U.O.P.W.A.'s petition.[37] Philip Murray praised the
decision as a "ruling [that] fully sustains the validity of the Constitutional amendment, adopted at the last CIO convention . . .
barring Communist dominated unions from continued affiliation
with CIO." On February 15, 1950, the C.I.O. expelled the United
Office and Professional Workers of America "whose policies followed and continue to follow exactly, without deviation, the program of the Communist Party." The expulsion became effective on
March 1.[38]

CHOOSING UP SIDES

About a month after the C.I.O. expelled the union, Allan Haywood wrote in his column: "Reports are that UOPWA, as well as
PW [Public Workers] are getting desperate and calling conventions.
While they 'bark' CIO marches on!"[39] And howl the U.O.P.W.A.
leaders did! In one of their first public utterances after the expulsion
the union leadership stated that their members "repudiated the
phony and biased trial and the kangaroo court proceedings of the
CIO." Durkin accused the national C.I.O. of inciting to religious
intolerance, of resorting to bribery and intimidation and of "playing
into the hands of employers in their efforts to company unionize the
white collar workers." Pointing out that the U.O.P.W.A. contracts
were still in effect, the union officials announced that they would
hold a convention in May for the purpose of strengthening union
democracy, defending union contracts and seeking wage increases.
One union leader tried to silence the critics by prejudging them. He
said: "Anyone who opposes or stands in the way of these fundamental aims and constitutional objectives of our union is an enemy
of our members and an obstacle to their welfare and security."[40]

The U.O.P.W.A. delegates assembled in Atlantic City on May 15,
1950. The union's insurance division went into the convention with
the Metropolitan, Hancock, Boston Mutual and other insurance

[37]*James Durkin* v. *Philip Murray,* 90 F. Supp. 367, D.D.C. (1950).

[38]*C.I.O. News,* February 13, 1950, p. 2.

[39]*Ibid.,* March 27, 1950, p. 11.

[40]*U.O.P.W.A.,* March 14, 1950, uopwa #16-1.

company agreements intact. During the course of the proceedings, the delegates, to no one's surprise, condemned the C.I.O. and the Taft-Hartley Law. As an antidote to further defections among the insurance membership they pledged themselves to greater unity. And in response to the C.I.O.'s reference to their union's failure to organize the white collar industry, the delegates approved a vaguely worded resolution establishing a strike fund of approximately one hundred thousand dollars. On the final day of the meeting all voted unanimously to return Durkin and Mooney to high union office.[41]

Nothing had changed. If anything, the union's leadership repeated all the trite phrases with increasing vigor. Apparently acting under instructions, a union publication carried an article from the *Daily Worker,* which proposed to show that American participation in the Korean War was a clear violation of that country's sovereignty. The copy read in part:

> We can demolish the Korean people, but we cannot win them. All we can do is get out. The Russians didn't call them "gooks." They treated the Koreans as equal human beings. The Russians didn't make Communists of the Koreans. The Japanese did — and we did.[42]

If the U.O.P.W.A. was bowing out of the labor picture in pitiful style, the C.I.O., in Haywood's words, was "marching on." The national union had granted charters to insurgent groups of agents under the title of "local industrial unions," and it planned to merge them into a Committe. On April 23 and 24, 1950, the national leadership convened a meeting of former U.O.P.W.A. insurance members in Philadelphia. This move was more easily contemplated than carried out, for the C.I.O. recognized that it was unable to furnish a union with an experienced insurance leadership for those men. The C.I.O. also realized that the A.F. of L. Insurance Council was beckoning these agents and that it had a union ready made for their purpose. Accordingly, the C.I.O. offered the agents the carrot of compromise: seasoned veterans of the national union's organizational battles would operate a committee of agents until such time as the men could stand alone.

[41]*Career,* May 31, 1950, p. 1. This issue of the newspaper contained the Abbreviated Proceedings of U.O.P.W.A. Constitutional Convention, Atlantic City, New Jersey, May 15-19, 1950.

[42]*U.O.P.W.A./*18, reprinted from the *Daily Worker,* July 24, 1950.

The agents who wanted to stay within the C.I.O. had little choice in the matter; they accepted the plan. As chairman of the group the C.I.O. proposed Allan Haywood. This already overburdened man had shown enormous interest in the insurance division of the expelled U.O.P.W.A. and had, in fact, helped the union on numerous occasions. Haywood was acceptable to the agents. In the role of secretary-treasurer, the C.I.O. cast Harold Ash. He had recently served as a leader of the Communications Workers Organizing Committee. His experience in the insurance field was negligible, but the agents approved of his appointment. The C.I.O. looked around for an insurance debit agent for the vice chairman's position and decided upon Simon Helfgott, a man with a varied background in the old Local 30, U.O.P.W.A., New York. (After his split with the union, Helfgott became first president of the C.I.O.'s newly chartered Local 1706 in New York City.) Elected to the executive board were debitmen, all of whom had wide experience in insurance unionism.[43]

Searching for a name for the new organization proved difficult, for some agents, no doubt influenced by the A.F. of L. Insurance Council's form of organization, wanted a union for insurance agents only. The national C.I.O. disagreed, and its opinion prevailed. At the request of the C.I.O. the agents decided to call the new group the Insurance and Allied Workers Organizing Committee, thereby upholding the C.I.O.'s demand for an affiliate that would eventually enroll insurance company office workers.

After the formation of the Committee, the most important business of the meeting centered around the Hancock and the diminutive Metropolitan contracts. Although the U.O.P.W.A. was in a shambles, it still possessed these contracts and without them the Committee could not possibly hope to survive. Therefore, it decided to capitalize on the union's expulsion and the reasons for it. In a

[43]*C.I.O. News,* May 1, 1950, p. 11.

[44]"Don't Be Fooled!" I.A.W.O.C., C.I.O.

[45]*Career,* March 15, p. 3; and June 15, p. 1 (1950). The Hancock contract expired on December 31, 1948. The U.O.P.W.A. defeated the A.F. of L. in a subsequent election. Between the time of the expulsion and the formation of the C.I.O. Insurance Committee, John Hancock received a court order entitling it to withhold payment of the agents dues to the U.O.P.W.A.

leaflet entitled, "Don't be fooled," the C.I.O. presented evidence that the majority of the U.O.P.W.A. officials had signed various petitions and protests in behalf of the Civil Rights Congress, a group on the Attorney General's list of subversive organizations.[44]

In addition to this, the C.I.O. Committee distributed cards bidding the agents go off dues deduction in Metropolitan and Hancock.[45] Furthermore, it tried unsuccessfully to defeat the U.O.P.W.A. in an N.L.R.B. election in the Boston Mutual Life Insurance Company. This incident led to further complications which will be detailed later on in this history.[46]

Meanwhile, the U.O.P.W.A. was moving in a new direction. In an effort to strengthen its position against Hancock, Metropolitan, and other firms, and the C.I.O. as well, the union's officers decided to join forces with two small labor organizations.

THREE SMALL UNIONS MERGE

At a meeting of the executive board of the United Office and Professional Workers of America on August 28, 1950, the union's highest officers voted to merge their union with the Distributive Workers' Union, which had seceded from the C.I.O., and with the Food, Tobacco, Agricultural and Allied Workers, which had been expelled from the C.I.O. James Durkin, president of the U.O.P.W.A., told the press that the merger was in no sense "a third labor federation."[47]

Of the three organizations, the Distributive Workers' Union (D.W.U.) was the largest, and it was financially solvent. Founded as an international in February 1950, the union had a stated membership of 36,000, half of whom were in the organization's Wholesale and Warehouse Local 65 in New York City. The union's history actually dates from 1937 when Arthur Osman founded the Local. Affiliated to the C.I.O.'s United Retail, Wholesale and De-

[46]*Ibid.*, June 15, 1950, p. 2.

[47]At the 1949 C.I.O. Convention Mike Quill, president of the Transport Workers, said: "If anyone tells me a third Federation of Labor was not planned, it is wrong, because I used to travel in very good circles . . . in the month of January, 1947, Bill Foster told me that the National Board of the Communist Party had decided to form a third Federation of Labor, the same as they did the Henry Wallace Third Party." cf. 1949 C.I.O. *Convention Proceedings*, p. 273.

partment Store Union, Local 65 has been described as "one of the most completely Communist-controlled trade unions in the entire United States."[48] When the Retail Union decided to clean house in 1948, the Osman group had no choice but to leave the C.I.O. It undertook this action because of what it termed the national union's "dictatorship and undemocratic practices." At the time of its merger with the U.O.P.W.A. and the Food, Tobacco and Agricultural Workers, the Distributive Workers' leaders maintained that ninety-six per cent of the rank-and-file had paid their dues in full.

The Food, Tobacco, Agricultural and Allied Workers resembled the U.O.P.W.A. in that it had been expelled from C.I.O. for Communist domination. Its president, Donald Henderson, stated that the union had a membership of 35,000 and that it had contracts with such firms as R. J. Reynolds, Campbell Soup, the Quaker Oats Co., Van Camp and the Growers and Shippers Association of California.[49]

On October 6 and 7, 1950, the three unions merged and called the new organization the Distributive, Processing and Office Workers of America (D.P.O.). The U.O.P.W.A. entered the merger with an imposing list of credentials. The Hancock agreement was intact, although the union's relationship with Metropolitan was not so secure; the union had lost all of its jurisdictions in the company, with the exception of Greater New York and New Jersey. The union also possessed a number of smaller insurance company agreements.[50] Other divisions of the union had contracts with the following firms: M.G.M., 20th Century Fox, Columbia and Paramount Pictures' offices in New York; C.B.S. Radio and two local New York radio stations; the publishing firms of Alfred Knopf, Random House and Viking; the retail stores of Lerner's, Gimbel's and Bloomingdale's; and the technical employees in the Cutter Laboratories in Oakland,

[48]Kampelman, The Communist Party vs. the C.I.O., p. 33.

[49]Champion, September 7, 1950, p. 3. cf. also, Official Reports . . . C.I.O., "Expulsion of FTA," pp. 23-33, and Kampelman, The Communist Party vs. the C.I.O., pp. 173-75.

[50]These firms included Boston Mutual, the Southern Aid Society, the Golden Eagle Life, Pioneer Life, Supreme Liberty Life, Provident Home, Home Life, and the Monumental Life in Ohio and Missouri.

California.[51] The U.O.P.W.A.'s Union News' membership in Boston had recently bolted to the right-wing Retail, Wholesale and Department Store Union, but the organization preserved its contract with the New Jersey branch of the company.

To impress the other two parties to the merger still more, the union announced that it had about 27,000 members and a cash fund of some $20,000.00. The statistics must have impressed the Food, Tobacco, and Agricultural Workers, since this union had no treasury at all, although the Distributive Workers, with its great financial resources, must have considered the U.O.P.W.A. an impoverished organization.[52]

When the three unions met, the delegates elected by acclamation the following individuals to high office: Arthur Osman, president, James Durkin, secretary-treasurer and Donald Henderson, administrative director. After he was sworn, the new president said that the merger brought together delegates representing eighty thousand members. Reflecting on the difficult times of the past months, Osman observed:

> We are part of the industries that C.I.O. considered unorganizable. But C.I.O. and A.F. of L. leaders are exposed by us, for without their betrayals, the conspiracy would not have succeeded. We are incorruptible. We became a source of embarrassment to the traitors in the labor movement and the object of their union busting tactics.[53]

The theme continued. With small modesty, Osman told the delegates to pattern their future on the old Distributive Workers' Union Local 65. Osman ended his speech with the cry: "Build, build, build!"[54]

The delegates then voted on a new constitution, based on the D.W.U.'s, with relatively few changes. Of interest is the constitutional phrase granting local unions the right to secede from the national organization provided the local's membership approve. There likewise was enacted a provision that "there be full respect

[51]*Union Voice*, October 22, 1950, p. 2.

[52]Distributive, Processing and Office Workers of America, *Founding Convention* (New York, N.Y., 1950), p. M1.

[53]*Union Voice*, October 22, 1950, p. M1.

[54]*Ibid.*

for diverse opinions and all shall have freedom of expression." Per capita tax was determined on the basis of paid employment.

The new union also provided for eight vice presidents. The former Office Workers' union picked up two of the posts, for the delegates elected John Stanley and Victoria Garvin as vice presidents. And among the members of the union's executive board the following were one-time U.O.P.W.A. officers: Norma Aaronson, Leon Berney, Max Lefkowith, Aaron Schneider, Osborne Landix and Bernard Segal.

The merger was far from a happy one. In May 1951 Durkin was at work in Winston-Salem in charge of reorganizing the employees of the R. J. Reynolds Tobacco Co.[55] But he was not slated to remain at this task for long. Congress had passed the Subversive Activities Control Act in 1950, over the veto of President Truman, and in the summer of 1951 a Senate investigating committee began to look into the affairs of certain former C.I.O. unions. At these hearings Osman, Henderson and Durkin were identified as Communists. One witness, Harvey Matusow, said that the New York County branch of the Communist Party was directing the newly merged union, the Distributive, Processing and Office Workers of America.[56] Another witness, Louis Budenz, said of Durkin: "James Harvey Durkin I know to be a Communist from having met him, though the occasions are not fresh in my memory at the moment. They are not many."[57] And Victor Riesel obliged the committee members with the following observation:

> I have seen Mr. Durkin lead the Communist contingent on the floor of the CIO, have had personal jousts with him when he espoused the Communist Party line . . . he is known in New York and in national CIO as one of the men chosen by the Communist Party to lead the fight against Phil Murray.[58]

[55]*Ibid.,* June 3, 1951, p. 8.

[56]Subcommittee of the Committee on the Judiciary, *Hearings* . . . Distributive, Processing and Office Workers of America, p. 162.

[57]*Ibid.,* p. 2.

[58]*Ibid.,* p. 5. Riesel confirmed the statement of Mike Quill concerning the formation of the Third Labor Labor Federation. He said: "The *Daily Worker* on October 10, 1950, made the point that the merger of the three unions [U.O.P.W.A., the Distributive Workers and the Food and Tobacco Workers] was going to be a Third Federation outside A.F. of L. and C.I.O., a Communist Party Federation in the United States."

None of the D.P.O. leaders were called to testify that summer.

On October 24 the union's executive board reviewed the first year of the merger and decided that a "more democratic union was needed." The former U.O.P.W.A. had, it seemed, doctored its membership figures and had gone into the merger with four or five thousand dues paying members, instead of the 27,000 it had initially claimed. The board therefore devised a proportional representation formula whereby "every leader of D.P.O. must come from a substantial group of members." As a result of the new ruling the board dismissed the entire slate of former U.O.P.W.A. officers, with the exception of Osborne Landix who stayed on as an organizer of Negro insurance agents in the New Orleans area. (The organization publicly emphasized that the American Negro was desperately in need of labor organization.) Donald Henderson replaced James Durkin as secretary-treasurer, and David Livingston, the chief executive officer of Local 65, was appointed vice president. The board replaced most of the organizers at the Reynolds plant at Winston-Salem, including James Durkin. Those who wished to stay on were to join District 65.[59]

On February 15, 1952, Durkin appeared before the Senate subcommittee. Although he spoke freely about his role as an organizer with the United Office and Professional Workers of America, he took the fifth amendment on every occasion involving his career as president of that organization and as secretary-treasurer of the Distributive, Processing and Office Workers of America. When the committee completed its questioning in that area, Durkin was asked to describe his whereabouts since Winston-Salem. Again he responded, and his answers possess the element of high tragedy. He told the committee that he had worked in a Newark, New Jersey, factory during the latter part of 1951 and that, at the time of his appearance before the committee, he was employed by the Dutch Mustard Company in Brooklyn.[60]

With Durkin's eclipse, he and his union, the latter with one glaring exception, faded from view.[61]

[59]*Union Voice,* November 4, 1951, p. 13.

[60]Subcommittee of the Committee on the Judiciary, *Hearings* . . . D.P. O.W.A., p. 157.

[61]The Food and Tobacco Workers were also expelled and were no longer heard from. cf. D.P.O., *Convention Proceedings,* 1953, p. 1 The Distributive Workers subsequently sought re-affiliation with the C.I.O.

The John Hancock Case

When the U.O.P.W.A. merged with the Distributive Workers and the Food and Tobacco Workers, it represented the agency force of the John Hancock Mutual Life Insurance Company. These agents were intensely loyal to the principles of trade unionism, even though several thousands of them had defected from the union. In the summer of 1950 the Insurance and Allied Workers Organizing Committee, C.I.O., along with the U.O.P.W.A., asked the company to increase the agents' wages, a necessity, both groups maintained, in view of the rising living costs occasioned by the outbreak of war in Korea. One C.I.O. source pointed out that Paul Clarke, the president of Hancock, advised the union that the pending Labor Board election ruled out any thought of bargaining at that time. The same source further related that the C.I.O. was dissatisfied with Clarke's response and, as a consequence, sent a delegation to Boston to try to convince him that the C.I.O., in theory, represented the company's agents. If the C.I.O. even theoretically represented the debit men, then the company would grant the increase, or so the C.I.O. reasoned. Clarke necessarily rejected the argument.[62]

In the latter part of 1950, it appears that Hancock unilaterally granted its agents an increase of $250.00 per year, promising to begin payment of the first installment on January 17, 1951, and to complete the deal when the contract expired in December. The Distributive, Processing and Office Workers Union, which by then had inherited the Hancock agreement, merely expressed dissatisfaction with the size of the increase.

Leon W. Berney, the chairman of the union's insurance division, took note of another dissatisfying development. He stated that the Hancock force had been "seriously split and that, among the agents generally, there has been no widespread, consistent demonstration of strength as union members."[63] This was an interesting and realistic observation, for Berney was at last admitting that his possession of the Hancock agreement was tenuous to say the least. Although he held the contract, this meant nothing if the company was granting

[62]"What Can We Believe? Vote IAWOC-CIO," Insurance and Allied Workers Organizing Committee, Washington 5, D.C.

[63]*Union Voice,* January 14, 1951, p. 3.

wage increases without consulting him and if the agents were "seriously split."

Between late 1950 and May 1951, Berney undertook a series of calculated risks, none of which assured the preservation of his influence or of his job. His first plan was to surrender over to the C.I.O. the Hancock contract but with the reservation that he keep his job. Accordingly, he met with Haywood who, in turn, laid down certain conditions for Berney's return to the C.I.O. He demanded that Berney break with his associates in the Distributive, Processing and Office Workers Union and that he sign the non-Communist affidavit. Berney agreed. However, at their next meeting Berney advised Haywood that he could not commit himself. Haywood then washed his hands of Berney.

Yet Berney did not lose hope of re-entering the C.I.O. He made contact with Simon Helfgott, the president of the newly chartered C.I.O. insurance local in New York, and prevailed upon him to plead his cause with Haywood. However, Haywood's first answer was final. He planned to obtain the Hancock contract without the aid of Berney.[64]

During this time increasing numbers of Hancock agents were joining the C.I.O. Insurance Council. In an effort to deny the Council the contract, Berney consulted with George Russ of the A.F. of L. Insurance Council on the possibility of taking his followers into the Federation. Russ is alleged to have considered the matter with the national A.F. of L., but just whom he contacted is a matter of some dispute. One source has it that he asked George Meany for a charter for the agents. Meany, suspecting Berney, merely promised to study the problem.[65] Another viewpoint holds that Russ went directly to William Green, who allegedly offered to make provision for the Hancock agents.[66]

Whichever of the two versions of the story is correct, Berney and Russ obtained certain guarantees from the A.F. of L. and went ahead with plans for the amalgamation. In essence, it was decided that Berney would enter the National Federation of Insurance

[64]Interview with Kenneth Young, former Research Director, Insurance Workers of America, C.I.O., June 18, 1959.

[65]*Ibid.*

[66]Heisel, Interview. It should be noted that Russ was a paid employee of the A.F. of L. during the time under consideration.

Agents Council, A.F. of L., as a vice president and that the merger would occur at the founding of a new A.F. of L. insurance union in May 1951.

Early in that year Berney withdrew from the Distributive, Processing and Office Workers Union and took the loyal Hancock agents with him. He established an organization called the United Insurance Agents of America.[67] The Russ-Berney detente might have succeeded had not certain A.F. of L. insurance men, such as Charles Heisel and Max Shine, discovered its existence. Both men had held executive posts in the former U.O.P.W.A. and had known Berney well. And, more importantly, they had defected from the union when the Communist issue became irresolvable. As a result of this complicated and unhappy experience both men told Russ that neither their union nor the A.F. of L. should have dealings of any kind with Berney.[68] Their arguments were such that they apparently convinced Russ.

Moreover, the I.A.W.O.C., C.I.O., publicized the Russ-Berney agreement. In making the pact known, the C.I.O. resorted to a crude maneuver: it informed the Hancock agents that Berney despised the A.F. of L. and quoted chapter and verse from old U.O.P.W.A. literature to prove it.[69]

While these developments were taking shape, the Labor Board announced its decision to hold a mail ballot election among Hancock agents. The A.F. of L. protested and asked for a postponement. Hancock likewise objected because of what it termed insufficient investigation of the case. The Board disregarded both objections and handed down a decision which noted that about half of the 5,800 Hancock agents had joined the C.I.O.'s Insurance Committee.[70] The Board therefore determined that the ballots should be mailed not later than May 10, 1951.

When all of the results were tabulated, the Insurance and Allied Workers Organizing Committee, C.I.O., won the election, although

[67]*CIO Insurance News Letter, IAWOC,* January 28, 1952, "The Year in Review—May, 1951," p. 3.

[68]Heisel, Interview.

[69]Young, Interview.

[70]*C.I.O. News,* March 19, 1951, p. 11. cf. also, *John Hancock Mutual Life Ins. Co.,* N.L.R.B. Case no. 1-RC-1654.

Berney's United Insurance Agents of America performed remarkably well. Out of about 5,400 eligible votes, a little over three thousand men voted for the C.I.O., while 1,499 agents chose Berney's union. For all practical purposes, the C.I.O. routed the A.F. of L. Insurance Council, since only 692 Hancock agents voted for it. In all only seventy-eight debit men voted for no union.[71]

However, Leon W. Berney was not beaten yet. He had one more chance to hold on to his position. When the National Federation of Insurance Agents Council, A.F. of L., held its convention in Chicago, a group of Hancock agents loyal to Berney gathered in the same city and asked Russ, the president of the Council, to recognize the United Insurance Agents of America. Russ merely promised to keep the group in mind.[72]

With this incident the United Office and Professional Workers of America, then a part of the Distributive Workers' union, disappeared as an effective force in the insurance field. Only once more would the embers of the old "militancy" revive, for the Distributive Workers had the Boston Mutual Life contract and intended to keep it. In the end these men too would disappear with Berney, Durkin, Merrill, Stanley and all the rest, their deeds relegated to the dustbin of lost causes.

That their union was Communist-dominated can scarcely be questioned. That the ghost of the old United Office and Professional Workers of America walked the earth and haunted the right-wing C.I.O. insurance organizers is also part of the continuing story. A true evaluation of this union and its leaders cannot be put down so easily. Although it was a small organization, as Philip Murray had taunted, it achieved what no other union, large or small, had been able to accomplish. It brought into the union fold insurance agents of the Metropolitan, Prudential and Hancock companies. One can pause and wonder what the U.O.P.W.A. might have done had its leaders not been trapped by an ideology that was foreign to American trade unionism. But the union made its mark on the labor movement. For better or for worse, the C.I.O. and A.F. of L. insurance unions would have to follow in its footsteps.

[71]*C.I.O. News,* May 28, 1951, p. 11.

[72]Adapted from various sources.

CHAPTER 7

THE NEW C.I.O. UNION: A RECORD OF SURVIVAL

THE INSURANCE AND ALLIED WORKERS
ORGANIZING COMMITTEE, C.I.O.

Nineteen hundred and forty-nine was the year of decision for the C.I.O. The organization finally faced up to the critical issue of left-wing unionism and, although it sustained a substantial loss in membership, expelled eleven Communist dominated unions. Yet, more was required than the elimination of such affiliates, for the C.I.O. committed itself to the formation of right-wing unions for those workers who never fell prey to the blandishments of the Party line. Forces and counter forces were at work to make the transition a difficult one.

The United Office and Professional Workers of America is a case in point. In spite of Philip Murray's condemnation of the union, the U.O.P.W.A. had pioneered the organization of certain segments of the American white collar industry. The C.I.O. recognized this and desperately wanted to fill the vacuum created by the expulsion of the U.O.P.W.A.; at the same time, the C.I.O. attempted to hold on to as much of the Office Workers' organizational advantage as possible.

To accomplish this goal the C.I.O. needed time, and it required a fresh approach to the mentality of the insurance agents and of white collar workers in general. Charles Heisel, a leader of the Prudential secessionist faction, gave the C.I.O. no time. Because of the pressure of events, the labor organization could not form a union for insurance agents in the brief period Heisel and others allotted it. Consequently, he accused the C.I.O. of procrastinating and took about 5,000 Prudential agents into the A.F. of L.[1] As a result of Heisel's move, the C.I.O. lost the advantage that had made the U.O.P.W.A. unique. No longer was there a national union that could lay claim to representing the majority of the insurance agents in Prudential and John Hancock and a substantial number in Metropolitan, the firms which had come to be known as the "Big Three" industrial life insurance companies.

Organized labor's appreciation of the white collar mentality posed quite another problem. From the beginning of its existence

[1]*Supra,* pp. 118-19.

the C.I.O. was aware of the dilemma, although it never fully discovered the basic tool for organizing the professional employee. When the U.O.P.W.A. was expelled, the C.I.O. possessed men with experience, such as Allan S. Haywood, who had worked with the Office Workers' union from its infancy. While Haywood never agreed with the dominant faction in the union, he considered the U.O.P.W.A.'s structure basically sound. According to his way of thinking, there was need for a catch-all type of organization, one which could grow and prosper because its members had a common interest and a common goal. Since the C.I.O. had the utmost confidence in Haywood, it was to him that the national union turned to fill the void created by the disruption of the U.O.P.W.A. In appointing him, the C.I.O. was indicating the importance it attached to the new Committee and was, in reality, putting its reputation on the line; after Murray himself, Haywood was the most important person in the union. If he failed, the C.I.O. might just as well wash its hands of the white collar worker.

The majority of the organized insurance agents dismissed Haywood's viewpoint about the basic soundness of the U.O.P.W.A. These men believed that the organization had been structurally defective from the beginning, precisely because the leftwing founders had been able to preserve control over its divergent elements. Since the agents carried the major portion of the union's financial obligations, they considered themselves entitled to a stronger voice in union affairs than they in fact possessed. It has already been shown that any effort on the part of the insurance division to minimize the power of the ruling faction was vetoed by members of the other sections who enjoyed the same rights and privileges as the agents. As a result of this experience, these men came to distrust the white collar union member who was not employed in the insurance industry; they expressed this fear knowing full well that their own division was not without fault by any stretch of the imagination. However, they believed that they had a better than even chance of controlling fellow unionists whose basic work and interests were the same.

For many of these C.I.O. trade unionists there was also a certain appeal in the slogan of the National Federation of Insurance Agents Council, A.F. of L.: it advertised itself as an organization "of, by and for insurance agents." Nevertheless, they had come to value the C.I.O.'s methods and were not prepared to branch out into the unfamiliar territory of the Federation in any case.

When the C.I.O. established the Insurance and Allied Workers Organizing Committee in April 1950, then, it was forced by circumstances to grant the agents almost everything they wanted. Allan Haywood, the founder and first chairman of the Committee, was responsible for inserting the C.I.O.'s one condition. Believing that the agents could never succeed in dealing with the companies unless they had allies among the office personnel, he insisted that the charter include a provision for the organization of the entire insurance industry work force. However, according to Haywood's reasoning, this was a compromise solution at best; to the end of his life he would preserve the goal of using the new union as a base on which to form a labor organization for most of America's white collar workers.[2] That this viewpoint was not Haywood's exclusively will be shown later.

The formative period of the Insurance and Allied Workers Organizing Committee (I.A.W.O.C.) was burdened over conflict of policy between the agents and the national C.I.O. The debit men desired all the help the C.I.O. could offer, yet they wanted to run the organization themselves. From the beginning Haywood insisted that the C.I.O. appoint all the Committee's officers and that his group be the final arbiter of the many organizational difficulties confronting the fledgling union.

Among those C.I.O. personnel to whom Haywood entrusted the I.A.W.O.C. was Richard Leonard. Leonard's background in the insurance industry was a modest one; in 1941 he negotiated a pension plan for the United Automobile Workers with John Hancock. Since he was available and willing, Haywood made him his top administrative assistant.[3]

With one exception, Haywood offered the remaining posts in the new union to C.I.O. organizers. Harold Ash became the first secretary-treasurer of the I.A.W.O.C. and Fred Pieper one of its principal organizers. Haywood chose Simon Helfgott, a book carrying agent and a founder of Local 1706, New York, as the

[2]Insurance and Allied Workers Organizing Committee, *Report of the Proceedings of the Second and Third Annual Conference*, 1951 and 1952.

[3]Interview with Richard Leonard, Assistant to Walter P. Reuther, I.U.D., AFL-CIO, June 18, 1959.

vice-chairman of the Committee, a move which helped to appease the more critical insurance men.

Haywood resigned the chairmanship of the I.A.W.O.C. in 1952 and recommended that Richard Leonard succeed him. His promotion of Leonard vindicated his faith in a man about whom he said: "Your accomplishments of the past year are all his doing."[4] Haywood had established his last organizing committee, and both out of respect for his wishes and because of their genuine admiration the agents abided by his request. Haywood also advised the agents to re-elect Helfgott and to choose James Brisbane as the secretary-treasurer in place of Harold Ash who had recently resigned. Though not an agent himself, Brisbane had found employment in the national C.I.O. as an accountant and had come to Haywood's attention during the course of his career with the labor union. The debit agents elected both Helfgott and Brisbane to the national leadership of their organization.[5]

Haywood's estimate of Leonard was accurate, for his accomplishments were many. He ruled a numerically small union — there were approximately seven thousand members in the I.A.W.O.C. at the time — and he succeeded in pacifying all of the differing elements within the organization, divergencies resulting from company affiliation, geography and organizational technique.

Leonard also led the I.A.W.O.C. in negotiating contracts with seven of the smaller companies, in achieving a union shop agreement in Hancock and in winning an election in Metropolitan Life in Greater New York, New Jersey and Pennsylvania. Leonard's leadership ability is well illustrated in the battle the Organizing Committee conducted against Metropolitan for union recognition. In 1949, the United Office and Professional Workers of America had won elections among the company's agents in Greater New York and New Jersey, but the Metropolitan management refused to bargain with the union because it had failed to comply with the Taft-Hartley Law. The union protested the company's action to the N.L.R.B. In 1950, the Board ruled "administratively" that the union had complied and ordered elections in six states, all of which proved inconclusive or were lost by the U.O.P.W.A.[6]

[4] I.A.W.O.C., *Conference Proceedings* (Philadelphia, Pa., 1952), p. 13.

[5] *Ibid.*

[6] *The Metropolitan Life Insurance Co.*, 90 N.L.R.B. 935 (1950). The states were: Connecticut, Massachusetts, Pennsylvania, Michigan, Indiana and Illinois.

Meanwhile, the C.I.O. formed the I.A.W.O.C. and began raiding the U.O.P.W.A.'s Metropolitan membership in Greater New York, New Jersey and Pennsylvania. Since the C.I.O. believed it had fallen heir to these organized agents, it found itself in the awkward position of siding with Metropolitan in asking the Labor Board to "open the record" with regard to the U.O.P.W.A.'s jurisdiction in Greater New York and New Jersey. In the fall of 1950 the Board denied the petition and ordered the company to bargain with the U.O.P.W.A.[7]

The company refused to abide by the Board's decision. Its task was eased by the fact that the U.O.P.W.A. had entered into an alliance with the Distributive Workers and the Food and Tobacco Workers Union in September 1950, and its jurisdiction became cloudy at best. Seizing upon the U.O.P.W.A.'s bankruptcy, the C.I.O. all but took over its jurisdiction in Greater New York, New Jersey and Pennsylvania by the summer of 1951. The Committee then petitioned the Board for an election. Convinced that the I.A.W.O.C. did in fact possess sufficient strength in these areas the Board ordered a representation election that same year.

Metropolitan officials then let it be known they were in earnest when they refused to deal with the U.O.P.W.A.; and, according to the *C.I.O. News,* they refused to deal with the I.A.W.O.C. as well. The newspaper reported that the company management protested the Labor Board's decision and showed their antipathy by promising compensation increases to those agents who did not vote in the election. The Metropolitan agents, however, paid little heed to the company's proposal, for on November 30, 1951, the majority of the insurance men chose the I.A.W.O.C. as their bargaining representative.[8]

Negotiations followed and the company, in spite of its initial refusal, signed a notable agreement with the union. For the first time in its bargaining history the Metropolitan consented to the elimination of the no-strike clause in the contract and to the payment of a guaranteed weekly minimum of $60.00.[9]

Armed with its tri-state victory the I.A.W.O.C., C.I.O., leaders

[7]*The Metropolitan Life Insurance Co.,* 91 N.L.R.B. 473 (1950).

[8]*C.I.O. News,* December 10, 1951, p. 11.

[9]*C.I.O. Debit News,* I.A.W.O.C., C.I.O., April 7, 1952, p. 1.

sought out the company's agents in Ohio, Connecticut and Massachusetts. A conflict, totally extraneous to the I.A.W.O.C.-Metropolitan campaign, entered into the picture and, according to a union spokesman, cost the Committee the three states. It was at this time that the Insurance Agents International Union, A.F. of L., struck the Prudential, and the adverse publicity surrounding the dispute caused the Metropolitan agents in these states to question the need for union representation and to vote against the union.[10]

To this explanation the I.A.W.O.C. added a more penetrating reason: the Metropolitan was against a labor union for its insurance agents *in se*. In expressing its position, the company naturally could not publicly state its opposition. What it did, according to many union sources, was to raise the specter of Communism in all three campaigns. The I.A.W.O.C. considered the charge unfair, because its members, although they had formerly belonged to the U.O.P.W.A., had never subscribed to the left-wing tenets of the leadership. However, Metropolitan was able to use this issue against the union and, thereby, frighten off those agents who were not convinced of the need for union membership, or at least by the policy of the I.A.W.O.C.[11]

However, to this evaluation the company might just as easily have reminded the I.A.W.O.C. that it had for too long felt the whiplash of half-truth and unjust criticism during the days of U.O.P.W.A. dominance. And an institution such as the Metropolitan no doubt squirmed under the abusive title "Mother Met," a phrase the union organizers used with abandon. Since the company management was in no mood to forget the days of the U.O.P.W.A., and since it considered itself a citadel of the free enterprise system, it kept the union at a safe, comfortable distance, and all the power of the national C.I.O. was unable to render the company amenable.

The I.A.W.O.C. was, however, better equipped to tackle the John Hancock Mutual Life Insurance Company. Under Haywood's leadership the union wrested control of the company's agents from the U.O.P.W.A. By sheer force of numbers the union was thereby capable of dealing with this firm on a more equal footing. It is this phase of the C.I.O. insurance union's history that must now be considered.

[10]The Prudential strike will be discussed in the next chapter.

[11]Adapted from interviews granted the writer.

THE LAW VS. THE UNION CONTRACT

In August 1951 the I.A.W.O.C. negotiated a union shop agreement and higher commission rates with Hancock. In early 1952 union officials requested that the company increase its agents' compensation so as to cover the rising costs of the Korean War period. Hancock negotiators rejected the proposal, asserting that they had "nothing left to pay our agents under the New York Law."[12]

To appreciate the complexity of the bargaining position of both parties certain salient features of the "expense limitation" section of the New York Insurance Law must now be considered. The "expense limitation" section of the law is numbered 213. It contains a subdivision numbered 213a, which defines the extent of a debit agent's compensation. These sections pertain to "ordinary" and "industrial" life insurance respectively.[13] Each section regulates the operating expenses of companies selling "ordinary" and "industrial" insurance in New York, and, by extension, in the rest of the states as well. A company's operating expenses in turn are regulated on the basis of certain marginal requirements, the margin in this instance signifying the difference between the "amount of money a company spends on selling and servicing life insurance, and the expense ceiling imposed by the New York Law."[14] A company determines its operating expenses on basic actuarial formulae, the most important of which must reflect the amount of its premium income, the amount of insurance in force at the beginning of the year, and the amount of insurance issued during the year and in

[12]C.I.O. News, Insurance Edition, July 28, 1952, p. 1.

[13]Since 1954 the word "industrial" was deleted from Sections 213 and 213a of the New York Insurance Law. As the law exists today, Section 213a is applicable to "Debit Life Insurance," which means "all life insurance with premiums payable monthly or more frequently normally collectible by an agency force organized to make systematic house to house collection of premiums." New York Insurance Law, Section 213-a, "Debit Life Insurance," (1), p. 47, as amended, 1954. Rather than remove the word "industrial" from the text, the writer has preferred to keep the original designation.

[14]"An Explanation of the New York Expense Law: The Purpose of the Memorandum is to Answer Questions which have been asked about Section 213 and 213a of the Insurance Law of New York," (Newark: Prudential Insurance Co. of America), p .2.

force at the end of the year.[15] In computing its operating expenses, then, a company must total the three previously listed items and work within the ceiling established by the New York Insurance Department, the administrative agency of the Law. Obviously, the "expense limitation" section of the Law is intended to protect the policyholder's money.

Part of a life insurance company's operating expenses consists in paying agent compensation. It has already been pointed out in this study that, since the end of the Great Depression, sales of "industrial" life have fallen relative to the sale of "ordinary" insurance and that unions of debit agents were founded partly to protect those men who sold the "industrial" policy. As a consequence, any labor organization would naturally be more concerned with the industrial life phase of the "expense limitation" section of the New York Law, that is, with 213a.

Section 213a was added in 1940. The New York State Legislature included under this not only Weekly Premium Insurance, but also so-called 'Intermediate' Monthly Premium Insurance issued since 1938 in the amounts of less than $1,000.00 (It should be pointed out that prior to 1938, 'Intermediate' was considered a part of Ordinary insurance and was placed under Section 213. Subsequent to the enactment of Section 213a only larger Intermediate policies issued since 1938, plus all issued before that year, came within Section 213.) While this arrangement in no way affected the over-all payment of an agent's compensation, a labor union had a stake in the Intermediate policy since its members sold this type of insurance as well.[16]

It therefore follows that because of the "expense limitation" section of the New York Law a life company is legally bound to maintain an agent's compensation rates and other commissions within the margin prescribed by the New York Insurance Department. By the same token, union agitation for a wage increase must be circumscribed by the same marginal requirements.

At the time the I.A.W.O.C. petitioned Hancock for a wage adjustment, the debit agent was receiving an average of thirteen cents on every premium dollar collected during the first year of the

[15]Adapted from various sources.

[16]*New York Insurance Law,* Section 213 (12).

policy life and a lesser amount in renewal commissions during a subsequent, but specified, time period.[17] This figure, coupled with the company's amount of insurance in force at the beginning of the year and the amount issued during the year and in force at the end of the year, brought the agent's total salary in Hancock to well over the $60.00 minimum the union was agitating for. However, union officials believed that the size of the commission was too small, particularly because of the inflationary spiral caused by the Korean War.

Hancock management insisted that the company could not increase the compensation rates since it had come dangerously close to depleting its margins. To do so would make the company liable to a violation of the New York Law. Hancock officials could draw only one conclusion: to raise his earnings the debit agent must sell more insurance.

The I.A.W.O.C. refused to accept the company's evaluation of the compensation issue. Through its attorney, Irving Abramson, the union petitioned the New York Insurance Department for a ruling on the case. Department officials replied that the law must remain the basis for determining Hancock's operating expenses, part of which included the agent's compensation.

Dissatisfied with the ruling, Abramson decided to take the dispute to the New York Supreme Court and to name as defendants both the company and the New York Insurance Department. He formulated his argument on the following basic premise: during inflationary times collective bargaining cannot obtain a decent standard of living for insurance agents if a law placed a ceiling beyond which collective bargaining could not go. He argued that the New York Insurance Law hindered the process of collective bargaining, with the result that insurance agents could not obtain a decent standard of living.

Abramson then quoted several precedents in confirmation of his plea. The United States Supreme Court in the *South Eastern Underwriters'* case declared insurance to be interstate commerce, he wrote, and, although congress continued the regulation of insurance by the states in the *McCarran Act,* it specifically prohibited the states from interfering in labor relations. He then attempted to prove that section 213a of the New York Insurance Law was unconstitutional

[17]"An Explanation of the New York Expense Law . . .," Prudential, p. 12.

on the theory that it violated both the Supreme Court's decision and the *McCarran Act*.[18]

In the hope of making his case airtight, the I.A.W.O.C. counsel asserted that the New York Law was unconstitutional for still another reason: it was in contravention of the Labor Management Relations Act of 1947. He said that this law was formulated to promote free collective bargaining and that it did not exclude insurance agents from its coverage.[19]

In September 1952 Abramson obtained from a justice of the court a temporary injunction, prohibiting Hancock the use of the "expense limitation" provision of the law.[20] Both the company and the New York Insurance Department appealed the ruling to the full court; and Hancock management did something more. The Insurance Committee's newspaper reported that the company disregarded its plea of poverty and granted its clerical force a cost-of-living increase of five per cent.[21]

In November the New York Supreme Court ruled on the case. Declining to pass judgment on the constitutionality of the New York Insurance Law, the court decided that "no controversy" existed between the company and the union. Since Hancock did not exceed its expense margin, the justices ruled, there was nothing to judge.[22]

As a result of the decision Abramson counselled the I.A.W.O.C. to lobby for an amendment that would remove the agents' com-

[18]*Memorandum as to the Proposed Legal Action Against Sections 213 and 213-A of the New York State Insurance Law*, by Irving Abramson, January 30, 1952.

[19]*Ibid.*

[20]*C.I.O. News, Insurance Edition*, September 29, 1952, p. 1.

[21]*Ibid.*, November 3, 1952, p. 1. The I.A.W.O.C. had two locals of Hancock white collar workers at this time. Commenting on C.I.O.'s efforts at organizing the insurance agents of the various departments of the State Farm Insurance companies, Alexander Picone observed that the insurance firms might be able to raise commissions within the limits of the New York Law and thus divert the C.I.O. from any further attempts to use the Law. Alexander Picone, "Big CIO Drive to Organize 150,000 Life Insurance Agents," *The Journal of Commerce*, March 11, 1952, p. 19.

[22]*C.I.O. News, Insurance Edition*, December 1, 1952, p. 1.

pensation from the strictures of the law.[23] He also urged the union to create a controversy by "forcing" Hancock to exceed its expense margins.

Accordingly, the union negotiators — the so-called Hancock "Streamlined Committee" — met with company officials and attempted to "force" a wage increase in excess of the New York Law. Hancock negotiators declined the bait, but they did offer a number of concessions in the welfare provisions of the contract and a guaranteed $60.00 weekly minimum. These improvements were all within the legal limits of the New York Law.[24]

The new pact did not meet with universal approval, for, when the contract was submitted to the Hancock membership for ratification, only two-thirds of the men voted to accept the new provisions, with the majority of the New York contingent voting against ratification. New York's rejection was of great significance, and it came to play a prominent role in the unfolding history of the C.I.O.'s insurance union.

THE INSURANCE WORKERS OF AMERICA, C.I.O.

In June 1953 the I.A.W.O.C. became an international union and its members called the new organization the Insurance Workers of America, C.I.O. In granting the international charter the C.I.O. officials hoped to make two points crystal clear. In the first place, Walter Reuther appeared before the convention to settle the dispute concerning the union's jurisdiction. He stated that the Insurance Workers of America (I.W.A.) was established "for insurance workers only."[25] Reuther's stipulation thus brought to a conclusion the controversy that Allan Haywood had started at the time of the founding of the Organizing Committee. As was expected, certain members of the new union expressed dissatisfaction with Reuther's decision; they wanted an organization for the agents exclusively.

[23]cf. New York, *Report of the Joint Legislative Committee on Insurance Rates and Regulation* (1955), c. 814, no. 56. This document contains the revised version of the Law. Because the revision failed to remove agent compensation from the "expense limitation" section, the C.I.O. disapproved the amendment.

[24]*C.I.O. News, Insurance Edition,* February 2, 1953, p. 1.

[25]Insurance Workers of America, C.I.O., *Report of the Proceedings of the First Constitutional Convention* (Cleveland, O., 1953), p. 36.

Nevertheless, they accepted the final compromise, relieved that the C.I.O. would not build their union along the lines of the United Office and Professional Workers of America.

A second source of discontent revolved around the agents' hostility toward the C.I.O.'s conduct of union affairs. Even though Richard Leonard had performed his job well as chairman of the I.A.W.O.C., the debitmen considered themselves capable of governing their own organization. To put a stop to the criticism Leonard announced, before the convention opened, that the insurance men should select candidates from their own ranks. And he added: "No representative of C.I.O. is, or will be, a candidate for any office at the forthcoming convention."[26]

Such tactics removed from the convention proceedings areas of controversy that might have disrupted the gathering but, by the same token, gave the delegates more time to express other grievances. Uppermost in the minds of the delegates was the power of the large eastern locals representing insurance agents from Hancock and Metropolitan. During the regime of the national C.I.O., this power was held in check, and each area of the country and each company delegation had received the assurance that their voice would be heard. With the C.I.O. out of the picture there was no guarantee that a balance of power would be preserved. To those men not aligned to the power centers the future of democratic unionism did not appear bright.

Two factions were jockeying for position at the founding convention. They created an issue over the role of the first vice president of the union and both submitted reports designed to promote their own interests. The majority report, backed by the national C.I.O., favored a strong president, assisted by two vice presidents whose activities were to be performed under the direction of the president. The authors of the minority report (in the main, these were members of the eastern locals) believed that such a restriction would make the vice president an office boy at best. The eastern group wanted the first vice president to be in sole charge of organization, and they wanted him to be an Easterner.

Tempers flared, but in the end the majority report was accepted without compromise or amendment. Behind the thinking of the minority there lurked the fear that eastern influence would wane in

[26]*C.I.O. News, Insurance Edition,* May 4, 1953, p. 1.

the event a first vice president were chosen who was not sympathetic to their objectives. Since the East gave the union its greatest financial support and was the largest numerical group within the organization, the authors of the report wanted the power to reside where they thought it belonged.[27]

A related dispute was occasioned by the Greater New York delegation. In this instance, the agents went into the convention pledged to elect two of their members to the union's general executive board. Since New England, with fewer members, had two representatives on the board, the New Yorkers argued, they were entitled to the same consideration. Their protests were so strongly worded that they alienated their sister power-center, the New England delegation. Fred Pieper, the administrative director of the former I.A.W.O.C., spoke to the New York delegates at this point and was able to convince them that they should drop the proposal in the interest of unity. However, the agents were unhappy with the outcome and planned to assert themselves at the next convention.[28]

A final upsurge of discontent occurred on the final day of the meeting. It was a well known fact that the C.I.O., in spite of its withdrawal from union affairs, had hand picked a slate of officers for the new organization. When these men were nominated, the minority offered names of its own choosing. The move failed, leading many of the agents from the large eastern locals to believe that the C.I.O. would not untie the apron strings. However, they agreed to go along with the majority for the time being at any rate.

Elected to the office of president of the Insurance Workers of America was Kenneth O'Dell, a Prudential agent from New Jersey who had chosen to stay on in the C.I.O. when that company's agents went into the A.F. of L. Simon Helfgott, a leader of the New York faction, was elected first vice president of the union, and Robert Nicholson, a Hancock agent from Greater Boston, was chosen second vice president. The incumbent secretary-treasurer, James Brisbane, continued in the post.[29]

THE HANCOCK "STREAMLINED" COMMITTEE

Throughout their term of office the new leaders of the I.W.A.

[27]I.W.A., *Convention Proceedings* (Cleveland, O., 1953), pp. 57-67.

[28]*Ibid.,* pp. 81-90.

[29]*Ibid.,* pp. 135-43.

sensed that the power struggle had not ended with the founding convention and that their opposition was ready to make political hay out of their mistakes. It is true that the national officers blundered in their conduct of negotiations and that their sense of timing was off. Whether their error was due to lack of experience or to subterfuge, as their accusers put it, or to a combination of both, is open to question.

President O'Dell recognized as well as anyone else that his small union was walking a tightrope. The companies under contract were tough competitors, and the legal obstacles created by the New York Insurance Law made meaningful negotiations extremely difficult. A case in point occurred in January 1954 when the national officers submitted demands to John Hancock for a new contract. The New York Law had not been amended at that time, so O'Dell decided to follow the suggestion of Irving Abramson, the union's lawyer, to force the company into granting a compensation increase in excess of the "expense limitation" section of the law.[30]

The members of the I.W.A. applauded O'Dell's militancy, but Hancock rejected the proposal as insulting. O'Dell then effected a compromise with the company, the outcome of which was used as an excuse by the opposition to unseat all but Helfgott at the next convention.

The national officers conducted negotiations with Hancock along the lines laid down by the union's constitution. At the time of the founding convention the delegates desired to make the new organization as democratic as possible. To this end they incorporated in the constitution an article which specified that the business of writing and negotiating contracts be the responsibility of two committees. They called one the "General Bargaining Committee" and the other the "Policy Committee," and each was to be divided along company, numerical and geographic lines. Since the union was already divided into nine regions, the delegates specified that each area was to select one agent to serve on the "General Bargaining Committee;" if a particular company did not operate in one or several of these regions, a provision was made to eliminate these sections from the Committee. The delegates further decreed that any region having membership in excess of a specified number had the right to elect additional members to the same Committee.

[30]*The Insurance Worker*, February, 1954, p. 2.

161

The "General Bargaining Committee" had as its purpose the task of writing contract proposals. Once this goal was achieved the group "streamlined" itself into the second committee, the "Policy Committee." This latter was designed to undertake the actual negotiations with the company. Both committees were immediately subject to the supervision of the I.W.A.'s executive board whose members were also *ex officio* members of each committee.[31]

Prior to the January negotiations with Hancock the company's agents chose the members of the "General Bargaining Committee." New England, with the largest number of Hancock agents, had the highest representation on the Committee, while Greater New York and Eastern Pennsylvania sent two members, and the remaining sections of the country were represented by one member each. After formulating the bargaining proposals the Committee "streamlined" itself and went into negotiations under its proper title, the Hancock "Policy Committee."[32]

Consisting of seventeen members, it was this group that had initially attempted to force Hancock into exceeding the expense margins imposed by the New York Law. Since their plan was unsuccessful, the members of the "Policy Committee" were themselves "forced" to accept a compensation award that preserved the Law's requirements. The "Policy Committee" members at length signed a contract, and in June 1954 the I.W.A.'s national officers urged the Hancock membership to ratify the new agreement.

However, ratification was not easily achieved, and in attemptir g to obtain the agents' consent O'Dell and his fellow officers committed their first tactical blunder. The story begins in the Hancock "Policy Committee" where six of the seventeen negotiators rejected the company's compensation award and published their reasons for doing so. It should be noted that all six men represented the eastern bloc whose local leadership seemingly opposed the national officers as a matter of principle. One year after the founding convention these agents continued to harbor the suspicion that the C.I.O. had railroaded them into accepting national leaders whose backgrounds and opinions were alien to their own.

Joseph Raab was one of the "Policy Committee" members who

[31]I.W.A., *Convention Proceedings* (Cleveland, O., 1953), pp. 146-47.

[32]*C.I.O. News, Insurance Edition,* December, 1953, p. 1.

was outspoken in his criticism of the contract. At a meeting of Local 5 in Philadelphia Raab accused President O'Dell of conspiring with members of the Hancock "Policy Committee" to control the vote on contract approval. Raab asserted that the new agreement contained only fringe benefits and that the Committee's acceptance of this form of relief betrayed the agents' trust.

Raab's speech so inflamed the Philadelphia agents that they demanded a strike vote against the company, a solution that he and the Local's president, William Gillen, realized would settle nothing. Both men no doubt had the wisdom to understand that a work stoppage could not alleviate an internal problem.[33]

The position of Raab and others could not be maintained, however. Basically, the union's constitution weighted the vote against them. The national officers wanted the contract approved, and with the votes of members from other regions on their side, they could easily show the Hancock membership the need for ratifying the contract.

And there was another reason for the opposition's defeat. An insurance man does not look for a fight if he can avoid one. The majority of the Hancock agents interpreted the "Policy Committee's" lopsided vote as a plea for discretion. If the company failed to grant the union's demands this time, the majority reasoned, the national officers could try again. Furthermore, most of the agents considered their compensation adequate.[34]

Undaunted by defeat, the dissidents waited for another opportunity to discredit the national leadership. It soon came from an unexpected source. The national officers were so angry that the six members of the "Policy Committee" should broadcast the dispute that they circulated a petition of censure against the men "for engaging in activities detrimental to the membership."[35] The plan was

[33]*C.I.O. Reporter,* Local 5, Philadelphia, June, 1954, p. 4.

[34]*The Insurance Worker,* August, 1954, p. 1. The vote on contract ratification was as follows: 2,764 voted in favor while 1,748 voted against the contract.

[35]*Ibid.,* August, 1954, p. 1. It should be noted that Simon Helfgott, the first vice president of the I.W.A., played an ambiguous role in this affair. It was well known that he was at odds with his fellow officers, although publicly he had to agree with them. His ambivalence helped him to preserve his office at the 1955 convention.

successful but the long range effect of the censure was disastrous. The national officers only solidified their opposition and, what was worse, dismayed their own followers.

President O'Dell and his fellow officers aided their opponents in still another way. Sometime prior to the 1955 convention they convened the Hancock "Policy Committee" for the purpose of drafting bargaining proposals to be submitted to the convention delegates. Curiously, these proposals paralleled the very program that the minority was seeking. When the meeting ended, the Committee issued a statement that at first reading appears ingenuous. It read in part: "A study of negotiations since the original contract in 1951 indicates that the major benefits were obtained in the so-called fringe issues."[36] It is useless to speculate here, but the writer believes that the statement contains not an admission of defeat but an attempt on O'Dell's part to placate his opposition. He knew from the beginning that the contract was not a good one. But he also realized that both his union and the company were hampered by the New York Law and that all the arguments in the world could not enjoin the law's violation.

By calling together the "Policy Committee" members, O'Dell thought he might take the lid off the conspiracy that was ranged about him. In this move he again miscalculated, for the so-called "streamlined" committee only further disrupted the relationship between the two groups.

Defeat in Detroit

The time for the long awaited convention arrived and O'Dell's opposition controlled the proceedings from the start. In an effort to make peace, O'Dell addressed himself to the problem of the "streamlined" committee straight away. He put his ideas in this manner:

> In the past relatively hasty decisions have been made by comparatively small groups as to what should be the union's demands . . . . There is a real need to function as a unit on whatever may be the final collective bargaining proposals rather than have a number of demands each of which may enjoy a high degree of popularity in a given area but would differ in important respects from equally popular proposals coming from some other areas.[37]

[36]*Ibid.*, February, 1955, p. 2.

[37]I.W.A., *Convention Proceedings* (Detroit, Mich., 1955), p. 14.

He again referred to the question of the fringe benefit, and he asserted that a compensation scale in Hancock had to be achieved on an industry-wide basis. To achieve this goal required a consensus, O'Dell said, which in turn necessitated greater education of the rank-and-file.

However, his opponents were not interested so much in long range goals as they were in unseating him as president. They berated his performance as chief officer of the I.W.A. and demanded that the assembly elect a man who would be militant in spite of the New York Law, the companies, and those insurance men who wanted to preserve the placid ways of the O'Dell administration.

On the first day of the convention, the opponents of O'Dell and of his fellow officers, Robert Nicholson and James Brisbane, questioned the voting procedure and argued strongly in behalf of greater representation for the larger regions. They were voted down, but only because their plan had been tried before and the other delegates were primed.

The question of the bargaining and policy committees then came up for discussion. Naturally, O'Dell's opponents wanted a greater hearing on these committees. A delegate tried to compromise by offering a resolution whereby the national officers would have less opportunity to control the committees. But the opposition wanted no compromise. One of the leaders of the group, William Gillen, noted the handiwork of the national leadership in the writing of the constitutional article and announced that many points within the amended constitution had been voted on by what he termed the "now familiar 5 to 4 vote."[38]

Delegate after delegate asked that the entire article be returned to committee. President O'Dell objected, stating that discussion of the issue was necessary for the preservation of democracy within the union. At length, Robert Ponsi, a member of the executive board and an ally of O'Dell, brought to light the meaning of the dispute. He said: "As one of the members of the Hancock Negotiating [sic] Committee, we felt it necessary to spell this out because of a certain situation which occurred during the Hancock negotiations with which I think most of you are familiar."[39] Needless to say, the article was returned to committee.

[38]*Ibid.*, p. 56. Gillen was president of I.W.A. Local 5, Philadelphia.

[39]*Ibid.*, p. 62.

165

Next morning the Metropolitan Life membership further complicated the proceedings. The largest group working for this company came from Greater New York, and they revived the question of greater representation for the Metropolitan agents. In particular, certain of the area's delegates demanded a larger part in formulating and executing the work of the Metropolitan "Policy Committee." As the New Yorkers presented their case there were shouts of "cry babies," an expression that so angered the delegation that they threatened to walk out of the convention.

O'Dell prevailed upon them to stay and in so doing failed to reckon with the strategy of the opposition. The New York agents were doing just what the other power structures within the union dreaded; they were confusing the question of committee representation by inserting extraneous material into the debate. The question at hand concerned the Hancock committees specifically, and the opposition did not want to scatter its strength so that O'Dell and the other two national officers could take control of the union again. Had O'Dell recognized the aim of these groups he might have permitted the New Yorkers to leave the convention, regained the presidency for himself, and later on healed the wounds of the Greater New York delegates. He succeeded in pacifying the New York group and lost everything in the bargain.

Sometime that afternoon the constitutional committee of the I.W.A. returned to the hall with a provision that sought to vest complete control in O'Dell's opposition. The committee reported that the union's general executive board was to be relieved of its powers in regulating the "Bargaining" and the "Policy" committees and that they, too, would have to stand for election in order to serve on these committees. The delegates approved the resolution.[40]

With this victory in its collective pocket the opposition next turned its gaze upon the leadership of the I.W.A. Aware that such would be their ultimate move, Richard Leonard, who attended the convention *ex concesso*, tried to bring the opposing sides together. His efforts were useless, and the proceedings of the last day of the meeting showed just how much O'Dell's enemies wanted to control the union. Leonard told the agents that their union was too small to endure internal warfare, and he said: "This fight, this valiant fight for jobs may result pretty soon, unless we get together, in

[40]*Ibid.*, p. 151.

having nothing to fight over, and that is the possibility you have."[41]

In an attempt to keep the organization united, Leonard suggested that the convention establish a committee composed of members of each of the opposing factions, which in turn would present a united slate of candidates to the assembly. After Leonard had completed his remarks, O'Dell was on his feet and asked for an immediate vote on the resolution. His action was precipitate, to say the least, for after a show of hands and a flurry of "ayes," he pronounced the Leonard resolution accepted. He convinced few persons, however. Agents from every corner of the hall demanded a roll call on the resolution. O'Dell had to back down and agree to the roll call. With this act he saw his chance for re-election defeated as the delegates voted overwhelmingly against the proposal.[42]

The convention then swiftly ran its course. O'Dell's group placed in nomination all of the incumbent officers with the exception of Helfgott, the first vice president of the union; by this time he was firmly allied to the eastern locals. In his place they proposed Robert Ponsi, a Metropolitan agent from New Jersey and a member of the I.W.A.'s general executive board.

Before accepting the nomination O'Dell said:

> I had offered to withdraw in the interest of unity and with the expectation and hope that the result of that act would to a degree bring unity in this convention . . . . Now my hopes have not been attained in this respect. I feel that the office of president, the highest office in the union, is one that should not go by default. Therefore, I humbly accept the nomination as president of IWA.[43]

O'Dell might have saved his words. His opposition was ready for him and offered the convention a set of names all representing the eastern division. For the office of president they offered William Gillen, president of the strong Local 5 in Philadelphia. For the post of first vice president they nominated Simon Helfgott who had occupied this position during the past two years and who, more importantly, had high connections in the largest local in the union, Local 1706, in Greater New York. The opposition assigned to the

[41]*Ibid.*, p. 183.

[42]*Ibid.*, p. 186.

[43]*Ibid.*, p. 193.

position of second vice president William MacDermott, a power in the Greater Boston area. And the final post, that of secretary-treasurer, went to Arthur Higginson, the president of the Rhode Island state group of insurance locals.

The voting was held and the delegates selected an entirely new slate of officers. Gillen, Helfgott, and MacDermott defeated the incumbent officers by a large margin; Higginson also unseated Brisbane but won the office by less than five hundred votes.[44]

O'Dell's opposition jubilanty left the hall while the old-timer, Simon Helfgott, tried to cool tempers by leading the group in a half-hearted rendering of "Solidarity Forever."

From the viewpoint of the losers Helfgott's song was a mockery. They feared the power of the East and considered the union's new leaders, in words that President Gillen would later coin, "wild-eyed radicals . . . who were completely erratic."[45] These agents believed that the spirit of democratic unionism had been lost in Detroit and that it could never be regained.

Gillen, however, set out to prove them wrong. Immediately after his election he wrote an article in the union's newspaper, *The Insurance Worker,* trying to repair the damage done to the morale of a large number of agents at the convention. In his remarks he might have been thinking of a statement that Kenneth O'Dell had made at the Detroit gathering, for he wrote:

> One thing is very obvious. Our union needs a greater exchange of viewpoints. We have to start thinking somewhat alike in New York and DeMoines, in Boston and Oakland. We cannot afford the luxury of continual divisions along geographic lines.[46]

Gillen succeeded fairly well in healing the division within the I.W.A. By visiting every local in the organization he convinced at least the majority of the members that he and the new officers were earnestly striving to promote harmony and that their interests were not regional. That he succeeded is attested to by the praise both Leonard and Irving Abramson lavished upon him at a later date.[47]

[44]*Ibid.,* pp. 213-17.

[45]Ibid., I.W.A., *Convention Proceedings* (Buffalo, N.Y., 1957), p. 7.

[46]*Ibid.,* p. 6.

[47]*Ibid.,* pp. 76 & 135.

Gillen and his fellow officers, MacDermott and Higginson, accomplished a great deal in spite of an additional handicap. Some time after the convention Simon Helfgott, the first vice president, became gravely ill and was forced to retire from active service. Since he was widely known and highly regarded, his absence from union affairs increased the burden of the other officers.[48] However, it seems fair to report that they did the best they could to pick up the pieces after a convention that rocked the union to its foundation.

The Insurance Workers of America, C.I.O., thus managed to survive a stormy period in its short history. While the internal struggle was a trying one, the work of its competitor, the Insurance Agents International Union, A.F. of L., caused the union far more trouble. Nevertheless, by the middle 1950's the C.I.O. insurance men could pronounce their small labor union a qualified success.

[48]Helfgott resigned at the June 1957 convention and died the following September.

CHAPTER 8

THE A.F. OF L. UNION: A RECORD OF DISSATISFACTION

The American Federation of Labor played an indifferent role during the formative period of insurance unionism in the United States. After recovering from the shock of recognizing the C.I.O.'s success in this area, the Federation chartered groups of agents who were unsympathetic to the C.I.O. and placed them in a council which by executive decree possessed a minimum amount of authority. That the A.F. of L. acted against a longstanding policy in establishing the council is obvious; as late as 1937 William Collins, the national union's eastern representative, told members of the Bookkeepers' Local that the organization was as strongly opposed to the industrial insurance system as it was in 1901, the year it finally prohibited union membership to industrial insurance agents.

The A.F. of L. founded the insurance council along the traditional lines of the craft union principle, establishing it for the agents exclusively and granting the local affiliates almost complete autonomy. The concept of exclusiveness appealed to those men who either rejected the C.I.O.'s brand of organization or who, as onetime members of the U.O.P.W.A., considered themselves helpless among their many clerical and white collar associates. By the same token, the autonomy of the Locals created a lack of direction in the Council, whose officers exercised such relatively insignificant functions as presiding over occasional conferences or appealing to the locals for funds in organizing campaigns. The main difficulty with this setup was that it developed a spirit of caution among those A.F. of L. insurance officials who could have made a far greater contribution to the agents at a time when they were ripe for organization.

In addition to this, the A.F. of L. kept the agents in a council-status for almost fourteen years. By treating the men as perennial adolescents, the Federation only compounded the frustration of the Council's leadership. In view of all of this, it is quite remarkable that the Council was able to accomplish as much as it did.

When the Prudential agents opted for the National Federation of Insurance Agents Council, A.F. of L., in the 1949 election, they discovered that the organization had achieved a limited, though authentic, bargaining experience with their company. As early as

1943 the Industrial and Ordinary Insurance Agents Council, the N.F.I.A.C.'s forerunner, had negotiated labor union contracts with Prudential in Maryland, Virginia, Delaware, the District of Columbia and Toledo, Ohio.

However much this fact might have impressed the agents, they found it difficult to reconcile themselves to the Council's conservative ways. To cite a case in point: shortly after the election the men began to pressure George Russ, the Council's president, for a wage increase. They believed they were entitled to a reward for the job they had done in defeating the U.O.P.W.A. and in handing over to the Council a large increase in membership.[1] A somewhat plodding man, Russ preached restraint, asking the agents to permit the organization sufficient time to become accustomed to its new found strength. The men had little sympathy for Russ' problem and eventually compelled him to form a negotiating committee which would, they hoped, obtain the compensation increase from the company.

The committee labored with Prudential negotiators for three months, and in November 1949 both parties signed a two-year agreement. It was a sorry affair. The company granted the union an increased vacation allowance and a special disability clause, and that was all.[2]

Angry and disillusioned, the agents condemned Russ and the committee. Their irritation deepened when the N.F.I.A.C. failed to consolidate within the newly acquired 31-state Prudential bargaining unit, Maryland, Delaware, Virginia, the District of Columbia and Toledo.[3]

Meanwhile, Matthew Hogan, the secretary of the N.F.I.A.C. and a leader of the Baltimore local, had openly challenged the authority of Russ and Charles Heisel, a director of the Council and the man most responsible for bringing the Prudential agents into the A.F. of

[1]When the Prudential agents voted for the N.F.I.A.C., it had already signed eighteen contracts with the smaller companies. The Council had a membership of about 2,500 agents at the time of the election; the Prudential force increased this number to about 12,000. In all, the Council represented some 20,000 men.

[2]*N.F.I.A.C. Reporter,* February, 1950, p. 3.

[3]*The Prudential Insurance Company of America,* 80 N.L.R.B. 1583 (1949). Supplemented by *Prudential,* 81 N.L.R.B. 295 (1949).

L. Aware of the agents' discontent, Hogan advised many of them to strike the company, predicting that Prudential was ill prepared for a walkout at that time. He conducted a poll of the agents' sentiment for the strike and, when the majority registered approval, presented it to Russ and Heisel. Both men thought the plan ridiculous and told him so. However, their political noses soon made them reconsider; they agreed to cooperate with Hogan.

The trio misjudged the national A.F. of L.'s reaction, however. When word of the strike proposal reached the Federation's hierarchy, Harry O'Reilly, the director of organization, called the men together and compelled them to cancel the strike preparations. Since O'Reilly was the immediate superior of all three men, they had no choice but to retreat.[4]

Hogan's action made him a temporary hero among the Council's Prudential members, and it also served to indicate the absence of authority in the N.F.I.A.C. The latter observation is further illustrated by an event that occurred in 1950. In that year the Council's leaders permitted the New York Prudential Local to establish a so-called "Steering Committee," which wrote a set of separate bargaining proposals for the forthcoming negotiations with the company. In effect, these proposals went far beyond national union policy. The New York agents demanded an immediate wage increase and threatened to strike the company for it, a solution that Russ considered both ill-advised and poorly timed. In spite of his opposition he lent the Local some of the funds he had on hand in order to carry out its program.[5]

Russ did something more; he attempted to use this development to consolidate his position within the N.F.I.A.C. In October 1950 he wrote to the Prudential management requesting an increase in salaries based on the cost of living. His letter contained no threats. Sensing that the New York Local was creating an issue for its own purposes and that the A.F. of L. would never countenance a strike in any case, he decided to scotch the ambition of the Local's officers. He informed the company that he would accept the wage increase in the form of either a higher commission rate or an expense allowance. In specifying alternatives, Russ allowed the company room to

4Interview with Matthew Hogan, August 6, 1959.

5N.F.I.A.C. Reporter, November, 1950, p. 4.

work around the restrictions of the New York Insurance Law and, at the same time, showed the agents that he was as interested in their welfare as the New Yorkers were.

As expected, Prudential rejected both proposals and, according to the Council's newspaper, submitted one of its own. It urged the N.F.I.A.C. to accept a non-contributory pension plan, estimating that the device would add three dollars a week to the agents' take home pay. Russ turned down the suggestion, adding that the agents' personal contributions to the existing pension plan afforded them greater security.[6]

Meanwhile, the New York "Steering Committee" had branched out into other parts of the country and, in conjunction with certain Prudential local union officials, began to prepare the agents for strike action. Leaders of the various groups concluded that a "mass disability" was the most effective means for securing the wage increase; they proposed this technique knowing full well that it was in direct violation of the contract and of A.F. of L. procedure.

This time Prudential was fully prepared for any action the agents might undertake. The company's officials informed Russ that they knew of the plan, and they told him to discourage the agents. Furthermore, they promised to find a way to appease the men.

William Green likewise heard of the "mass disability" proposal, but he was less conciliatory than Prudential. He dictated a letter to Russ and told him to transmit it to all the agents; it demanded that they respect the contract and call off the "disability."[7]

Green's prohibition went unheeded. On the morning of January 8, 1951, about five hundred Prudential agents walked off their jobs in the Pittsburgh area. According to *The New York Times,* this particular work stoppage occurred over a dispute concerning the filing of the "debit report," the agent's statement of business conducted during a specified time period. The agents refused to hand in the report, and in their view, the office manager "retaliated" by suspending thirty-two of the men. The agents then took matters

---

[6]*Ibid.,* December, 1950, p. 1. The plan was unsatisfactory from the union's viewpoint for two reasons: first, the contributory plan offered the agent a reserve on which he could draw should he leave the company; and second, under the contributory plan social security payments were added to the agent's contributions to the fund.

[7]Hogan, Interview.

into their own hands, insisting that the report was not required at the time of the suspension. They also said that the manager had deliberately used the submission of the report to provoke an incident.[8]

On the following day agents in Newark, Boston, Providence, and New York City joined in the dispute; they reported "sick" and failed to collect their debits. Lest the public misinterpret the "disability," Prudential placed ads in the press informing its policyholders that the agents had violated the contract by engaging in a "wildcat" strike. The company also told the policyholders that they were legally bound to continue paying their premiums regardless of the walkout.[9]

President Green was disgusted and told Russ that he had better settle the dispute as soon as possible. Accordingly, Russ met with Prudential officials, who promised to reinstate the suspended agents provided they turn in their "debit reports." Most of the debit men complied and the "mass disability" was discontinued. Calling off the strike placed Russ in the unenviable position of having to take the blame from both sides. He had little direct control over the Council, yet President Green held him responsible and the Prudential agents looked upon him as an even less militant leader than they had originally believed. Russ was at last coming to the end of a long sought goal, and he did not want to lose it because of the role he had to play in settling the wildcat strike. All signs pointed to his assumption of the presidency of the international union the A.F. of L. would create in a few short months; to achieve this position he would have to show the agents he was a militant labor leader. The maneuver required Russ to go along with the majority view of the Prudential membership, a view that came to be called "No Contract — No Work." He conformed and was elected president.

AN INTERNATIONAL UNION AT LAST

As the seeds of disharmony occasioned by the wage dispute continued unabated, the A.F. of L. conferred the long coveted international charter on its insurance council. The historic event took place at the final N.F.I.A.C. conference in May 1951, and the agents named the new organization the Insurance Agents International

[8]*The New York Times,* January 9, 1951, p. 21.

[9]*The New York Daily News,* January 10, 1951, p. 10.

Union, A.F. of L. As has been recorded, the delegates elected George Russ president; they also chose Charles Heisel and Max Shine, the vice president and secretary-treasurer respectively. (Shine was the first of a line of agents who quit the U.O.P.W.A.) Among its foremost acts, the new union voted a "No Contract — No Work" resolution for the Prudential, a proposal it intended to carry out if the company persisted in withholding the wage increase.

In August 1951 Russ wrote to Orville Beal, a vice president of Prudential, to urge that the company fulfill its obligations towards the agents and to propose that both sides meet no later than October 1 to discuss a new contract. Beal replied that the company would take the letter under consideration.

It may very well be that Prudential management reflected on other things as well. Since the agents had chosen the A.F. of L. union — with the company's support — there had been a deterioration in the labor management relationship. The threatened strike in 1949, the mass disability, the convention resolution, all pointed toward a showdown with the new union. There was one bright spot in an otherwise bleak picture, however. The Insurance and Allied Workers Organizing Committee, C.I.O., which up until then had concentrated on the Hancock and Metropolitan agents, had manifested interest in the Prudential and was preparing a petition for an N.L.R.B. election. The company might well have imagined that pressure for the wage increase would ease off while the A.F. of L. fought the C.I.O.'s Organizing Committee in a representation election.

George Russ was well aware of the C.I.O. encroachment. Phrasing his thoughts on the matter in the strongest words possible, he said: "Anyone attempting to deny Prudential agents the fruits of their labors after many years of organizing is an enemy of the Prudential agents and shall be treated accordingly."[10] Russ' words apparently had no effect on the C.I.O. Committee, and, if the reports of its activity among the Prudential agents are accurate, he was bluffing. However, the I.A.W.O.C., C.I.O., decided to postpone the presentation of the election petition out of respect for what it termed "the agents' wishes." Its action was prompted by the agents themselves, who wanted to see what the company would offer by way of a wage increase at the pending negotiations. According to the C.I.O.'s

[10]*The Insurance Agent,* August, 1951, p. 1.

account of the episode, the agents promised to join the I.A.W.O.C. if Prudential either denied the increase or failed to propose a sum they considered adequate.[11]

The I.A.W.O.C.'s withdrawal temporarily lessened the burden on George Russ and his new associates, Charles Heisel and Max Shine. At the union's request, these men met with Prudential on October 1 and proposed the following demands for the new contract: a $20.00 across the board increase, a collection commission of 18 per cent for weekly premium business and a guaranteed weekly minimum of $75.00. For a man who began as a conservative, Russ did not manifest any caution in these proposals. Prudential negotiators merely listened and then recessed the meeting.

Both sides met again on October 18, and this time Prudential officials offered a counter proposal. They told the I.A.I.U. that the company could arrange a package deal totalling $5.38 per agent per week. In proposing the concession the company used the same argument Hancock was to use later on: it could not pay its agents a higher compensation award because of the restrictions of the New York Law. Prudential officers also reintroduced the non-contributory pension plan. This time the union negotiators recessed the meeting.

The company and the union met intermittently until November 26. By that date the majority of the Prudential agents voted to strike the company, and any last minute negotiations proved useless.[12]

AN UNSUCCESSFUL STRIKE

On December 1, 1951, the I.A.I.U., A.F. of L., struck Prudential. The dispute was to become the largest, and longest, of its kind in the annals of the American labor movement. The strike lasted seventy-eight days, and, when it finally came to an end, Prudential seems to have suffered less than the union.

From the I.A.I.U.'s standpoint, the strike can best be described as a fizzle. The agents had little money and only token support from the A.F. of L., although the enthusiasm of the striking agents in the early days of the walkout amply compensated for this lack. But the strike failed, and that for several reasons.

In the first place, the agents were not united. Although more than

[11]Adapted from various sources.

[12]*The Insurance Agent,* November & December, 1951, p. 1.

half of the agency force joined in the work stoppage, there was little sentiment for the strike in western and southern sections of the United States.[13]

The strike failed for another, and perhaps more important, reason. The I.A.I.U. specifically excluded the insurance clerical force from membership, a point that has already been made. When the strike occurred, the union's prohibition played against its objectives. For instance, an early morning demonstration in Newark failed to produce the desired effect. On January 4, 1952, a large group of agents picketed the Prudential home office, hoping to prevent the office staff from entering the building. The girls simply crossed the picket lines, feeling little concern for the plight of their co-workers, and watched the proceedings from the comfort of a warm building.[14]

The union gained nothing from the walkout for yet another reason. Striking a company like Prudential involved a good deal more planning than the debit men were capable of. An industrial insurance strike differs from any other type of labor dispute by reason of the relationship that exists between the agent and his company. In dealing with the public the agent is, for all practical purposes, the company, and one of his main tasks is to prevent the lapsing of policies through the non-payment of premiums. Realizing his position as a representative of the company and knowing the importance to his company, and to himself, of the amount of insurance in force, the agent instructs the policyholder on the absolute necessity of keeping the policy in force. When he strikes his company the agent is in fact indicating to the policyholder that lapsing a policy is not so grave after all. A striking debit man obviously does not collect his client's premiums and, if the dispute continues long enough, the policy will technically lapse. As a consequence, the policyholder will show little sympathy to a striking agent, and he will also make sure his premiums are paid, no matter how.

During the course of the long strike the I.A.I.U. garnered a surprising amount of support from the Prudential policyholders. Yet the very length of the walkout dampened the union's efforts to explain the meaning of the dispute and to relieve the policyholders'

[13]"The Evolution of a Strike," *The Spectator,* January, 1952, p. 20. About 10,000 out of an estimated 16,000 debit men participated in the strike at one time or other.

[14]*The New York Times,* January 11, 1952, p. 15.

fears about lapsing their policies. A group of interested citizens appealed to the New York Insurance Department for a ruling on this thorny problem, there being no precedent to speak of. Even though there had been strikes against the smaller companies in the past, none had lasted so long and none seemed so difficult to resolve. The State's Superintendent of Insurance allowed himself ample time to respond, and his answer was as ambiguous as could be. He assured the policyholders that their policies would not lapse, but, in the same breath, he urged them to continue paying their premiums. Prudential took advantage of the ruling and of the increasing apprehension of its clients. It has been reported that the company spent in the vicinity of five million dollars on advertising alone, trying to convince its policyholders that they must continue their premium payments in spite of the strike.[15]

Throughout December and January mediators brought the disputants together, and occasionally it seemed that the walkout might be ended. On January 12, 1952, for example, both sides met, and the union, no doubt alarmed at the intransigence of the company, substantially lowered its demands; it decreased its original $20.00 to $7.50. Prudential persisted in its initial deal, however, again appealing to the expense limitation section of the New York Law, and the strike went on.

As the strike continued into late January more and more of the agents returned to their jobs, a development that forced the I.A.I.U.'s negotiators to lower their demands still further. When the union officials realized that they were fighting a hopeless battle, they met again with company negotiators and announced a settlement on February 16, 1952.

President Russ signed the new two year agreement, calling it "as good a contract as exists in the insurance field."[16] While his words might be accurate, and this is debatable, they hide the obvious fact that Prudential held the line. By way of concession the company withdrew the offer of the non-contributory pension plan, and that is about all it had to withdraw.

For the union's part, it found itself in the ridiculous position of

[15]*Ibid.*, December 12, 1951, p. 12; and "The Evolution of a Strike," *The Spectator* p. 20.

[16]*A.F.L. News Reporter*, February 20, 1952, p. 4.

accepting a compensation award two cents less than the company's original offer. The final agreement spelled out that the unionized agents were to receive an increase of $5.36 per week, and a lump sum bonus of $150.00 as reimbursement for a single year's contribution to the pension plan.

Of some importance was Prudential's agreement to compulsory arbitration of work rules, dismissals and certain other sections of the contract. This technique occasioned much conflict in later years, as will be shown.[17]

The vast majority of the agents were totally dissatisfied with the new contract. Many had quit the union during the course of the long strike; others defected when they saw their labors rewarded by a contract they considered shameful. These men were also disgusted with the half-hearted support the strike received from President Green and the A.F. of L. unions. What little sentiment they bore the Federation and the I.A.I.U. was destroyed when Russ signed with Prudential.[18]

A Schism Is Started

Lack of unity about the contract and loss of membership were manifestations of the agents' displeasure that were susceptible of solution. But neither bore the marks of the personal animosity that had built up within the union since the A.F. of L. had incorporated the thirty-one state Prudential contract in 1949. The dispute centered around Matthew Hogan, a vice president of the National Federation of Insurance Agents Council, and Charles Heisel, a director of the organization. In 1950, both men ran for national office, and Hogan defeated Heisel for the post of secretary. Heisel continued in his work, biding his time and enlisting the support of the Prudential agents and of President Russ. His chance occurred in May 1951. He ran against Hogan for the office of vice president at the founding convention of the Insurance Agents International Union and, with the active support of George Russ, defeated him.[19]

Unsettled by the defeat and also by the fact that he received no national office at the convention, Hogan quit the union. He re-

[17]*The New York Times,* February 18, 1952, p. 21.

[18]Adapted from various sources.

[19]N.F.I.A.C., *Minutes of Special General Executive Board Meeting* (Chicago, Ill., 1951), p. 10; and *The Insurance Agent,* June, 1951, p. 1.

turned to the Maryland local where he became assistant editor of the union newspaper for a time. Ultimately he became president of the Local. He then convinced the Maryland agents that they should withdraw from the I.A.I.U., stating that their organization was still an autonomous local. He argued that since at the time of the Prudential election the N.L.R.B. had decided that the locals in Maryland, Virginia, etc. were to remain separate and autonomous, they should not be consolidated into the Prudential 31-state bargaining unit.

On October 1, 1951, the I.A.I.U. entered into negotiations with Prudential. President Russ attempted to write a master contract for his union and the five unit area, part of which included the Maryland Local. All but the Hogan organization agreed to Russ' plan. The I.A.I.U. then struck Prudential. However, under orders from Hogan the Maryland agents refused to join the walkout.

Hogan's temerity shocked Russ, and when the strike was settled he decided to punish him. In March 1952 he urged the N.L.R.B. to consolidate the Maryland Local with the I.A.I.U. The Board canvassed the Maryland agents and shortly thereafter informed Russ that the men preferred autonomy. Russ then asked the debit men to return to the I.A.I.U. voluntarily; they rejected him again.

During this time an event took place which only widened the split between Hogan and the national officers of the I.A.I.U. After the strike settlement Prudential informed the organized agents that it would sell a new form of insurance known as "Sickness and Accident." The I.A.I.U. officers forbade the agents to sell the insurance, since its terms of sale had not been incorporated into the contract. Hogan disagreed, negotiated the terms of sale with the company, and the Maryland agents began to offer the insurance to the public. The I.A.I.U. promptly told Hogan that the separate negotiations had emasculated its position and that his attitude only helped the company. Hogan and his local responded by selling more "Sickness and Accident."

In November 1952 the executive board of the Insurance Agents International Union issued an ultimatum to Hogan: either he and his union return to the national union or be expelled. Hogan then called a meeting of the Maryland agents, and the men voted not only to preserve their autonomy but also to form a new union which they called the Association of Life Insurance Agents. The I.A.I.U.

expelled the dissidents and attempted to salvage a bad situation by rechartering the old Maryland Local under new officers.

Meanwhile, Prudential was caught in the middle of the dispute. The company refused to bargain with the Association and, since the I.A.I.U. and Hogan could not settle their differences, petitioned the N.L.R.B. for a ruling on the appropriate bargaining unit. After some investigation, the Board dismissed the company's petition, concluding that the Association had succeeded to the Prudential contract and that it was the proper administrator.[20]

The I.A.I.U. then began a series of moves designed to bring about the return of the Maryland agents. The union's executive board members calculated that the Maryland insurance men were suffering as much as other Prudential agents under what they termed company "pressure." The Prudential's tactics would, therefore, soon force the Association into seeking the I.A.I.U.'s assistance. Accordingly, in 1954 the latter organization's executive board set up a list of conditions under which a reconciliation might take place; and they were stringent. The Association, the board members decreed, could return to the I.A.I.U. provided its members expel Hogan. As for Hogan himself, he could seek readmission to the union as an "individual" insurance agent.[21]

Neither Hogan nor the Association accepted the terms of surrender at that time. However, as the years went by and Prudential's "pressure" increased, the Association applied for affiliation to the I.A.I.U.; and Hogan returned as an "individual" in 1957.[22]

The Prudential Strike Aftermath

Whether the word "pressure" best describes the Prudential's activities during the years following the strike is a moot question. If an organized Prudential agent were quizzed about his working life he would concur in the opinion that the company was renewing the "pressures" of pre-union days. However, a Prudential official would refer to his company's program as one of "dynamic expansion," meaning that the economics of the industry required the company to increase its sales.

[20]*The Prudential Insurance Company of America,* 106 N.L.R.B. no. 55 (1953).

[21]*The Insurance Agent,* December, 1954, p. 3.

[22]I.A.I.U., *Convention Proceedings* (Cleveland, O., 1957), p. 278.

Union officials were as much aware of the competitive quality of the insurance business as anyone else. They recognized that the sale of "industrial" life insurance had peaked just before America entered the Second World War and that there had set in a long term decline in the sales of "industrial" relative to the sale of "ordinary," "group life," and all the rest. What the I.A.I.U. leaders objected to was the promotion campaign Prudential management undertook to keep the company competitive. The Prudential's introduction of "Sickness and Accident" insurance was a case in point. The union's officers had nothing against the offering of this type of insurance *per se.* However, they wanted a voice in the terms of sale, and they wanted those terms written down in the labor contract.

Accordingly, the I.A.I.U. began to circulate the notion that Prudential was reintroducing all of the pressure tactics of the 1930's, such as the blackboards, the contests, the placards and the speed-up. All of these "gimmicks" purposed expanding sales of insurance, the I.A.I.U. officers agreed, but they were unworthy of the members of a labor organization.[23]

The union also protested the use of pressure to the company. As early as December 1953, Russ wrote to the Prudential suggesting that the use of pressure constituted a violation of the contract. His argument was succinct. Since the agreement contained a grievance and arbitration clause, each time Prudential fired an agent for poor production without first granting the I.A.I.U. recourse to the grievance and arbitration clause, the company stood in violation of the contract. He therefore urged the company to respect the contract. .Moreover, he demanded that Prudential grant the agents an immediate compensation increase based on the cost of living.[24]

Prudential replied that only increased production could satisfy the money needs of the agents. The company flatly denied that its incentive system was indicative of pressure; it stated that promotional campaigns were designed rather to help the agent increase his sales. Although certain agents were fired or quit their jobs for failure to meet company standards, Prudential argued, this development had nothing to do with the contract.

Both sides attempted to reconcile their differences during January

[23]*The Insurance Agent,* July, 1952, p. 1.

[24]*Ibid.,* March, 1954, p. 2.

and February 1954. Before long it became apparent that the Insurance Agents International Union was willing to strike the company again, for in mid-February the agents authorized the union to institute a work stoppage if necessary. Only the last minute efforts of a federal mediator brought about a peaceful settlement. Both company and union signed a new two-year contract on February 28.

Union officials called the new agreement a poor substitute for the needs of the times. Prudential refused to grant a wage increase, although it did agree to the terms of sale of "Sickness and Accident" insurance and to a more stringent grievance and arbitration clause.[25]

The contract was no sooner signed than the union accused Prudential of violating the grievance and arbitration procedure. In a case involving the termination of an agent the union took the company to court for failure to comply with the terms of the agreement. The union was unable to preserve the man's job because the federal judge, in effect, sustained the dismissal, ruling that the dispute was an internal problem.[26]

The I.A.I.U. then engaged in a rather childish form of retaliation. Delegates to the union's 1955 convention passed a series of resolutions calling into question Prudential's right to manage; the most important of these was entitled "All Go or None Go." By this resolution the delegates intended to implicate the company in fostering a spirit of rivalry among the agents for invitations to company-sponsored business conferences. This, the agent delegates decreed, was a form of pressure and had to be eliminated.[27]

Needless to say, Prudential management told the union to mind its own business. Moreover, the company sought to repay the union in kind by resorting to a prank of its own. Shortly after the I.A.I.U.'s convention adjourned, Prudential brought suit against the union in the federal district court in Louisville, requesting an injunction to restrain the union from carrying out the "All Go or None Go" resolution. The game became serious when the federal judge granted the company a temporary restraining order in December.[28]

25*Ibid.*

26*Prudential Insurance Co.* v. *Insurance Agents International Union,* D.C. EP., 122 F. Supp. 8 69, August 6, 1954.

27I.A.I.U., *Convention Proceedings* (Louisville, Ky., 1955), p. 342.

28*The Insurance Agent,* January, 1956, p. 1.

Sometime in January 1956, the company and the union went into negotiations to work out the terms of a new contract. Since they could not reach agreement by March 18, the date on which the old pact expired, the union's membership once more authorized their national officers to strike the company. Instead of carrying out the authorization the I.A.I.U. negotiators decided upon a policy of "Work Without a Contract," a scheme that was to include mass picketing, late reporting, sit-ins, a refusal to write new business and the like. The Prudential agents approved and, for the next three months, periodically engaged in all of these forms of harassment.[29]

Central to the conflict was Prudential's new approach to an insurance agent's bread and butter, his debit. Prior to the 1956 negotiations the company had assured the I.A.I.U. that each agent's debit would remain intact and that his geographic area of operation would be cut only with the written consent of the agent. This all changed in 1956. Prudential officials brought to the bargaining table the proposal that the agent's debit was not sacrosanct, that, in fact, the company could scale down the size of a debit without an agent's consent any time it pleased.

It should be noted that the Prudential management proposed the debit cutting procedure as part of its overall policy of expansion. Certain agents, these officials reasoned, were working debits that were too large, with the consequence that they could not cover a specific territory within a given period of time. The company, therefore, proposed to cut the debit, giving part of the area to a new agent, who, if a hustler, would receive a portion of another location contiguous to his new debit. On the basis of the theory he could increase his sales still further.

In reforming the debit system the company negotiators were acting realistically; sales of "industrial" life insurance had settled on a plateau since 1940. To remain competitive the company management considered itself forced to reduce the size of the debit area and, by hiring new agents, hoped to obtain greater production out of the agency salesmen.

The only trouble with Prudential's plan was that it placed the Insurance Agents International Union in a dilemma all out of proportion to its staying power. For one thing, membership in the union had never regained its pre-strike levels, and the hiring of new

[29]I.A.I.U., *Convention Proceedings* (Cleveland, O., 1957), p. 27.

agents raised the ever difficult question of organization. Would these new men embrace the labor union?

To Prudential's debit-cutting program must be added the union's strategy of "No Contract — No Work," a policy which posed another and basically different problem for the I.A.I.U.'s national leadership. When the contract expired the automatic check-off ceased at the same time; the national officers therefore depended upon the good will offerings of the membership. As time went on fewer of the agents paid their dues, and the union was fast becoming financially strapped.[30]

Faced with this twofold crisis, the union's national leaders began to circulate the idea that the union would have to settle with Prudential even though the terms of agreement would include the debit-cutting article. Soon after this unpleasant news became known, Russ assembled his union's executive board and the Prudential bargaining committee to discuss the company's proposal and the dues payment situation. It is difficult to know just exactly what went on during these meetings. According to Joseph Pollack, the president of the Prudential Local in New York City and a member of the board, Russ approached the emergency obliquely. First of all, he is supposed to have reinterpreted all of the resolutions passed at the 1955 convention. He said that the "All Go or None Go" resolution, for example, did not mean what it intended; that the wording of the resolution merely implied that no agent could forbid another to attend the company conferences. There were other changes that need not be supplied here. Russ' action was, according to Pollack, a contravention of the I.A.I.U.'s constitution, which made the convention the supreme governing body of the union. By misinterpreting the resolutions Russ was taking supreme authority unto himself.[31]

Russ, of course, denied Pollack's accusation. More importantly, none of the board or committee members sided with Pollack in his evaluation of Russ' action. They simply agreed with Russ that something had to be done to bail the union out of the crisis. Russ believed that acceptance of the debit-cutting article was the only alternative to continued strife.

Accordingly, in June 1956 the union signed a new agreement with

[30]Hogan, Interview.

[31]Letters from Joseph Pollack, President of Local 19, I.A.I.U., AFL-CIO, June 29 & July 9, 1956.

Prudential whereby the company paid the agents a $7.63 weekly increase in exchange for the hated debit-cutting article. When he offered the contract to the members for ratification, Russ exclaimed: "I have never experienced a more trying time, not even during the strike of 1951."[32]

However, the negotiations and intra-union discussions were but a prelude to the even "more trying" events that arose out of the Prudential agents' voting over contract ratification.

ANOTHER REVERSE ON THE HOME FRONT

When Russ submitted the new agreement to the I.A.I.U.'s Prudential membership, about one-third of the agents voted against acceptance, with Local 19, New York, rejecting the contract by an overwhelming majority.[33]

Joseph Pollack, the president of the large New York Local, was at work. He not only kept his own Local out of Russ' camp but tried to spoil the vote for contract ratification in the other locals as well. As soon as Russ asked the Prudential agents to accept the new agreement, Pollack addressed letters to every local president, repeating his indictment of Russ and suggesting that the entire union membership reject the contract.

Russ countered Pollack's charges with letters of his own. He insisted that he was not guilty of violating the union's constitution and tried to show that the conflict with Prudential could not wait upon the general convocation of the agents. He accused Pollack of indulging in half-truth. Pollack, he wrote, had failed to inform the local presidents that the union's executive board had agreed to accept the debit-cutting article, that he was unable to convince the board members of a contrary position and that he did not vote against the article but merely abstained. Russ concluded his correspondence with the threat that Pollack's action could destroy the union. To prevent this outcome he urged the Prudential members to approve the contract.[34]

[32]I.A.I.U., *Convention Proceedings* (Cleveland, O., 1957), p. 27.

[33]*The Insurance Agent,* August, 1956, p. 1. The vote in the New York local was 753 against and 184 in favor.

[34]Letter from George Russ, President of Insurance Agents International Union, AFL-CIO, July 6, 1956.

Pollack then became the central character in a rather bizarre episode in union politics. After investigating the agents' sentiment about the contract, he concluded that the majority of the men would favor Russ' position. In an effort to thwart Russ he sought a temporary restraining order from a federal district court in Washington, D.C. to postpone voting on the contract. He named as defendants the three national officers of I.A.I.U., Russ, Heisel, and Max Shine. The judge took Pollack's petition under deliberation and shortly thereafter dismissed the motion, declaring that the dispute concerned a purely internal union matter and was therefore outside his jurisdiction.[35]

Since the majority of the Prudential agents ratified the contract with its debit-cutting article, their approval afforded Russ the opportunity of dealing with Pollack. He waited until the I.A.I.U.'s executive board meeting in November 1956. Pollack was present and Russ permitted him the right to defend himself, which he did. In spite of his plea the board found Pollack guilty of an unwarranted attack on the integrity of the national leadership, expelled him as board member for one year and fined him $100.00. The board members also judged Local 19 guilty of conspiring with Pollack and fined it $500.00. Before the meeting adjourned both Pollack and representatives of his Local announced that they would appeal the conviction to the union's national convention.[36]

This incident caused a crisis within the I.A.I.U. of far greater consequence than Hogan's defection. Pollack controlled the largest Prudential affiliate in the union, a fact he never failed to mention at conventions and board meetings. He believed his strength alone would buy him exoneration, and he said as much at the 1957 convention.

> I have been told and have been given to understand that the stand we take on this appeal will greatly affect many things that are going to happen at this convention. We stand on our record . . . . We have been put in a spot for reasons which are of no consequence in this talk. We ask the delegates to find us not guilty.[37]

[35]*The Insurance Agent,* August, 1956, p. 1.

[36]I.A.I.U., *Convention Proceedings* (Cleveland, O., 1957), pp. 42-6.

[37]*Ibid.,* pp. 519-20.

Pollack was really asking for the moon. To many of those present he had abused his authority as president of Local 19 by his attack on Russ. Furthermore, he antagonized delegates of every other local union by his repeated demands for greater representation for Local 19 at union conventions and on the general executive board. (On this point, the I.A.I.U.'s New York Local was very much like its counterpart in the C.I.O. insurance union.) Pollack's appeal for clemency, therefore, afforded the delegates the opportunity of putting him in his place, and they did just that. They rejected his appeal, but, interestingly enough, they did so by a small margin, a fact that more than anything else tempered Pollack's reaction to defeat. As a result of the vote, he retired from the executive board for one year, retroactive to November, 1956; he also paid his fine, as did Local 19.[38]

Their honor avenged, the national leaders once more took control of the I.A.I.U., content in the knowledge that Pollack was a good loser. They could turn their attention to the increasingly vexing relationship with Prudential.

A LANDMARK DECISION FROM THE HIGH COURT

Shortly after George Russ signed the contract with Prudential, he expressed amazement at the speed with which the company began to cut the agents' debits. In December 1956 he wrote to the company for information on the number of debits cut and the number of times it reduced debits with the consent of the agents. He also inquired about the company's future plans in this area.

Prudential officials replied that Russ' questions were too cumbersome to answer and that the future arrangements of debits were the sole responsibility of management.

Russ tried to enlist the support of the delegates to the 1957 I.A.I.U. convention in ruling favorably on a resolution censuring Prudential for its debit-cutting program. The delegates disappointed him as they refused to have anything to do with the condemnation.[39] Russ then returned to his letter writing and to receiving stereotyped replies from the company.

The Prudential management was in no mood for a game of cat and mouse. While Russ was composing his letters, the N.L.R.B.,

[38]*Ibid.*, p. 562.

[39]*Ibid.*, p. 428.

after investigating an unfair labor practice charge filed by the company, decided that the I.A.I.U. was guilty of "bad faith" bargaining during its "No Contract — No Work" period of 1956.[40] The ruling caught Russ off balance momentarily. He ultimately decided to fight those whom he termed the "Eisenhower" members of the Board.

Along with most labor leaders of the time George Russ felt he had a mission to instruct the Republican members of the N.L.R.B. in the subtleties of the labor-management relationship. Using all the resources at his command — they were not considerable — he appealed the Board's decision, only to be repulsed by a lower court. He then took the case to the United States Court of Appeals. This branch of the judiciary ruled in favor of the union, declaring that it had not technically engaged in "unprotected harassing tactics" during the "No Contract — No Work" episode and, consequently, that it did not violate Section 8 (b) (3) of the National Labor Relations Act.[41]

However, the Prudential officials were as convinced of the correctness of the N.L.R.B.'s decision as Russ was of its defect. The company therefore undertook an immediate defense of the Board, asking for a "declaratory judgment" from a United States District Court on a material violation of the contract. A justice of the court brought Prudential management to grief because he denied the request.[42]

With this decision the combatants prepared their weapons for the final phase of the battle, an appeal to the United States Supreme Court. The court decided the case in 1960, and Justice William J. Brennan, writing for the majority, observed that the "use of economic pressure is of itself not at all inconsistent with the duty of bargaining in good faith." He concluded his remarks with the thought that the "Board's approach involves an intrusion into the

[40]*The Prudential Insurance Co.,* 119 N.L.R.B. 768 (1957).

[41]*Insurance Agents International Union* v. *N.L.R.B.,* 260 F. 2d 736 U.S. Ct. of Appeals (1958).

[42]*The Prudential Ins. Co.* v. *Insurance Agents International Union,* D.C.S.D.N.Y., 169 F. Supp. 534 (1959).

substantive aspects of the bargaining process."[43]

Leaving aside the fact that the high court ruled in favor of the I.A.I.U., the decision represents, in the words of Justice Brennan, an important declaration on the scope of the N.L.R.B.'s authority under Section 8 (b) (3).[44] It would be interesting to pursue this question further; however, such a procedure clearly exceeds the purpose of this dissertation.

When the Supreme Court handed down the decision, the I.A.I.U. was no longer in existence. George Russ, his national officers and the A.F. of L. insurance agents finally agreed to merge with the C.I.O. union. It is this important development that will now be traced in the history of the organized insurance agents.

[43] *N.L.R.B.* v. *Insurance Agents International Union,* 361 U.S. 477 (1960). Justices Frankfurter, Harlan and Whittaker joined in a separate opinion. Agreeing that the action taken by the Board was not tenable, they nevertheless proposed that the case be remanded to the Board for further investigation.

[44] *Ibid.*

CHAPTER 9

TWO SMALL UNIONS MERGE

During the 1940's the leaders of the various insurance agents' unions preached the gospel of unity. Periodically officials of the United Office and Professional Workers of America contacted George Russ, the president of the A.F. of L. insurance agents' council, and tried to convince him of the need for one jurisdiction. Both the U.O.P.W.A. leaders and Russ in turn attempted to lure into their respective folds the Milwaukee-based independent, the International Union of Life Insurance Agents. There was no question in the minds of these men that separate unions worked to the disadvantage of the insurance agents. However, their efforts ended in failure.

When the U.O.P.W.A. disintegrated, George Russ was quick to realize that all of the disparate elements in the insurance field might be brought together under the banner of the American Federation of Labor. In May 1951 his council became an international union, and he used the occasion to extend invitations to the founding convention to the C.I.O. Organizing Committee, to the independent union and to the shaky newcomer, the United Insurance Agents of America, headed by Leon W. Berney. The C.I.O. rejected the proposal, and old-time U.O.P.W.A. agents, by then members of the A.F. of L., having discovered Russ' alliance with the Berney group, rejected any such merger. The plan for one large union was scotched.[1]

Russ persevered, however. Shortly after the convention he journeyed to Milwaukee to consult with William Harper, the president of the I.U.L.I.A. This small independent union constituted a special prize, as Harper was the leader of 1,500 Prudential agents in several Midwestern states, and the acquisition of this membership would have assured Russ' supremacy in the Prudential jurisdiction. Again the plan collapsed; the I.U.L.I.A. agents and their leaders preferred autonomy.[2]

There were other unions of insurance agents right in George Russ' bailiwick, yet his efforts to bring them into the new union were as

[1]*N.F.I.A.C. Reporter,* May, 1951, p. 1.

[2]*The Insurance Agent,* June, 1951, p. 3.

unproductive as his contact with Harper. It has been recorded that Matthew Hogan and the Maryland Prudential Local left the I.A.I.U. shortly after the founding convention and that it took Russ years to reunite the two groups. He met with similar opposition from the Maryland Local of Metropolitan agents who defected from the A.F. of L. insurance council in 1950 over the matter of dues deduction. In Detroit a number of agents of the Life Insurance Co. of Virginia had received a federal charter from the Federation in the late 1940's, and these men, too, spurned Russ' overtures.[3] For one reason or another, it seemed that many groups of agents, once they achieved an independent status, did not want to surrender their autonomy to the Russ international.

In his relationship with the newly formed Insurance and Allied Workers Organizing Committee, C.I.O., Russ had scant opportunity to reflect upon the merits of unity. From the start Russ and the C.I.O. waged a no-holds barred campaign, using its contracts with the various companies to show that the agents were victims of unenlightened trade union leadership. Each staged raids on the other's members with the express purpose of cleansing the debit men from the contamination of competing policies.

In March 1952, for example, I.A.W.O.C., C.I.O., agents raided the I.A.I.U.'s Local 12 in Philadelphia. Founded a decade earlier, the Local had fifty-six members and operated along strictly company lines, the men belonging to the Philadelphia United Mutual Insurance Co. Russ was furious at the intrusion and, to restore order, placed the Local in trusteeship and suspended those agents who were responsible for the C.I.O.'s success. Sometime afterwards the N.L.R.B. ordered a representation election. Russ protested the decision, stating that his union had signed a three year contract with the company and that it would not expire for another year. In an interesting rebuttal, the Board ruled that the three year contract was not an established practice in the insurance industry. When the election took place, the I.A.I.U., A.F. of L. won it, although its

[3]Insurance Agents International Union, A.F.L., *Report of the Second Biennial Convention* (Louisville, Ky., 1955), pp. 25-6. The Detroit agents of Virginia Life affiliated to the I.A.I.U. in March, 1956. cf. I.A.I.U., *Convention Proceedings* (Cleveland, O., 1957), p. 37.

margin of victory was a narrow one.[4]

In spite of this distasteful encounter the I.A.I.U. left the way open for merger talks between the two unions. Commenting on the election, a member of the A.F. of L. organization wryly observed that the companies had enjoyed the fracas, watching both unions spend time and money fighting each other.[5] Yet, it seems likely that the dispute occasioned the first official meeting between the I.A.I.U. and the newly chartered C.I.O. union, the Insurance Workers of America. This occurred in December 1953, and out of the deliberations there resulted a joint statement to the effect that the two presidents would seek ways to promote mutual understanding.[6] Unfortunately, neither side was prepared to implement this noble sentiment. In fact, both unions were about to enter a period of belligerent activity and frustrating confusion; the battle was already taking shape when the chief officers issued their joint communique.

A MOST UNLIKELY OCCASION FOR UNITY

For several years after it expelled the United Office and Professional Workers of America, the C.I.O. tried to establish legal claim over the Boston Mutual Life Insurance Company contract.[7] Under the leadership of Frank Siegel, the agents had joined the Distributive, Processing and Office Workers of America and seemed immune to the C.I.O. Organizing Committee's raiding activity. The latter union twice petitioned the N.L.R.B. for an election to determine representation, and it twice failed to elicit the support of the company's insurance men.

[4]*The Insurance Agent,* February, 1952, p. 7. The case has an interesting conclusion. In 1954 the United Mutual dropped the general management system in favor of the general agency system, thereby removing the agents from the pale of unionization. Russ appealed the action to the N.L.R.B. The I.A.I.U. lost the case on the grounds that the Board could not prevent a company from changing its mode of operation. The United Mutual insurance local was dissolved in 1955, and the former unionized agents went to work for other companies in the Philadelphia area. cf. I.A.I.U., *Convention Proceedings* (Louisville, Ky., 1955), pp. 24-5.

[5]*The Insurance Agent,* June, 1952, p. 4.

[6]*Ibid.,* January, 1954, p. 1.

[7]Operating in Massachusetts, Rhode Island, New Hampshire and Maine, the company was incorporated on August 18, 1891, as the Boston Mutual Life Association and commenced business on February 15, 1892. It was reincorporated as a legal reserve company and changed its name to its present title on July 1, 1899. The company writes participating ordinary and industrial life insurance. Moody's, p. 1762 . The U.O.P.W.A. had first organized the company's agents in 1941.

In the spring of 1951 Siegel formed the Boston Mutual agents into one large local union; calling it Local 1282, D.P.O., he became its first president. When conditions within the D.P.O.W.A. began to deteriorate, Arthur Osman, the union's president, put out "feelers" about the possibility of returning to the C.I.O., and he used Frank Siegel as part of his advance section. In September 1953 Siegel wrote to Kenneth O'Dell, the president of the Insurance Workers of America, C.I.O., offering the support of Local 1282 in the former's organizing drive against Metropolitan Life in Massachusetts.[8] Moreover, the Siegel group started to call itself Local 1282, D.P.O./ C.I.O.

The contract between the Boston Mutual and Siegel's Local expired in October 1953, and Everett Lane, the company's president, refused to negotiate a new agreement unless the Local accept certain conditions on rates of pay and the like. It was at this time that the dispute took on a new dimension, involving both the A.F. L. and C.I.O. insurance unions in a bitterly contested battle over representation of the agents. The Russ organization promised to assist Siegel, and when the I.W.A., C.I.O., asked him to withdraw, asserting that it had a golden opportunity to wrest control of the Local from the Distributive Workers, he refused to do so.

Just why Russ chose to deprive the C.I.O. of victory is a matter of conjecture. It can be stated, for example, that he was not so upset over the Philadelphia United case as to forbid his editor the right to hold out the hand of friendship to the I.W.A. Furtermore, his statement of purpose over his own and O'Dell's signatures indicates that he believed that a unified labor union would profit the insurance men. Even the underhanded tactics of the C.I.O. during the days prior to the Prudential strike had occurred long enough ago to enable Russ to forgive and forget. Russ himself explained that the I.A.I.U.'s entry into the Boston Mutual dispute was part of his union's continuing effort to bring the "best" in trade unionism to insurance agents.[9] The unfolding of events in this history will make Russ appear less than altruisitic, yet they should not be interpreted in the same context as his early appearance on the scene of the Boston Mutual dispute.

[8]Letter from Frank Siegel, president of Local 1282, DPO, September, 1953.

[9]I.A.I.U., *Convention Proceedings* (Cleveland, O., 1957), pp. 72-3.

The presence of two national unions apparently emboldened Siegel and his fellow officers, for sometime in the late fall of 1953 the Boston Mutual agents voted to strike the company.[10] As if this action were not sufficient in itself, Local 1282, D.P.O./C.I.O., proved even more embarrassing to the C.I.O. when it became known that the Massachusetts Commission Investigating Communism planned to question Siegel about his conduct of union affairs. To complicate matters further, the C.I.O. affiliates in New England demanded that the national union inform Siegel that his use of the C.I.O. designation was unlawful; they also warned the Insurance Workers of America that any assistance to Siegel was ill-advised and in poor taste.

In spite of the interplay of these events, the C.I.O. was unable in late 1953 to wash its hands of Siegel. For one thing, President O'Dell of the Insurance Workers had made a speech at the recently adjourned national convention in which he left the door open to Siegel. Moreover, the national C.I.O. had granted permission to Local 65, the successor of the Distributive, Processing and Office Workers of America, to send fraternal delegates to the same convention. To make matters worse, the C.I.O. had begun to collect dues from the Local union and its affiliates.[11]

The Siegel affair was temporarily resolved in January 1954. The national C.I.O., acting under pressure from New England, forbade him the use of the C.I.O. designation in the official title of his Local, and it emphasized the prohibition by refusing him membership in the union. Siegel's reaction to the C.I.O.'s prohibition seems cautious. He contacted President O'Dell to request information on the I.W.A.'s official policy toward him and his Local. Moreover, he submitted a list of grievances against the C.I.O. union which, among other things, accused members of the I.W.A. of raiding his Local and of collecting dues from some of the Boston Mutual agents. For reasons that will become apparent shortly, Siegel did not consider the C.I.O.'s action final, because toward the end of his letter he asked O'Dell to address a strike meeting of Boston Mutual Agents

[10]Telegram from Arthur St. John, president of Local 11, I.W.A., C.I.O., Boston, Mass., December 6, 1953.

[11]Letter from Kenneth O'Dell, president of Insurance Workers of America, C.I.O., December 10, 1953.

on February 25, 1954.[12] O'Dell naturally refused, although it is not altogether clear why he did so. Perhaps he was not receiving accurate information from his Boston correspondents, and his refusal of the invitation was dictated by prudence.

On February 24, 1954, the day before the strike meeting, Frank Siegel appeared before the Massachusetts Commission Investigating Communism. During the course of the hearing witnesses developed a theme that has been sung before: they said that Siegel had taught at the Samuel Adams' School in Boston during the 1940's, that his Local had become the headquarters in Boston for the mimeographing and distribution of Communist literature, and that the Boston Mutual agents had been assessed for the defense of the so-called "Communist 11" in New York City. When the investigators asked Siegel to refute the allegations, he sought refuge in the Fifth Amendment.

Later in the same day, two more witnesses testified against him. The first was Everett Lane, president of the Boston Mutual, who was reported to have told the Commission that Siegel and his fellow officers had attempted to make Local 1282's members "hate the company." The other witness was Hugh Thompson, the New England Regional Director of the C.I.O. Because of the lack of documentation, his testimony against Siegel is extremely difficult to evaluate. The Commonwealth of Massachusetts published a brief report on the Siegel appearance, yet it furnished nothing of any value with regard to Thompson's testimony. In addition to this, the Boston press, while it covered the hearing in some detail, simply reported that Thompson read a statement from Walter Reuther to the effect that Siegel and his Local were not affiliated to the C.I.O.

This is of some interest because at a prior session of the investigation, witnesses tried to develop the idea that Arthur Osman, David Livingston and Jack Paley were Communists. (All three men were the chief officers of Local 65, the successor of the Distributive, Processing and Office Workers of America.) The Commission knew that Siegel was a member of the Local, and, when he was asked to comment on the sworn statements about the trio, he refused to

[12]Letter from Anne Kerrigan, secretary of President O'Dell, February 21, 1954.

incriminate himself.[13] Siegel's appearance, and the reference to Osman and the others, no doubt placed Thompson in an awkward position. It was generally well known that Local 65 was negotiating with the C.I.O. for a return to the national union, and it seems peculiar that the organization was offering an opportunity to the Local's chief leaders and at the same time denying the right of membership to one of the Local's more prominent officials, Frank Siegel.

The next day Local 1282 held the strike meeting at Worcester, Massachusetts. The majority of the Boston Mutual agents, disgusted with Siegel's performance before the Commission, were in no mood to listen to his tirade against the company, nor were they appreciative of the presence of Local 65 leaders on the platform. David Livingston, the secretary-treasurer of the union, had prepared a twenty minute speech urging the agents to remain united and to strike the company, but because of the heckling of the opposition, it took him two hours to complete his remarks. His perseverance payed off, however, since he was able to put across the important parts of his message. Among other things, he told the agents that Hugh Thompson had been "mistaken" about the Boston Mutual Local's affiliation to the C.I.O. and that he would furnish, within the week, "proof that C.I.O. will support us if we strike." Before adjourning the meeting, Siegel pledged that Livingston would make good his promise.[14]

Both Lane and Thompson decided to get tough with Siegel. On March 1 Lane wrote to the agents that he would no longer negotiate with their union. He stated that he had no objection to their joining the C.I.O., the A.F.L. or an independent, but that he could no longer "tolerate Siegel." He advised the insurance men not to strike the company, and he concluded his letter on a note that caused much concern among the agency force. Regardless of the outcome of the current dispute, Lane wrote, he would introduce a new compensation plan on April 1; the old method, based on a flat rate device, was to be replaced by a plan constructed on an incentive basis.[15]

[13]*The Boston Herald,* February 25, 1954, p. 1.

[14]*The Boston Daily Globe,* February 26, 1954, p. 1.

[15]Letter from Everett Lane, president of the Boston Mutual. The flat rate device amounted to $10.00 and was similar to a weekly guarantee.

Hugh Thompson took stock of the situation, and, perhaps for the first time, Thompson and all of the officials of the C.I.O., along with Kenneth O'Dell of the Insurance Workers, realized what was going on. He made up his mind that Siegel had to go and that Livingston would never obtain a statement of C.I.O. support for the Boston Mutual Local.

Thompson also decided that if any organization were to inherit the Boston Mutual's unionized agents it would be the C.I.O.'s own Insurance Workers. Accordingly, he sent his men to Siegel's next meeting which was held on March 4. They distributed a statement pledging the C.I.O.'s assistance in the coming fight with Lane, yet it would be granted on C.I.O.'s terms. The statement presented a bill of particulars about Siegel and ended with the sentence: "We cannot and refuse to recognize the present leadership of the Boston Mutual agents."[16]

Siegel got hold of the statement, rushed to the platform and denounced Thompson and the C.I.O. He begged the agents to repudiate it and came close to achieving this goal. There was a vote taken on the issue and, of those present, 116 favored the statement while 112 voted for Siegel.[17]

During this same meeting Thompson's men were able to engage the support of a group of Boston Mutual agents who tried to unseat Siegel as president of Local 1282. Their plan failed, but it so frightened Siegel that he felt obliged to explain his use of the Fifth Amendment at the recent hearings. He said:

I am not a member of the Communist Party . . . . I refused to tell this to the Commission because I do not like people who use threats and force and who have caused real harm to B/M agents and their families.[18]

Siegel left the meeting with a core of loyal followers. Bereft of C.I.O. support — David Livingston did not attend the meeting — he took about 120 members of Local 1282 into the Insurance Agents International Union, A.F.L. Although the latter organization had remained relatively quiet throughout the early part of 1954, Presi-

[16]Letter from Hugh Thompson, New England Regional Director, C.I.O., March 4, 1954.

[17]Letter from James Brisbane, secretary-treasurer of I.W.A., C.I.O., March 8, 1954.

[18]Statement from Local 1282, D.P.O.W.A., March, 1954.

dent George Russ had preserved contact with Siegel, and three days after the final Worcester gathering he announced that he had accepted Siegel into the I.A.I.U. He justified his course of action on the theory that company president, Everett Lane, had imperiled the bargaining position of the Boston Mutual agents. The editor of the A.F.L. newspaper in Worcester thought otherwise; he wrote that Russ was more interested in dues paying members than in the welfare of the Boston Mutual debit men.[19]

On March 18 the agents loyal to Siegel voted to leave the Osman group, to affiliate to the I.A.I.U., A.F. of L., and to transfer the Boston Mutual Local's funds to the Russ union. The latter endorsement was not easily accomplished, however, for, along with its ordinary balance, the Local held a sum of $7,000.00 which Siegel had collected from the agents in 1952. Although Siegel's critics in the Local had allowed him discretionary power over the fund, many of them were accusing him of having used part of the money to pay his legal fees in his appearance before the Massachusetts Commission Investigating Communism. These men subsequently brought suit against Siegel to retrieve their contributions to the fund. The case was tried on March 31. Siegel swore that most of the fund was still intact and that he had paid his lawyer from an outside source. The judge seemed satisfied with the explanation but decided that the money be placed in escrow.[20]

Meanwhile, the remnants of the Siegel Local were incorporated into the I.A.I.U. as Local 243; under the terms of the agreement the Local remained autonomous. Moreover, the N.L.R.B. had entered the dispute and decreed that an election take place on April 1. The vote was indecisive, for both the I.A.I.U. and the I.W.A., C.I.O., received one hundred eighty-five ballots each. The Board therefore ordered another election for April 15.[21]

On the day following the first election, Lane questioned Max Lefkowith, an officer in the new Siegel Local, about an article that appeared in the A.F.L. insurance publication. Lane accused Lefkowith of writing the piece that implicated Lane and the Boston Mutual attorney, Benjamin Gordon, in a deal that, according to the

[19]*The Worcester Labor News,* in a C.I.O. leaflet, March, 1954.

[20]*The Boston Daily Record,* April 1, 1954, p. 2.

[21]Letter from George Russ, President of I.A.I.U., A.F.L., April 2, 1954.

writer, Siegel and Lefkowith had turned down — but that the I.W.A., C.I.O., had swallowed "lock, stock and barrel." Lane told Lefkowith that he would fire him if he admitted authorship. The latter boasted that he would answer the charge after the runoff election.[22]

If either the C.I.O. or the Boston Mutual favored the I.W.A. it certainly was not apparent during the runoff campaign. On April 5 the national union announced that it had accepted back into the fold Osman, Livingston and Paley, the chief executive officers of Local 65, New York.[23] Seeking to excuse its own conduct, the A.F.L. insurance union made good use of the reinstatement and accused the I.W.A. and Thompson of hypocrisy.[24]

Far worse for the I.W.A. was the activity of Everett Lane. He campaigned for the union in a way that was bound to attract the attention of the N.L.R.B. For example, on April 7 he wrote to the Boston Mutual agents as follows:

> I have had no hesitation in the past few weeks of disclosing to you the dislike and contempt that your company has for the A.F.L. insurance workers union and its Local 243. I was of the opinion that I had made clear to all of you why your company had taken this stand, but it would appear from the tie vote that I may not have made our position clear to some of you.[25]

He then told the agents that a vote for the C.I.O. was the only possible way they had to show respect for themselves and for the company.

Lane wrote to the agents again, just two days before the election, stating that the law did not compel an employer to agree to an arbitration clause in a contract. His words were strong:

> It should be obvious that no company, in the exercise of good discretionary judgment, would agree to an arbitration procedure, if it had no respect for the representatives of the union

[22]Letter from Max Lefkowith, officer of Local 243, I.A.I.U., A.F.L., April 8, 1954.

[23]*The C.I.O. News,* April 5, 1954, pp. 2 & 11.

[24]Leaflet, Local 243, I.A.I.U., A.F.L., n.d.

[25]*The Boston Mutual Life Insurance Co.,* 110 N.L.R.B., no. 36, (1954).

with which it is to negotiate. If your company should refuse to agree to insert an arbitration clause in a collective bargaining agreement, then it retains the unrestricted right to terminate anybody for any cause.[26]

By these remarks Lane was adverting to more than just Siegel's demands for an arbitration clause if his union won the election. Lane had no intention of granting the request because there were agents like Siegel, Lefkowith and others whom he would dismiss if the occasion arose. However, he hoped that such a solution would be unnecessary, in fact, he intended to do all within his power to deny Siegel and the A.F.L. the Boston Mutual contract.

And the I.A.I.U., A.F.L., was just as intent upon seizing it. Referring to the events of the campaign, the officers of the union issued a statement that read in part: "We have followed the policy of never raiding another union or of courting friendship with a company."[27] The secret was out, for the words of the I.A.I.U. leadership reflect not only their bitterness towards Lane but go a long way in explaining the A.F.L. union's presence in the Boston Mutual dispute. Russ and his colleagues had never forgiven the C.I.O. insurance union for the raids on the Prudential and Philadelphia United Agents, and the Boston Mutual situation furnished them with the very sweet occasion for revenge.

Many of the Boston Mutual agents could not have cared less for the pique of the I.A.I.U. officers, and, when election day arrived and the I.W.A., C.I.O., obtained the majority of votes cast, these agents looked forward to more peaceful days. However, on the night of the C.I.O. victory Siegel met with the leaders of the I.A.I.U. and decided immediately to institute unfair labor practice charges against the company on two counts: Lane's interference in the campaign and his dismissal of Lefkowith (he fired this agent just as soon as the election results were in).[28]

Since Lane had clearly violated the law, the Labor Board had no choice but to investigate the charges and ultimately to set aside the runoff election. This development put the unionized insurance men in the difficult position of working without a contract for a still longer period of time. In an effort to assist the agents, the I.W.A.,

[26]*Ibid.*

[27]Letter from George Russ, April 8, 1954.

[28]"Time for a Change," C.I.O. leaflet, n.d.

C.I.O., officials approached Lane and asked him to preserve the union shop agreement and to maintain the old compensation plan. Lane replied that his hands were tied while the Board continued its investigation.[29]

Sometime in May the agents pleaded with Russ to drop the charges; they even promised to ask Lane to reinstate Lefkowith if that would resolve the conflict. Both Russ and Lefkowith ignored the request, and with good reason. By this time Lefkowith had replaced Siegel as leader of the Boston Mutual Local in the I.A.I.U., and, if the A.F.L. union dropped the charges, then the I.W.A., C.I.O., would have taken over the company's agents and Lefkowith could not tolerate such an arrangement.[30]

In June the Boston regional director of the N.L.R.B. decided that hearings on Lefkowith's dismissal be held the next month, but, as so frequently happens, the trial did not take place until September. On the basis of its findings, the full Board decided, on a three to two vote, that Lane's activities violated the law and that Lefkowith's dismissal was unwarranted. The Board ordered a new election.[31]

Both sides resumed the battle, and again the I.W.A., C.I.O., seems to have displeased the gods of labor elections. Since the second ballot had been cast, the Boston Mutual had terminated about forty agents and had hired fifty other men to take their place. The I.A.I.U. demanded that these insurance men be denied the right to vote in the coming election. The Labor Board agreed. When the balloting took place the agents chose I.A.I.U. by a substantial margin; 183 men voted for the A.F.L., while 132 voted for the C.I.O. It is apparent that the I.W.A., C.I.O., could have used the votes of the newly hired debit men.[32]

Lane's reaction to the I.A.I.U.'s victory was predictable; he refused to negotiate. Thereupon, President Russ sought to placate the agents who, by that time, had been working without a contract for fourteen months. In rather high-toned, statesmanlike language he told them: "It falls to each generation to fight for the liberty and freedom that we inherit . . . we fight either to preserve it or to regain

[29]C.I.O. leaflet, Local 1776, I.W.A., C.I.O., Boston, Mass.

[30]*The Insurance Worker,* May, 1954, p. 1.

[31]*The Boston Mutual Life Ins. Co.,* 110 N.L.R.B. no. 36 (1954).

[32]*The Insurance Agent,* November, 1954, p. 1.

it."[33] The agents opted for freedom and voted to strike the company. The immediate cause and the resultant conduct of the work stoppage were deplorable.

On February 10, 1955, the company management suspended an agent for an alleged immoral act against one of its policyholders. The agents in the man's district office petitioned Russ for permission to go out on strike. Russ granted their request, and the company promptly dismissed them. On February 14 the entire agency force walked off their jobs. Pickets were thrown around the company's home office in Boston and proved so effective that Lane decided to move his office equipment to another area. When the local teamsters' union refused to handle the job, the Boston Mutual management called in scab truck drivers. A fight broke out, and in the ensuing moments one of the truck drivers was accidentally killed. Less serious, but no less instructive, was the fact that an assistant manager of the company was given a three week jail sentence for striking an agent.[34]

Both sides tried to resolve the dispute. President Lane offered the debit men a deal on compensation which they rejected. George Russ appealed to the Governor of Massachusetts to intervene, a plea that was apparently rejected. And the strike went on.

Because outside assistance was not forthcoming, and because company and union were growing weary of the dispute, both sides decided to end the walkout on May 20, 1955, thus bringing to a close the longest strike a union ever waged against an insurance company. When George Russ signed the contract, he said that it "was not what we wanted," but, since he was as tired of the strike and of the Boston Mutual affair as anyone else, he accepted the company's proposals. Among the salient features of the new agreement, the agents received a five dollar increase in compensation, the elimination of the incentive salary program, the union shop, and most importantly, a grievance and arbitration clause.[35]

The man who caused so much of the trouble, Max Lefkowith, also had enough. When the agreement was signed he collected the back pay settlement the I.A.I.U. negotiated for him and quit the company. In commenting on his departure Russ said that he asked

[33]I.A.I.U., *Convention Proceedings* (Louisville, Ky., 1955), p. 172.

[34]*The Insurance Agent,* March & May, 1955, p. 1.

[35]*Ibid.,* June, 1955, pp. 1 & 5.

Lefkowith to remain, but that he did not want his job back and that "was his business."[36]

When the strike was over there were no cheeers, nor was anyone especially proud of his achievement in bringing Lane and the Boston Mutual to their collective knees. Most of the men involved would no doubt admit that the strike should never have occurred. The I.A.I.U. leaders had got their pound of flesh from the I.W.A., C.I.O., and did not know what to do with it; in fact, the assistance the latter union rendered during the course of the strike caused the A.F.L. organization some embarrassment. The I.W.A. supported the striking agents more than any other union, furnishing free of charge approximately 22,000 pieces of literature and daily manning the picket lines.[37]

In spite of the bitterness of the pre-election campaigns, neither Russ nor President O'Dell seem to have forgotten the joint statement of purpose of December 1953. Shortly after the final election both leaders decided to reopen the quest for unity.

A Prolonged Series of Fits and Starts

The officers of the I.A.I.U. and the I.W.A. got together in October 1954 after contacting the national presidents of the A.F.L. and the C.I.O. In November of the same year the leaders of each insurance union instructed their respective executive boards to explore ways of untangling the troublesome technicalities that kept the two organizations apart. During the November executive board meeting of the I.A.I.U., an important decision was made; aware of the many causes surrounding the union's defeat in the Prudential strike, the board members examined the question of the nonunion office worker in the insurance industry. The plan was not well received by all, for certain old-line A.F.L. insurance men could not envision a union that would include office personnel among its members. But the leadership of the I.A.I.U. proved that if the union were to merge with the I.W.A., C.I.O., this important issue had to

[36]I.A.I.U., *Convention Proceedings* (Louisville, Ky., 1955), p. 49. Lefkowith had a brokerage of his own and seems not to have wanted for money. C.I.O. leaflet, Local 1776, I.W.A., C.I.O., Boston, Mass.

[37]*The Insurance Worker,* March, 1955, p. 5.

be faced and resolved.[38]

After the meeting adjourned Russ studied the proposals of the special merger subcommittee and contacted O'Dell whose own committee had likewise submitted its findings. Both sides met in Washington on March 24 and 25, 1955, and soon realized that good will was not enough, for, in order to merge the unions, grave problems such as the following had to be faced and, hopefully, resolved: the number of national officers, the amount of per capita tax due the national union, the method of voting at conventions, the manner and method of establishing collective bargaining committees, the number of executive board members and the jurisdiction of the local unions. Yet, the meeting showed that both sides could sit down together, and, although the difficulties seemed insurmountable, each knew what they were and heard them stated publicly.[39]

Another meeting was held in late April 1955, and a temporary solution to the problem of local union jurisdiction was agreed on. The negotiators considered this a good start and decided to postpone any further meetings for the immediate future since each union was about to have its biennial convention.

Fraternal expressions of good will were much in evidence at both gatherings. O'Dell congratulated Russ for his union's victory in the Boston Mutual, and Russ in turn pledged his union's support to the I.W.A. in its strike against the Provident Home Life Insurance Company. However, not every convention delegate was pleased with the prospect of merger. One A.F.L. agent, for instance, accused his national leadership of "selling out" the smaller locals in the union. Terming the merger proposal a "monstrous thing," he called it a plan for giving the I.W.A. greater voting power in the united organization and said that if the union wanted to join with the A.F.L., it would have to come in under the I.A.I.U.'s terms. He concluded his speech with this thought: "Let us not destroy our unity and run the little locals out of this union just because somebody wants to gain power and prestige."[40]

[38]*The Insurance Agent,* December, 1954, p. 1. The I.W.A. had two locals of white collar workers at this time; one in Detroit was made up of clericals in the Maccabbees, a fraternal organization, and the other was composed of the office staff of the Denver branch of the National Farmers Union.

[39]*The Insurance Worker,* April, 1955, p. 1; and I.A.I.U., *Convention Proceedings* (Louisville, Ky., 1955), pp. 100-01.

[40]I.A.I.U., *Convention Proceedings* (Louisville, Ky., 1955), p. 528.

205

The I.W.A., C.I.O., lost more than power and prestige at its convention. It has already been recorded that the delegates replaced every officer with the exception of Simon Helfgott. Fortunately, the new leaders were as interested in the merger as their predecessors, and in January 1956 they initiated talks with the I.A.I.U. hierarchy about the possibility of introducing a joint bill in the New York Legislature to exempt policyholders from payment of premiums during an insurance strike.[41]

Throughout 1956 and part of 1957 there were periodic meetings, but nothing tangible was achieved because both sides feared the reaction of their memberships. The delegate to the 1955 convention of the I.A.I.U., for example, was expressing more than just a personal opinion when he spoke of the small local. Members of these locals and of the small companies as well had always expressed some apprehension about the eastern group, a fact that has been documented in this work. Since this and other fears had been expressed by the memberships of each union, the national officers had of necessity to approach the question of unity with great caution. Nevertheless, the presidents of both unions presented the record of achievement to their 1957 convention delegates. George Russ catalogued the important points, stressing that the issue of voting at the national convention remained the heart of the problem. However, he could report that the merger committees had tentatively established the make-up of the executive board, with each union receiving a share in both membership and voting power in proportion to their numbers. Since the I.A.I.U. was the larger union, it would have more members on the board and greater voting power.

Russ also informed the delegates that the union would have to decide on the question of organizing office workers. He stated further that special consideration would be shown the smaller companies in that a special convention would take place among delegates of the smaller firms so that they might elect a member to the executive board.

Russ then introduced William Gillen, the president of the I.W.A., C.I.O. Gillen indicated, as Russ had done before him, that the question of voting at the national convention was the fundamental difficulty in the path to merger. He stated that his executive board had authorized a change in the per capita voting that the I.W.A.

[41]*The Insurance Worker,* February, 1956, p. 1.

had used at its conventions. He concluded with the remark that George Meany, the president of the AFL-CIO, expressed the hope that there would soon be only one union in the insurance field. In addressing himself to Meany's expectations, Gillen of course implied that neither union could have explored the merger issue in any detail unless the A.F.L. and the C.I.O. had first showed the way.

When Gillen completed his statement, Russ opened debate on the merger question. There was immediate disagreement, for a group of agents tried to scuttle the work of the merger committee, asserting they were opposed to unity on principle. The Russ forces quickly introduced a resolution favorable to the merger, and this was approved. They went further; they wanted the assembly to resolve to convene a special convention twelve months after it approved the merger resolution. The majority of the agents defeated the motion, thereby leaving Russ with little besides the resolution approving the merger agreement. But that was enough.[42]

Over at the I.W.A. convention the C.I.O. insurance agents voted approval of the merger. However, the gathering failed to accept the compromise resolution on voting at conventions. The New York bloc tried to complicate the issue by again asking for increased representation on the union's executive board. Their motion was defeated after a delegate, speaking for the majority, said: "This has been one of the barriers in the eyes of the I.A.I.U. in merging with this union. They are a union that respects the small unions, we have been a union that respects membership."[43]

Like Russ, Gillen had his mandate to pursue the merger issue. After the conventions he met periodically with Russ and the merger committee of the I.A.I.U. The difficulties surrounding the number of officers in the merged union, their salaries, dues, initiation fees, the make-up of the executive board, the jurisdiction of the local unions, the amending of the constitution, all were discussed and their acceptance reasonably assured. However, the procedure of voting at conventions presented an obstacle that seemed insurmountable. Both Russ and Gillen met with George Meany in the fall of 1958 to seek his advice on this problem. Meany suggested a solution, and both

[42]I.A.I.U., *Convention Proceedings* (Cleveland, O., 1957), pp. 53, 101-05 & 311.

[43]Insurance Workers of America, *Report of the Proceedings of the Third Constitutional Convention* (Buffalo, N.Y., 1957), p. 105.

men called together their merger committees to discuss the proposal.[44]

Meanwhile, George Russ was busy working on the leaders of the independent International Union of Life Insurance Agents. The latter held its convention in October 1958, and Russ sent greetings, along with the reminder that his union and the I.U.L.I.A. represented eighty-five per cent of the Prudential agents. He suggested that both internationals join together "in an endeavor to restore to the agent the job security which he is entitled to and to help us make further advances in his behalf."[45] The officials of the independent expressed gratitude; they also expressed their desire to remain autonomous.

Russ and Gillen met again during the last part of January 1959. They agreed to submit the results of their decisions to the executive boards of their respective unions. On February 20, 1959, the Joint Merger Committee, composed of members of both organizations, signed a joint merger agreement, approving the proposed constitution for the merged union, and, on the same day, the executive boards of both unions affixed their signatures to the document.[46]

Later on, in April 1959, Russ and Gillen sent out the convention call, and both men extended invitations to the officers of the independent I.U.L.I.A. and to President Bauer of the Metropolitan Life Local in Baltimore. As it turned out, neither group was amenable to the merger.[47]

The Insurance Agents International Union, AFL-CIO, and the Insurance Workers of America, AFL-CIO, held special conventions in May 1959. The plan called for a voice vote on the compromised issues and the immediate convoking of the founding convention of the merged unions. The I.A.I.U. went through the business at hand in record time; the delegates were ready to meet with the I.W.A. agents by noon of the second day. Just before he brought down the gavel on the final convention of his union, George Russ managed to find the right words in expressing his sentiments:

[44]*The Insurance Agent,* November, 1958, p. 4.

[45]*Ibid.*

[46]Insurance Workers International Union, AFL-CIO, *Report of the Founding Convention* (Chicago, Ill., 1959), p. 127.

[47]*The Insurance Agent,* May, 1950, p. 1.

I feel like a June bride, not knowing what to expect, but nevertheless we will do the best we can and see how it works out in this marriage.[48]

Russ' elation was nowhere in evidence at the I.W.A. conclave, however. There the delegates were apprehensive and spent the better part of the second session in acrimonious debate over the seating of a delegate. The handling of the dispute was used as the occasion for venting personal dislike against two of the national officers, both of whom were in danger of losing their jobs.

Prior to the convention Joseph Raab, the chief officer of the Philadelphia Local, had a falling out with President Gillen over a matter of union policy. Raab asserted that Gillen was not offering the organization the militant leadership it required and was, therefore, announcing his own candidacy for the top job in the I.W.A. If Raab had received no support the matter might well have been dropped. However, William MacDermott, who had moved up to the post of first vice president of the union in 1957 and who had never agreed with Gillen, lent the power of his office to Raab. After they polled the anti-Gillen factions in the New York, Philadelphia and Boston locals, they decided to contest his leadership, even at the risk of subverting the merger.

To complicate matters still further, the New York agents attacked the leadership of Arthur Higginson, the secretary-treasurer of the organization.

On the afternoon of the second day, nominating speeches were made. MacDermott placed Raab's name before the convention, explaining that Gillen had failed as leader of the union and that Raab alone was worthy of the job. When the vote was counted, Gillen defeated Raab by a slim margin.

Ignatius Brennan of the Pittsburgh Local then went to the platform and nominated Eugene LeFebvre, vice president of the New York Local, for the office of secretary-treasurer. He said he had nothing against Higginson personally, but that a large local, such as New York, deserved the distinction of having the union's secretary-treasurer from its ranks. The delegates voted against the Brennan-New York coalition and chose Higginson by a large majority.

The other officers, MacDermott and Robert Ponsi, returned to their posts unopposed.

[48]I.A.I.U., *Convention Proceedings* (Chicago, Ill., 1959), p. 24.

Both Gillen and Higginson were visibly shaken by the rebuff. Yet, they asked the delegates to preserve the unity of the I.W.A. and, while they could not rise to the heights of happiness that characterized Russ' speech to his union, they did manage to ask the I.W.A. insurance men to support the merger and to meet with the I.A.I.U. delegates the following morning.[49]

MERGER AT LAST

Central to the fact of merger was the prior amalgamation of the A.F.L. and the C.I.O. The insurance unions subscribed to the new national organization's "no-raiding" pact, thus preparing the way for the talks that culminated in their own merger. The Insurance Agents International Union, AFL-CIO, and the Insurance Workers of America, AFL-CIO, brought their tiny forces together in Chicago on May 27, 1959.[50] The convention delegates voted to call the new organization the Insurance Workers International Union, AFL-CIO. They also approved all of the compromised resolutions on the new union's structure, including the difficult matter of voting at conventions; with certain minor changes the I.W.A. merger committee agreed to adopt the voting procedure of the I.A.I.U.

According to the terms of the merger agreement, George Russ became the first president of the Insurance Workers International Union and William Gillen its first secretary-treasurer. The new organization was to have five vice presidents; Charles Heisel and Max Shine, formerly of the I.A.I.U., and Arthur Higginson, William MacDermott and Robert Ponsi, formerly of the I.W.A., assumed these positions. The delegates chose the members of the executive board as planned and retained in office all those clerical personnel who had labored for the separate national unions.

When the convention finally got under way the several hundred delegates present realized that they had written a small but significant chapter in the history of the American labor movement. Their separate organizations were never very large; at the time of the merger the I.A.I.U. had a little over 13,000 members and the I.W.A.

[49]I.W.A., *Convention Proceedings* (Chicago, Ill., 1959), pp. 47-61, 89-101.

[50]*The AFL-CIO News*, February 7, 1959, p. 1. The insurance unions were the second set of separate jurisdictions within the larger body to merge, the first occurring between the Paperworkers and the Papermakers unions.

had about 9,000.[51] In terms of numbers these unions counted for very little, but in terms of militancy they had come to enjoy varying degrees of success in both organizing and bargaining with three of the largest business enterprises in the United States, the Metropolitan Life, the Prudential and the John Hancock insurance companies. They had survived Communist domination, bitter and, at times, hastily called and useless strikes and inter-union warfare. The delegates to the founding convention knew as well as anyone else that difficult days were not behind them, that, in fact, the merging of the two unions created problems that might be insoluble. However, they could agree with their new president, George Russ, that this was a happy day.

[51]William Gillen, *Report of Officers*, A Report to I.W.A., AFL-CIO, May 25, 1959, p. 1.

CONCLUSION

The introduction of industrial life insurance selling in the United States is closely connected with the history of America's industrialization. Insurance firms grew up around the centers of industry, and enterprising executives, quick to note the worker's need for security, devised means whereby the family breadwinner might insure his life at little cost to himself. For this privilege the worker made small weekly payments on an industrial life policy, and upon his death his beneficiaries received a sum sufficient to cover his funeral expenses.

As the American labor force increased, there was a corresponding growth in the number of industrial life insurance policies issued. Seeking to widen the coverage of the low-income groups, insurance management introduced other forms of industrial insurance, such as endowment and monthly debit ordinary insurance. These new forms of insurance were simply low-yield variations of policies already sold to more affluent Americans, and each retained the basic element of the standard industrial life policy: at the termination date of the policy the insured received a small sum of money, financed through diminutive weekly or monthly premium payments.

During times of financial distress, many policyholders were unable to continue making premium payments on their life investment. As a consequence, large numbers of policies were permitted to lapse, causing hardship to the policyholder and to the insurance agent. The policyholder received only the cash surrender value of his policy, and the agent was faced with the unhappy choice of either preserving the policy in force, often at his own expense, or running the risk of losing part of his salary.[1]

The question of industrial lapses caused alarm among segments of the American public, although it was not until the late 1930's that the State of New York and the Temporary National Economic Committee investigated the extent of the practice. By that time the problem was largely academic, for a combination of circumstances and new forms of insurance soon freed both the policyholder and the insuring agent from the vagaries of the industrial insurance system. It was at this time that a large part of the American labor

[1]"Cash surrender value" is defined as "the amount available in cash upon voluntary termination of a policy before it becomes payable by death or maturity." cf. *Life Insurance Fact Book*, 1964, Institute of Life Insurance, New York, p. 117.

force became eligible for Social Security and that both labor and employer groups introduced such insurance features as health and welfare plans and group insurance. The individual worker also began to insure his family in various hospital and surgical programs. While none of these new plans fulfilled the specific role of the industrial policy, the American worker was becoming less and less dependent upon industrial insurance.

Today's American worker, as an affluent citizen, continues to purchase industrial insurance but at a much slower pace than in the past. Because of his increased earnings and on account of the availability of other forms of insurance, the sales of industrial life policies have levelled off. On the basis of present evidence there is reason to believe that the trend toward fewer purchases of industrial policies will continue.[2]

This dissertation has attempted to trace the history of labor unions of industrial insurance workers, placing its emphasis upon the efforts at combination of the industrial agents. While it is a common practice to speak of a white collar, pro-business mentality among insurance agents, such a description is not altogether accurate. In the giant firms of the industry, the Metropolitan Life, the Prudential and the John Hancock companies, there were large numbers of industrial agents who considered themselves victims of an economic system that caused policyholders to lapse their policies. These men believed that their interests would be best served by membership in labor unions, and, over the years, they made efforts at forming such organizations.

There is evidence to show that small groups of agents organized into labor unions as early at 1895. A delegate to the convention of the American Federation of Labor in that year presented the agent's case to the gathering and received a sympathetic hearing. By the turn of the century, however, the A.F. of L. "irrevocably" denied the agent the right to membership in the Federation on the grounds that industrial insurance agents were engaging in fraudulent practices in selling policies to industrial workers.

During the next three decades there were several unsuccessful attempts to organize the insurance agents. Notable among these were

---

[2]*Ibid.*, pp. 12-24, 29-30. It should be noted that in 1954 the term "industrial" life insurance was deleted and in its stead there was substituted the term "debit" life insurance.

efforts made by a New York Local of office workers, the Bookkeepers, Stenographers and Accountants' Union, Local 12646. This
small Local was affiliated with the A.F. of L., and it had a history
of radical unionism. On two occasions during the 1920's the
Federation's chief officers were obliged to purge the Local of its
left-wing leadership, and, until the union was dissolved, no one was
ever satisfied that the Bookkeepers' union was completely free from
radical domination.

During the fall of 1936, the Bookkeepers' Local once more began
to recruit insurance agents. The A.F. of L. reaffirmed its prohibition
against the men, stating that industrial insurance furnished scant
security to the industrial worker. The Federation also implied that
the office workers' union was controlled by left-wing leaders.

Because of the A.F. of L.'s hostility, the Bookkeepers' Local left
the Federation and sought a charter from the newly formed Committee for Industrial Organizations. John L. Lewis, the president of
the C.I.O., granted the request, and in May 1937 the Bookkeepers
joined with other locals of office workers in forming the United
Office and Professional Workers of America. This new group sought
to organize all segments of the insurance industry, as well as other
professional occupations.

With the C.I.O. actively engaged in organizing insurance workers,
the A.F. of L. had no choice but to grant charters to groups of
agents in various parts of the United States. In order to attract
agents to the organization, the A.F. of L. began to campaign around
its time-honored theme of craft unionism: the Federation promised
the men an organization that would be run for and exclusively by
insurance agents. Whatever the merits of the scheme the A.F. of L.
was never able to make the issue of craft unionism an attractive
selling point to great numbers of insurance agents.

The United Office and Professional Workers of America, C.I.O.,
however, stressed the importance of an "industrial " type structure,
and, from the beginning of its existence, the union enjoyed a
measure of success in organizing agents of the Metropolitan and
John Hancock companies. The new union convinced the agents
that they could never hope to achieve gains of any importance
without the assistance of the insurance company office workers.
Although the C.I.O. union used the point to its advantage, the
circumstances of the insurance industry have made the organization

of insurance clerical workers a near impossibility. It can be correctly stated that at the time of the merger of the A.F.L. and C.I.O. insurance unions, both groups were almost exclusively agents' organizations.

By 1943, the United Office and Professional Workers of America represented the majority of the insurance agents in John Hancock and Prudential and had made substantial inroads into the Metropolitan agency force. However, the union did not achieve this victory without dissension. This work has shown that the U.O.P.W.A., C.I.O., was an outgrowth of the Bookkeepers, Stenographers and Accountants' Union, and of other office workers' locals as well. The Bookkeepers, in particular, held a nucleus of office workers who had left the Trade Union Unity League at the time of its dissolution. When the United Office and Professional Workers of America was founded, these persons, and certain other individuals from various left wing social service unions, attempted to gain control of the union's administrative apparatus. Although they were unable completely to dominate the union at its founding convention, it seems fair to state that they were firmly in control at the time of the organization's fourth convention in 1942.

Such a conclusion seems justified on the basis of reports published at the time the C.I.O. expelled the United Office and Professional Workers. Acccording to the C.I.O., the leadership of the union adhered strictly to all the convolutions of the Communist Party line. Their pre-war propaganda rigidly followed Moscow directives, and their activity during the war consisted mainly in agitating for union proposals around the theme of the Second Front. At war's end, they demanded, among other things, the immediate demobilization of America's armed forces and advocated a foreign policy that in substance was a clear reflection of the Kremlin's program of world politics.

During the Second World War there were two large scale efforts at exposing the organization's left wing leadership. Insurance agents, both in and outside the union, eliminated the U.O.P.W.A. in the Prudential campaign in Ohio, and Hancock agents succeeded temporarily in disengaging the union's officers from the Boston area. Right wing agents precipitated a crisis at the United Office Workers' convention in 1948; it was at this time that the national officers announced their support of the candidacy of Henry A.

Wallace and their intention of refusing to sign the anti-Communist affidavit of the Taft-Hartley Law. A short time after the convention adjourned, half of the union's Prudential membership withdrew and joined the C.I.O.'s United Paperworkers Union. The Prudential agents asked C.I.O. president, Philip Murray, for a new charter; when he temporized, the agents left the Paperworkers and entered the A.F. of L.'s newly formed insurance unit, the National Federation of Insurance Agents Council.

The action of the Prudential insurance men placed the A.F. of L. in a unique position. From the beginning the union had limited success in organizing the agents, its labor board victories occurring chiefly among agents of the so-called smaller companies. With the desertion of the Prudential group from the C.I.O., the American Federation of Labor had a base on which to challenge the supremacy of the C.I.O. In 1948 the A.F. of L. Insurance Council won a Labor Board election among Prudential agents, and, overnight, its membership jumped from about two thousand to over thirteen thousand.

The Council then attempted to disrupt the C.I.O.'s hold on the Metropolitan and Hancock agents. In this effort it was unsuccessful, and that for two reasons. In the first place, the leaders of the Council were not free of A.F. of L. dominance and on major issues had to abide by the directives of the national organization. Secondly, the leaders of the Council overemphasized the theme of craft unionism and, in so doing, only succeeded in alienating the agents of Metropolitan and Hancock and, in certain instances, Prudential as well. It seems correct to assert that these men recognized the importance of the office worker in the over-all picture of insurance unionism.

The C.I.O. expelled the United Office and Professional Workers of America in 1950, over the loud protests of the union's leadership. Both Murray and Allan Haywood, a ranking C.I.O. organizer, explained that the C.I.O.'s move was prompted by the Communist control of the union. They further announced that the Office Workers' union had never amounted to an effective force in organizing insurance workers, and they tried to show that the major companies would never have negotiated contracts with the United Office and Professional Workers if the national C.I.O. had not been represented at the bargaining table.

This might well be true; both men no doubt wanted to expose the union's leadership. Yet the fact remains that the executive body of the United Office and Professional Workers' union carried out the day-by-day tasks of making the insurance agreements work. In spite of the union's alleged Communist domination, the United Office and Professional Workers of America was the first union in American history to deal effectively with such firms as the Metropolitan, the Prudential and John Hancock and to achieve a degree of security for the agents that was unheard of before its appearance on the labor scene. How much more effective and more successful it might have been if it had devoted its full energies to this task instead of diverting them to the pursuit of the Party's objectives can only be conjectured.

The union was in a state of decline even before its expulsion from the C.I.O. Aware of the agents' desire to preserve membership in a labor organization, the C.I.O. finally established the Insurance and Allied Workers Organizing Committee in April 1950, and Allan Haywood assumed control. During his term of office, Haywood tried to construct the new committee along the lines of the expelled U.O.P.W.A. Most of the agents disputed with him in this regard, arguing that while they wanted an organization that would include the clerical staffs of the companies, a larger group would degenerate as had the Office Workers' union before it. The agents insisted that the United Office and Professional Workers of America had lost its sense of direction precisely because it was too all-inclusive. Haywood seems never to have agreed with the agents on the question of the Organizing Committee's jurisdiction, and it was not until the Committee became a national union in 1953 that the dispute was resolved in favor of the agents.

During Haywood's administration the C.I.O. won representation elections among the Hancock agents, and it also achieved bargaining rights for Metropolitan agents in Greater New York, New Jersey and Pennsylvania. The record of the C.I.O. was, therefore, impressive, although the same judgment cannot be made about its competitor. In the winter of 1951-1952 the Insurance Agents International Union, A.F. of L., struck the Prudential Insurance Company of America, and, because of lack of support from the Federation officials and the company office force, the union nearly succeeded in writing itself off as an effective voice of the agents. As a result of the strike, the A.F. of L.'s insurance union lost almost four thousand of its Prudential membership and entered upon a period of bitter strife with the company.

Both small unions survived the crises caused by internal dissension and external pressures, and, when the C.I.O. granted its Organizing Committee a union charter in 1953, leaders of the new union, the Insurance Workers of America, and officials of the Insurance Agents International Union, A.F.L., began to explore the possibilities of merging the two organizations. At issue was the fact that their over-lapping jurisdictions brought about needless expenditures of time and money; union officials maintained further that this dissipation of forces benefitted only the employer. This argument was made abundantly clear in a useless clash between the unions over the representation of agents of the Boston Mutual Life Insurance Company in 1954 and 1955.

The merger of the A.F.L. and the C.I.O. paved the way for the amalgamation of the insurance unions. Each of the organizations received approval from the AFL-CIO to pursue those objectives that would make merger a reality. After several years of discussion involving such questions as voting procedures at conventions, local union jurisdiction and membership on the executive board, the two unions finally merged in 1959 under the title of the Insurance Workers International Union, AFL-CIO.

At the present time the merged union represents some thirty-five thousand insurance workers, the vast majority of whom are agents. The Insurance Workers International Union has found it necessary to hire a full-time organizer to study all phases of the so-called "white collar mentality," which often has been an obstacle to organization. As is true of all unionized professional workers' groups, the insurance union considers this task a difficult one, and, while there are many suggestions for resolving the problem, no one has as yet devised a technique for enrolling the great numbers of white collar workers into the ranks of organized labor.

The Insurance Workers International Union faces other areas of conflict in addition to this traditional one. In the first place, the union must contend with its background. Although the new organization is perfectly free from any un-American ideology, the memory of the old United Office and Professional Workers of America is such that certain segments of insurance management use this period in the organized agents' history to fight the present day union. Besides, many of the newer agents stay out of the union, holding it suspect for the same reason.

But more important to the Insurance Workers International Union is the situation of industrial insurance itself. Before the merger neither union had much success in organizing those men who sold high priced insurance, the so-called "ordinary" agents. Since the industrial agent has been the backbone of the union and since the demand for industrial insurance has fallen off, the new organization will have to find ways of attracting the "ordinary" agent. This problem is much the same as the one the union faces with the insurance company office girl. Neither group considers a labor union necessary.

The number of persons enrolled in the Insurance Workers International Union at the present time closely approximates insurance membership figures of the defunct United Office and Professional Workers of America. While such a statement speaks well for the success of the latter organization in organizing insurance workers, it can scarcely make the leaders of the new union optimistic. The vast majority of the union membership comes from the industrial life section of the insurance companies. Should the present downward trend in industrial insurance continue (and there is little reason to forecast an opposite pattern), it seems correct to conclude that the Insurance Workers International Union will remain a fairly static organization.

APPENDIX 1

CHRONOLOGICAL TABLE OF MAJOR EVENTS:

1895: The first reference is made to the existence of a labor union of insurance agents, the American Agents Association.

1901: The American Federation of Labor prohibits the chartering of labor unions of insurance agents on the grounds that they are not bona fide organizations.

1916: The Agents Protective Association strikes the Prudential Insurance Company of America.

1924: The A.F. of L. expels certain members of the Bookkeepers, Stenographers and Accountants' Union, Local 12646, for alleged Communist activities. The Bookkeepers' union is a fore-runner of the United Office and Professional Workers of America.

1927: The A.F. of L. again expels members of the Bookkeepers' union for left wing activities.
The Bookkeepers' Local attempts to organize the office workers of the Metropolitan Life Insurance Company in New York.

1930: Lewis Merrill, the future president of the United Office and Professional Workers of America, joins the Bookkeepers' Local in New York.

1937: Merrill, along with other members of the Bookkeepers' union, join with leaders of social service unions in New York to form the United Office and Professional Workers of America. John L. Lewis grants the new organization a C.I.O. charter.
The A.F. of L. establishes the Industrial and Ordinary Insurance Agents Council, and groups of Metropolitan and Prudential agents in Wisconsin form the independent labor organization, the International Union of Life Insurance Agents.

1938: The insurance division of the United Office and Professional Workers of America attempts to organize industrial agents of the Metropolitan and John Hancock companies.
The A.F. of L.'s insurance council and the independent organize insurance agents in various parts of the United States.

1939: The New York State Court of Appeals in a decision affecting the Metropolitan Life Insurance Company and the United Office and Professional Workers of America upholds the state's labor relations act.
The Temporary National Economic Committee investigates the insurance industry. The Metropolitan Life Insurance Company expels thirteen of its agents for fraudulently signing policyholders' signatures to ballots used in company elections.

1940: The leftwing faction of the United Office and Professional Workers of America is against American involvement in the European War.

1941: The union's officials demand that the United States declare war on the Axis powers.

219

The union begins a long campaign for representation of the agents of the Prudential Insurance Company of America.

1942: The left wing faction of the U.O.P.W.A. achieves complete control of the union's leadership at the fourth constitutional convention.

1943: The International Union of Life Insurance Agents, independent, defeats the United Office and Professional Workers of America in the Prudential election in Ohio. The latter union loses as a result of the Communist issue.

A group of Hancock agents in Boston temporarily defeat the United Office and Professional Workers and form an independent union, the National Industrial Insurance Agents' Union. Members of this group later join the Industrial and Ordinary Insurance Agents Council, A.F. of L.

1944: In the *Southeastern Underwriters'* decision, the United States Supreme Court declares that insurance companies are subject to the anti-trust laws of the United States. In another decision, *Polish National Alliance v. N.L.R.B.*, the court decrees that insurance companies are subject to the jurisdiction of the National Labor Relations Board.

1945: Congress passes the *McCarran Act* which permits the individual states to regulate the insurance industry, provided the states conform, within a three-year time period, to federal provisions regarding the sale of insurance.

The United Office and Professional Workers of America, C.I.O., begins to follow the Communist Party line to the letter.

The United Office and Professional Workers start to organize the Monumental Life Insurance Company agents.

1946: The Communist issue erupts over the Office Workers' attempt at organizing the Monumental Life Insurance Co.

The A.F. of L. charters the National Federation of Insurance Agents Council. George Russ is chosen president of the group.

The United States Supreme Court upholds the *McCarran Act*.

1947: The United Office and Professional Workers of America win a strike against the Monumental Life Insurance Co.

James Durkin replaces Lewis Merrill as president of the United Office and Professional Workers of America.

1948: Right wing insurance agents try to unseat the leadership of the Office Workers' at its convention. Thousands of Prudential agents leave the union and join the United Paperworkers Union, C.I.O. These men later chose the National Federation of Insurance Agents Council, A.F. of L., in an N.L.R.B. election.

At its convention the C.I.O. accuses the United Office and Professional Workers of America of Communist domination.

The National Federation of Insurance Agents Council, A.F. of L., wins the Prudential election.

1949: The C.I.O. convention votes to expel the United Office and Professional Workers of America for Communist domination.

1950: After months of litigation in the federal courts, the C.I.O. expels the United Office and Professional Workers of America.

The United Office and Professional Workers of America merges with the Distributive Workers Union and the Food, Tobacco, Agricultural and Allied Workers under the title, Distributive, Processing and Office Workers of America.

Leon W. Berney, former chairman of the insurance division of the Office Workers', tries to take the Hancock agents into the C.I.O. Failing that, he unsuccessfully attempts a similar move into the A.F. of L.

The C.I.O. charters the Insurance and Allied Workers Organizing Committee under the chairmanship of Allan Haywood.

1951: The A.F. of L. establishes the Insurance Agents International Union. George Russ is elected its first president.

Matthew Hogan, former vice president of the National Federation of Insurance Agents Council, quits the new A.F. of L. union over a policy dispute. He takes the Maryland Prudential agents out of the Insurance Agents International Union and later on forms the Association of Life Insurance Agents, with an A.F. of L. charter.

The Insurance Agents International Union, A.F. of L., strikes the Prudential Insurance Company of America.

1952: The Prudential strike ends after eighty-one days of conflict.

Allan Haywood steps down as chairman of the Insurance and Allied Workers Organizing Committee. He is succeeded by Richard Leonard, a national C.I.O. organizer.

1953: The C.I.O. charters the Insurance Workers of America as an international union. Kenneth O'Dell becomes the organization's first president.

The Insurance Agents International Union, A.F.L., has trouble with Prudential over the sale of "sickness and accident" insurance, and accuses the company of engaging in pressure tactics.

Frank Siegel, the leader of the Boston Mutual Life Insurance Co. agents in New England, approaches the Insurance Workers of America, C.I.O., about the possibility of merging his group with the C.I.O. Siegel possesses the last contract formerly held by the defunct United Office and Professional Workers of America.

Both the Insurance Agents International Union, A.F.L., and the Insurance Workers of America, C.I.O., meet to discuss the merger of the two organizations.

1954: New York state reforms the "expense limitation" section of its insurance law.

The Insurance Workers of America, C.I.O., wins a labor board election among agents of the Boston Mutual Life Insurance Co. Both Siegel and the A.F.L. insurance union protest the election.

The N.L.R.B. orders a new election in Boston Mutual, which the Insurance Agents International Union, A.F.L., wins.

1955: The Insurance Agents International Union, A.F.L., strikes the Boston Mutual Life Insurance Company.

William Gillen defeats Kenneth O'Dell for the presidency of the Insurance Workers of America, C.I.O.

1956: The Insurance Agents International Union, AFL-CIO, and the Insurance Workers of America, AFL-CIO, continue their quest for merger.

Joseph Pollack, president of the New York insurance local, brings suit against the three officers of the Insurance Agents International Union, AFL-CIO.

1959: The Insurance Agents International Union, AFL-CIO, and the Insurance Workers of America, AFL-CIO, merge under the title, Insurance Workers International Union, AFL-CIO. George Russ becomes the organization's first president.

1960: In a case involving the Prudential Insurance Company of America and the former Insurance Agents International Union, AFL-CIO, the majority of the Supreme Court of the United States decide that "use of economic pressure is of itself not at all inconsistent with the duty of bargaining in good faith."

APPENDIX 2

A LIST OF ORGANIZATIONS

OF INSURANCE WORKERS

1895:   American Agents Association, A.F. of L.

1901:   Insurance Agents Local Union, 8676, St. Louis, independent.

1916:   Agents Protective Association, independent.

1927:   Bookkeepers, Stenographers and Accountants' Union, Local 12646, A.F. of L. (Listed under this date because it made a first attempt to organize insurance workers.)

1937:   United Office and Professional Workers of America, C.I.O.
National Association of Industrial Insurance Agents, independent.
International Union of Life Insurance Agents, independent.
Industrial and Ordinary Insurance Agents Council, A.F. of L.

1943:   National Industrial Insurance Agents Union, independent.

194-?: Life Insurance Agents of Virginia, A.F. of L. Federal Local in Detroit.

1946:   National Federation of Insurance Agents Council, A.F. of L.

1950:   Insurance and Allied Workers Organizing Committee, C.I.O.
Distributive, Processing and Office Workers of America, independent.
United Insurance Agents of America, independent.
Metropolitan Agents of Baltimore, A.F. of L.

1951:   Insurance Agents International Union, A.F. of L.
Local 1282, Distributive, Processing and Office Workers of America.

1952:   Association of Life Insurance Agents, A.F. of L., Maryland.

1953:   Insurance Workers of America, C.I.O.

1959:   Insurance Workers International Union, AFL-CIO.

APPENDIX 3

MEMBERSHIP FIGURES OF THE

MORE IMPORTANT UNIONS:

(all figures are estimates)

Industrial and Ordinary Insurance Agents Council, A.F. of L.:
1938	1,000
1946	2,500

Insurance Agents International Union, A.F.L.:
1951	12,500
1953	9,400
1955	10,000
1957	10,000
1959	11,000

Insurance and Allied Workers Organizing Committee, C.I.O.:
1950	5,000
1951	7,000
1952	7,000

Insurance Workers International Union, AFL-CIO:
1959	20,500

Insurance Workers of America, C.I.O.:
1953	8,000
1955	8,500
1957	9,000
1959	9,500

International Union of Life Insurance Agents, Independent:
1938	500
1950	2,000
1959	2,000

National Federation of Insurance Agents Council, A.F. of L.:
1946	2,500
1948	12,500
1950	12,500

United Office and Professional Workers of America, C.I.O.:
1938	5,000
1944	20,000
1948	12,000
1950	*

---

* Unknown

BIBLIOGRAPHY

PUBLIC DOCUMENTS

COURT CASES:
German Alliance Ins. Co. v. *Lewis,* 233 U.S. 389 (1914)
Home Beneficial Life Ins. Co. v. *National Labor Relations Board,* CA 4 (1947)
James H. Durkin v. *Philip Murray,* 90 F. Supp. 367, D.C.D.C. (1950)
LaTourette v. *McMaster,* 248 U.S. 465 (1919)
Metropolitan Life Ins. Co. v. *James H. Durkin,* 276 App. Div. 394 (1950)
.... v. *James H. Durkin,* 301 N.Y. 376 (1950)
..................: v. *John P. Boland et al,* 257 App. Div. 950 (1939)
.... v. *John P. Boland et al,* 281 N.Y. 357 (1939)
.... v. *New York State Labor Relations Board,* Id. 255 App. Div. 840 (1938)
.... v. *New York State Labor Relations Board,* 280 N.Y. 194 (1939)
National Labor Relations Board v. *Phoenix Mutual Life Ins. Co.,* CA 7 (1948)
O'Gorman and Young v. *Hartford Ins. Co.,* 282 U.S. 251 (1931)
Paul v. *Virginia,* 8 Wall. 168 (1869)
Polish National Alliance v. *National Labor Relations Board,* 322 U.S. 643 S. Ct. 1196 (1944)
Prudential Ins. Co. of America v. *Benjamin,* 328 U.S. 408, 66 S. Ct. 1142, 90 L. Ed. 1342 (1946)
.... v. *Russ,* 22 CA 123 (1954)
.... v. *New York Supreme Court,* 23 CA 413 (1954)
.................., v. *National Labor Relations Board,* CA DC 260 F. 2d. 736 (1958)
.... v. *National Labor Relations Board,* DC SNY 169 F. Supp. 535 (1959)
.... v. *National Labor Relations Board,* 361 U.S. 477 S. Ct. 419 (1960)
Stipcich v. *Metropolitan Life Ins. Co.,* 233 U.S. 311 (1928)
United Ins. Co. v. *National Labor Relations Board,* 272 F. 2d 446 (1959)
United States v. *South Eastern Underwriters' Association,* 322 U.S. 533, 64 S. Ct., 1162, 88 L. Ed. 1440 (1944)

LAWS AND REPORTS:
Commonwealth of Massachusetts. *Acts and Resolves.* 164 A. General Court (1938). "An Act to Provide that no Insurance Agent shall be charged with decrease or deduction from his commission or salary on industrial life insurance policies lapsed after being paid on for three years."
State of New York. Acts of the Legislature passed at the session of 1906 upon the recommendation of the Joint Committee of the Senate and Assembly of the State of New York appointed to investigate the affairs of Life Insurance Companies . . . . May, 1906.
.... *Annual Report of the Superintendent of Insurance,* 1860-1962. New York Insurance Department. 1962.

.... "An Act to amend the insurance law in relation to the limitation of expenses on debit life insurance." Sect. 1, Subdiv. 213a, *New York Insurance Law.* 1953.

.... "An Act to amend the insurance law in relation to agents' commissions in connection with certain insurance." Sec. 1, Subdiv. 13 of 213 of Chap. 882 of 1939, *New York Insurance Law.* 1954.

.... *New York Insurance Law.* ¶213, subdiv. 13, amended, Chapter 555, 1946.

.... *New York Insurance Law*: Being the statutory revision of the laws affecting insurance companies enacted in 1892, with all amendments to and including 1906 . . . also the amendments . . . proposed by the Armstrong Committee. Prepared by Andrew Hamilton. 1906.

.... *Report of the Joint Legislative Committee on the Revision of the Insurance Law,* Legislative Document No. 77, 1938.

.... *Report of the Joint Legislative Committee on the Revision of Insurance Law,* Legislative Document No. 101, 1939.

.... *Report of the Joint Legislative Committee on Insurance Rates and Regulation,* Legislative Document No. 56, 1955.

.... *Report on the Examination of the Metropolitan Life Insurance Company, Special Study of Industrial Insurance,* State of New York Insurance Department, 1938.

.... Testimony taken before the Joint Committee of the Senate and Assembly of the State of New York to investigate and examine into the business and affairs of life insurance companies doing business in the State of New York. 1905-1906. 10 vols.

U.S. Congress. *Hearings before the Temporary National Economic Committee of the United States,* Part 4: *Life Insurance,* 76th Cong., 1st Sess., 1939; Part 10-A: *Life Insurance,* 76th Cong., 3rd Sess., 1940; Part 12: *Industrial Insurance,* 76th Cong., 1st Sess., 1939; Part 13: *Life Insurance,* 76th Cong., 1st and 2d Sess., 1939; and Part 28: *Life Insurance,* 76th Cong., 3rd Sess., 1940.

.... *McCarran Act.* 59 Stat. 33 (1945).

U.S. House of Representatives. Special Committee on Un-American Activities. *Investigation of Un-American Propaganda Activities in the United States,* vol. 1 and vol. 4. 75th Cong., 3rd Sess. 1938.

.... Report of the Special Committee on Un-American Activities. *Investigation of Un-American Propaganda Activities in the United States,* "Report on the C.I.O. Political Action Committee," Report No. 1311, 78th Cong., 2d Sess., March 29, 1944.

U.S. Senate. Subcommittee on Labor and Labor Management Relations. *Communist Domination of Certain Unions.* Doc. No. 89, 82d Cong., 1st Sess., October 19, 1951.

U.S. Senate. Subcommittee on the Committee on Labor and Public Welfare. *Communist Domination of Unions and National Security.* 82d Cong., 2d Sess., March 17-19, June 6, 11, 13, 17, 19, 27 & July 8, 1952.

—————————. Subcommittee to Investigate the Administration of the Internal Security Act and other internal security laws of the Committee on the Judiciary. *Hearings . . . ,* "On Subversive Control of the Distributive, Processing, and Office Workers," August 23-29, October 25-26, 1951, February 11, 13-15, 19-21 & March 7, 1952.

LABOR BOARD CASES:

John Hancock Mutual Life Ins. Co., Before the Labor Relations Commission (Massachusetts), Case No. CR 698 (1943)

Metropolitan Life Ins. Co., Before the Labor Relations Commission, (Massachusetts), Case No. CR 756 (1944)

—————————. Before the Labor Relations Commission, (Massachusetts), Case No. CR 757 (1944)

Boston Mutual Life Ins. Co., 57 N.L.R.B. 888 (1944)

—————————. 110 N.L.R.B. no. 36 (1954)

John Hancock Mutual Life Ins. Co., 26 N.L.R.B. 1024 (1940)

—————————. 57 N.L.R.B. 700 (1944)

—————————. 93 N.L.R.B. 778 (1951)

Metropolitan Life Ins. Co., 43 N.L.R.B. 962 (1942)

—————————. 54 N.L.R.B. 585 (1944)

—————————. 56 N.L.R.B. 1642 (1944)

—————————. 56 N.L.R.B. 1847 (1944)

—————————. 90 N.L.R.B. 935 (1950)

—————————. 91 N.L.R.B. 473 (1950)

Monumental Life Ins. Co., 60 N.L.R.B. 510 (1945)

—————————. 67 N.L.R.B. 244 (1946)

—————————. 69 N.L.R.B. 247 (1946)

—————————. 75 N.L.R.B. no. 93 (1948)

Polish National Alliance of the United States of North America, 42 N.L.R.B. 1375 (1942)

—————————. 72 N.L.R.B. 1382 (1947)

Prudential Ins. Co. of America, 46 N.L.R.B. 430 (1942)

—————————. 47 N.L.R.B. 1103 (1943)

—————————. 49 N.L.R.B. 450 (1943)

—————————. 50 N.L.R.B. 689 (1943)

—————————. 56 N.L.R.B. 1859 (1944)

—————————. 61 N.L.R.B. 1289 (1945)

—————————. 80 N.L.R.B. 1853 (1948)

—————————. 81 N.L.R.B. 295 (1949)

—————————. 106 N.L.R.B. no. 55 (1953)

—————————. 119 N.L.R.B. 768 (1957)

John Hancock Mutual Life Ins. Co., 3 S.L.R.B. 98 (New York) (1940)

—————————. 3 S.L.R.B. 654 (1940)

—————————. 4 S.L.R.B. 363 (1941)

—————————. 6 S.L.R.B. 113 (1943)

—————————. 8 S.L.R.B. 24 (1945)

Metropolitan Life Ins. Co., 1 S.L.R.B. 129 (1938)

—————————. 4 S.L.R.B. 215 (1941)

.... 4 S.L.R.B. 788 (1941)
.... 5 S.L.R.B. 458 (1942)
Prudential Ins. Co. of America, 4 S.L.R.B. 788 (1941)
.... 9 S.L.R.B. 636 (1946)
Workingmen's Cooperative Association, 1 S.L.R.B. 60 (1938)
John Hancock Mutual Life Ins. Co., W.L.B. (National War Labor Board),
    Case No. 111-1341-D (1944)
.... W.L.B. Case No. 111-13503-D (1945)
Metropolitan Life Ins. Co., W.L.B. (II). Case No. 11-D-11 (2733-D)
    (1943)
.... W.L.B. Case No. 111-5304-D (1944)
.... W.L.B. Case No. 2773-CS-B, 111-6436-D (1944)
.... W.L.B. Case No. 111-14499-J.B. (1945)
Prudential Ins. Co. of America, W.L.B. Case No. 11-2435 (1943)

BOOKS

American Federation of Labor. *History, Encyclopedic Reference Book.*
    American Federation of Labor, 1919.

Budenz, Louis F. *Men Without Faces: The Communist Conspiracy in the
    U.S.A.* New York: Harper & Bros., 1950.

Charters of American Life Insurance Companies: Being a Compilation of
    the Original Charters and all amendments thereto of thirty prominent
    companies operating under the legal reserve requirements with
    extracts from by-laws affecting contracts. New York: The Spectator
    Co., 1895.

Corwin, Edward S. (ed). *The Constitution of the United States of America*:
    Analysis and Interpretation, Annotations of cases decided by the
    Supreme Court of the United States to June 30, 1952. Library of
    Congress, Legislative Reference Service. Washington, D.C.: U.S.
    Government Printing Office, 1953.

Davis, Malvin E. *Industrial Life Insurance in the United States.* New York:
    McGraw-Hill, 1944.

Egbert, Donald Drew and Persons, Stow (ed). *Socialism and American Life.*
    Vol. 1: "The Background and Development of Marxian Socialism in
    the United States," by Daniel Bell. Princeton: Princeton University
    Press, 1952.

Fund for the Republic. *Digest of the Public Record of Communism in the
    United States.* New York: Fund for the Republic, 1955.

Galenson, Walter. *The CIO Challenge to the AFL: A History of the Amer-
    ican Labor Movement* 1935-1941. Cambridge: Harvard University
    Press, 1960.

Glazer, Nathan. *The Social Basis of American Communism.* New York:
    Harcourt, Brace & World, 1961.

Harris, Herbert. *American Labor.* New Haven: Yale University Press, 1938.

Kampelman, Max. *The Communist Party vs. the C.I.O.: A Study in Power
    Politics.* New York: Praeger, 1957.

Kauper, Paul G. *Constitutional Law: Cases and materials.* New York: Prentice-Hall, Inc., 1954.

King, Jerry, *et al. We Accuse (From the Record): A Factual History of the Seaman's Labor Movement,* New York: P.O. Box 63, 1940.

Labor Research Associates. *Labor Fact Book, III.* New York: International Publishers, 1936.

Life Insurance Fact Book, 1963. New York: Institute of Life Insurance, 1963.

Lorwin, Lewis and Flexner, Jean Atherton. *American Federation of Labor: History, Policies and Prospects.* Washington, D.C.: Brookings Institution, 1933.

Mason, Alpheus Thomas and Beaney, William M. *American Constitutional Law: Introductory Essays and Selected Cases.* Englewood Cliffs: Prentice-Hall, Inc., 1954.

Millis, Harry A. *How Collective Bargaining Works: A Survey of Experience in Leading American Industries.* New York: The Twentieth Century Fund, 1942.

O'Neal, James and Werner, G.A. *American Communism: A Critical Analysis of its Origins, Development and Programs.* New & rev. ed. New York: E. P. Dutton, 1947.

Perlman, Selig and Taft, Philip. *History of Labor in the United States, 1896-1932,* vol. 4: "Labor Movements." New York: Macmillan, 1935.

Peterson, Florence. *American Labor Unions: What They Are and How They Work.* New York: Harper & Bros., 3d. ed., 1945.

Saposs, David. *Communism in American Unions.* New York: McGraw-Hill, 1959.

Slichter, Sumner H. *The Challenge of Industrial Relations: Trade Unions, Management, and the Public Interest.* Ithaca: Cornell University Press, 1947.

Sourcebook of Union Government Structure and Procedures. New York: National Industrial Conference Board, 1956.

Taft, Philip. *The A.F. of L. in the Time of Gompers.* New York: Harper & Bros., 1957.

Thayer, James Bradley. *Cases on Constitutional Law, with notes,* vol. 1. Cambridge: George H. Kent, 1895.

Walsh, J. Raymond. *C.I.O.: Industrial Unionism in Action.* New York: Norton, 1937.

Warner, Colston E. *Yearbook of American Labor, vol. 1: War Labor Policies.* New York: Philosophical Library, 1945.

PAMPHLETS

Communist Party Independent Nominating Petition. Would YOU Sign This? Officers of the UOPWA Did! Prudential Press, November, 1948, no. 36725.

Fisher, Jacob. *The Rank and File Movement in Social Work,* 1931-1936. New York: New York School of Social Work, 1936.

Honig, Nathaniel. *The Trade Union Unity League Today: Its Structure, Policy, Progress and Growth,* rev. ed. 1934.

Official Reports on the Expulsion of Communist Dominated Organizations from the CIO, "United Office and Professional Workers of America." Congress of Industrial Organizations.

Pike, Sumner T. *Statement on Life Insurance Delivered February 28, 1941, Before the Temporary National Economic Committee.* Washington, D.C.: Government Printing Office, 1941.

The Workers' Party and American Trade Unions. Baltimore: Johns Hopkins University Press, 1928.

Articles and Periodicals

Berry, George R. "The Life Underwriters on the Debit," *The Life Underwriters' News* (May, 1952)

Broderick, John. "What Color is that White Collar, Mr. Durkin?" *Commonweal,* XLVI (August 22, 1947), 445-47.

Gillen, William. "Here's the Story of the Insurance Workers of America," *The American Federationist,* LXIV (June, 1957), 26-28.

Gompers, Samuel. "Letter to Albert F. Coyle," *The American Federationist,* XXIV (October, 1922), 777-78.

"The Insurance Agents Story," *The Electrical Workers' Journal,* LI (August, 1952), 36-40, 95.

Picone, Alexander, "Big CIO Drive to Organize 150,000 Life Insurance Agents," *Journal of Commerce* (March 11, 1952), 18-20.

Russ, George. "Insurance Agents' Progress," *The American Federationist,* LVII (August, 1950), 19 & 30.

Shlakman, Vera. "White Collar Unionism and Professional Organization," *Science and Society,* XIV (1950), 214-36.

————————. "Unionism and Professional Organizations Among Engineers," *Science and Society,* XIV (1950), 322-37.

————————. "Business and the Salaried Worker," *Science and Society,* XV (1951), 97-121.

————————. "Status and Ideology of Office Workers," *Science and Society,* XVI (1952), 1-26.

"The Evolution of a Strike," *The Spectator* (January, 1952), 18-20.

Stolberg, Benjamin. "Communist Wreckers in American Labor," *The Saturday Evening Post* (September 2, 1939), 5-7, 34-8.

Reports

American Federation of Labor. *Convention Proceedings:* 1890, 1895-1905, 1908-1909, 1911-1944.

Congress of Industrial Organizations. *Convention Proceedings:* 1941-1942, 1944, 1946-1950.

Distributive, Processing and Office Workers of America. *Convention Proceedings:* 1950 and 1953.

Industrial and Ordinary Insurance Agents Council, A.F. of L. *National 1945 Conference:* 1945.

Industrial Union Department, AFL-CIO. *Proceedings of Conference on the White Collar Worker,* "Labor Looks at the White Collar Worker," February 20, 1957.

Insurance and Allied Workers Organizing Committee, C.I.O. *Conference Proceedings*: 1951 and 1952.

Insurance Agents International Union, AFL. *Convention Proceedings*: 1953, 1955, 1957, 1959.

Insurance Workers of America, CIO. *Convention Proceedings*: 1953, 1955, 1957, 1959.

Insurance Workers International Union, AFL-CIO. *Convention Proceedings*: 1959 and 1961.

United Office and Professional Workers of America, C.I.O. *Convention Proceedings*: 1937, 1938, 1940, 1942, 1944, 1946, 1948.

United Office and Professional Workers of America. *Convention Proceedings*: 1950.

NEWSPAPERS

General:

    Boston Daily Globe
    Boston Daily Record
    Boston Herald
    Daily News (New York)
    The New York Times
    The Star-Ledger (Newark)
    World Telegram (New York)

Labor:

    Agents' Voice (Baltimore)
    AFL-CIO News
    AFL News Reporter
    AFL Weekly News Service
    Association News (Baltimore)
    Career (New York)
    Champion (New York)
    CIO Debit (New York)
    CIO News
    CIO News, Insurance Edition
    CIO Insurance Newsletter (Washington)
    CIO Reporter (Philadelphia)
    The Debit (New York)
    Debit Notes (Boston)
    Insurance Agent
    Insurance Agents' Progress (Washington)
    Insurance Career (New York)
    Insurance Worker
    The Ledger (New York)
    Life Insurance Reveille (Atlanta)
    Massachusetts CIO News

NFIAC Reporter
New England UOPWA News
New Jersey CIO Insurance News
19 *News* (New York)
Office and Professional News
Our Voice (Milwaukee)
Philadelphia Debit News
Union Voice (New York)
UOPWA News (New York)
UOPWA Local 30 *Agents News* (New York)
White Collar News (New York)

CORRESPONDENCE

General Executive Board, Local 30, UOPWA, CIO, to Lewis Merrill, April 4, 1939.

David Fay to Matthew Hogan, July 7, 1943.

American Federation of Industrial and Ordinary Insurance Agents of Greater New York to the Industrial Insurance Agents of Greater New York, n.d.

Association of Life Insurance Agents of Maryland to George Russ, February 14, 1953.

Frank Siegel to Kenneth O'Dell, September 14, 1953.

Joseph Baldwin to Everett Lane, October 27, 1953.

Everett Lane to Joseph Baldwin, November 2, 1953.

Arthur H. Higginson to Kenneth O'Dell, December 6, 1953.

Arthur St. John to Kenneth O'Dell, December 6, 1953.

Hugh Thompson to George Mooney, December 10, 1953.

Kenneth O'Dell to Hugh Thompson, December 10, 1953.

Kenneth O'Dell to Arthur Higginson, December 10, 1953.

Arthur Higginson to Kenneth O'Dell, December 11, 1953.

Kenneth O'Dell to Arthur Higginson, December 17, 1953.

Arthur Higginson to Kenneth O'Dell, December 21, 1953.

George L. Russ to Everett Lane, December 23, 1953.

Maurice Cauchon to Kenneth O'Dell, January 11, 1954.

Kenneth O'Dell to Frank Siegel, January 19, 1954.

Frank Siegel to Kenneth O'Dell, February 8, 1954.

Kenneth O'Dell to Frank Siegel, February 9, 1954.

Frank Siegel *et al.* to Kenneth O'Dell, February 21, 1954.

Frederick D. Higgins to Kenneth O'Dell, February 21, 1954.

Everett Lane to Boston Mutual Agents, March 1, 1954.

Insurance Workers of America, CIO, to Boston Mutual Agents, March 4, 1954.

Paul F. Tino to Kenneth O'Dell, March 6, 1954.

Hugh Thompson to Boston Mutual Agents, March 8, 1954.

James E. Brisbane to Paul Tino, March 9, 1954.

Kenneth O'Dell to George Russ, March 9, 1954.

Theodore F. Vecchione *et al.* to Boston Mutual Life Ins. Co., March 15, 1954.

Walter Reuther to Boston Mutual Agents, March 26, 1954.
Theodore Vecchione *et al.* to Boston Mutual Agents, March 27, 1954.
George L. Russ to Boston Mutual Agents, April 2, 1954.
Frederick Higgins to Kenneth O'Dell, April 3, 1954.
Max Lefkowith to Boston Mutual Agents, April 8, 1954.
George Russ to Boston Mutual Agents, April 8, 1954.
Louis Brooks *et al.* to Boston Mutual Agents, April 9, 1954.
Frederick Higgins to Kenneth O'Dell, April 17, 1954.
Theodore Vecchione to George Russ, May 3, 1954.
Robert J. Nicholson to Everett Lane, June 18, 1954.
Robert J. Nicholson to Boston Mutual Agents, August 2, 1954.
Robert J. Nicholson to Everett Lane, September 24, 1954.
Theodore Vecchione to George Russ, September 24, 1954.
Robert J. Nicholson to Boston Mutual Agents, November 4, 1954.
Joseph Pollack to International Officers and General Counsel of Insurance Agents International Union, AFL, June 29, 1956.
George Russ to Joseph Pollack, July 6, 1956.
George Russ to General Executive Board, Insurance Agents International Union, AFL, July 6, 1956.
Joseph Pollack to all local presidents, Insurance Agents International Union, AFL, July 7, 1956.
Joseph Pollack to General Executive Board and Presidents of IAIU locals, July 9, 1956.

INTERVIEWS

James E. Brisbane, former secretary-treasurer, Insurance Workers of America, July 16, 1959.
Charles Engelbrecht, former treasurer of National Federation of Insurance Agents Council, A.F. of L., July 30, 1959.
William Gillen, past president of Insurance Workers of America, CIO, and current president of Insurance Workers International Union, AFL-CIO, July 16 and 22, 1959.
Charles Heisel, former executive board member of United Office and Professional Workers of America and a vice president of Insurance Workers International Union, AFL-CIO, August 5, 1959.
Arthur Higginson, past secretary-treasurer of Insurance Workers of America, CIO, and a vice president of Insurance Workers International Union, AFL-CIO, July 16, 1959.
Matthew Hogan, former organizer of National Federation of Insurance Agents Council, A.F. of L., and past president of Prudential Insurance Agents Local in Baltimore, August 6, 1959.
Richard T. Leonard, past chairman of Insurance and Allied Workers Organizing Committee, June 18, 1959.
William MacDermott, past secretary-treasurer of Insurance Workers of America and Insurance Workers International Union, AFL-CIO, August 4, 1959.

Robert Ponsi, a former secretary-treasurer of Insurance Workers of America, CIO, and currently a vice president of Insurance Workers International Union, August 4, 1959.

George L. Russ, past president of Industrial and Ordinary Insurance Agents Council, AFL, National Federation of Insurance Agents Council, AFL, Insurance Agents International Union, AFL, and first president of Insurance Workers International Union, AFL-CIO, July 16, 1959.

Max Shine, past secretary of Insurance Agents International Union, AFL and a former secretary-treasurer of Insurance Workers International Union, AFL-CIO, December 2, 1958.

Kenneth Young, former Research Director, Insurance Workers of America, June 18, 1959.

Ruth Wiencek, International Representative for Clerical Workers, Insurance Workers of America, CIO, August 3, 1959.

MISCELLANEOUS

On the New York Insurance Law:

An Explanation of the New York Expense Law: The Purpose of the Memorandum is to Answer Questions which have been asked about Section 213 and 213a of the Insurance Law of New York, Prudential Ins. Co. of America.

Memorandum as to the Proposed Legal Action Against Sections 213 and 213-A of the New York State Insurance Law, Irving Abramson, Counsel for Insurance Workers of America, CIO, January 30, 1952.

Statement to Join Legislative Committee on Insurance Rates and Regulations, Robert E. Slater, Vice President and Controller, John Hancock Mutual Life Ins. Co., Boston, Mass., February 24, 1953.

Union Agreements:

Agreement Between John Hancock Mutual Life Ins. Co. and the United Office and Professional Workers of America, February 21, 1945.

Agreement Between Metropolitan Life Ins. Co. and the American Federation of Industrial and Ordinary Insurance Agents Union, no. 23322, A.F. of L., (State of Maryland), March 17, 1944.

Agreement Between Metropolitan Life Ins. Co. and Insurance Workers of America, AFL-CIO, (Pennsylvania), October 1, 1956.

Agreement Between the Prudential Ins. Co. of America and Associated Life Insurance Agents of Maryland, April 19, 1954.

Agreement Between Insurance Agents International Union, AFL-CIO, and the Prudential Ins. Co. of America, July 2, 1956.

Agreement Between the Prudential Ins. Co. of America and National Federation of Insurance Agents Council, A.F. of L., November 28, 1949.

Agreement Executed by and Between Golden State Mutual Life Ins. Co. and Insurance Workers of America, AFL-CIO, September 16, 1957.

Collective Bargaining Contract Executed by and Between John Hancock Mutual Life Ins. Co. and Insurance Workers of America, AFL-CIO, July 1, 1958.

Collective Bargaining Agreement Between Boston Mutual Life Ins. Co. and Insurance Agents International Union, AFL-CIO, January 2, 1958.

Collective Bargaining Contract Executed by and Between Insurance Workers
of America, AFL-CIO, and the Home Life Ins. Co. of America,
August 28, 1956.

Contract Between American National Ins. Co. and Insurance Agents International Union, AFL-CIO, February 8, 1957.

National Agreement Between Prudential Ins. Co. of America and United
Office and Professional Workers of America, CIO, February 1, 1943.

Union Publications:

American Federation of Labor:

Brief in Opposition to Motion to Consolidate Unit, filed by Local 10, Insurance Agents International Union, AFL, Baltimore, April 10, 1952.

"AFL and Local 1282 Agree to Affiliate," March 7, 1954.

"Debunking the Bunk About Security Fund," Local 243, IAIU, AFL, April
6, 1954.

"Defend Your Security Fund," Local 243, IAIU, AFL, March 22, 1954.

"Record of Everett Lane," IAIU, AFL, April 15, 1954.

Statement of David Greene, Boston Mutual Agent, 1952.

"Will B/M Bargain with Local 243, AFL?" Local 243, AFL, IAIU, March
22, 1954.

Constitution of Insurance Agents International Union, AFL, (1951, 1953,
1955, 1957).

Congress of Industrial Organizations:

"B/M Agents are on the Hot Seat," Local 1776, IWA, CIO, Boston.

"CIO Wins Met Election," IAWOC, CIO.

Constitution of Insurance Workers of America, CIO, (1953 & 1955).

"Dear Met Agents," IAWOC, CIO.

"The High and the Mighty," Boston CIO Agents.

Insurance and Allied Workers Organizing Committee, CIO, "Field Fact,"
1952.

Insurance and Allied Workers Organizing Committee, CIO, "Union Affairs,"
1952.

"Let's Look at the Record," Local 1776, IWA, CIO, Boston.

"Leftists in UOPWA," IAWOC, CIO.

Memorandum, James E. Brisbane to Executive Board Members, IWA, CIO,
March 10, 1954.

"Pardon Our Pride," IAWOC, CIO.

"Prudential Agents, Remember This . . . Now You are in the Same Position
Again," IAWOC, CIO.

"Time for a Change," IWA, CIO.

"To All Hancock Agents," IAWOC, April, 1953.

United Office and Professional Workers of America:

Amendments to the Constitution Proposed by the Administrative Committee
to the Delegates at the Sixth Constitutional Convention of United
Office and Professional Workers of America, CIO, Cleveland, February, 1946.

Amendments to the Constitution Proposed to the Delegates to the Seventh
Constitutional Convention of UOPWA, 1948.

Banquet Menu, UOPWA, CIO, Seventh Constitutional Convention, Hotel St. George, Brooklyn, N.Y., March 4, 1948.

Call to Special Convention, United Office and Professional Workers of America, Atlantic City, N.J., March 14, 1950.

Constitution of United Office and Professional Workers of America, CIO, 1937, 1940, 1942, 1944, 1946, 1948.

"Convention Call," to Founding Convention of UOPWA, April 4, 1938.

Leaders' Bulletin, UOPWA, CIO, No. 7, July 1, 1948.

————————, March 8, 1949.

"Lynn North Shore Agents Expel Leo Wallace! Protest Paperworkers' Raiding to Murray," June 15, 1948.

Officers' Report to Sixth Convention, UOPWA, CIO, February 18, 1946.

"Questions and Answers on Taft-Hartley Anti-Communist Affidavit," UOPWA, 1949.

Resolutions Submitted for Consideration by the Seventh Constitutional Convention, UOPWA, CIO.

Statement by UOPWA, CIO, to CIO, December 19, 1949.

"United We Will Win!" Statement by General Executive Board, UOPWA, March 14, 1950.

Statement to Members of United Office and Professional Workers from their Delegates to CIO Convention, 1949.

"To the Paperworkers of Sandusky: Don't Scab on Us!" UOPWA, Cleveland.

"Why Should I Join UOPWA, the Insurance Agents Union: Here's Why," 1944.

A

Aaronson, Norma, 3, 123, 141
Abramson, Irving, 128, 155-56, 160, 167
Agent, industrial debit insurance, cf. industrial debit insurance agent
Alfred Knopf, 139
"All Go or None Go" resolution, 182, 184
Aluminum Workers Union, 55
American Agents Association, 1
American Arbitration Association, 35-6
American Association of Social Workers, 51
American Communications Association, 110
American Federation of Labor, 1-14, 19, 22, 30-2, 33, 38-9, 42, 47-8, 49, 56, 58-9, 69, 70, 72, 73, 103
  Communism of U.O.P.W.A., 69-70
  Prudential contract, 126-29
  Resolution against agents, 2, 9
  Starts insurance union, 12-4
Anderson, Olin, 86
Appelate Division of New York Supreme Court, 24
Armstrong Investigating Committee, ix, xv, 78
Arthur Murray Dance Studios, 104
Ash, Harold, 149
Association of Catholic Trade Unions, 101-02
Association of Life Insurance Agents, 179-180

B

Banks of Athens, 6
Bankers Trust Co., 6

Bargaining unit,
  N.L.R.B. on, 31, 34, 37-8
  New York Labor Board on, 30
Baron, Sam, 9, 53, 54
Bauer, President, 207
Beal, Orville, 116, 121, 128, 174
Beirne, Joseph, 130
Berenholz, Anne, 92
Berne, Lewis Alan, 97, 110, 122, 131
Berney, Leon W., 9, 27, 28, 36, 39, 40, 46, 47, 58, 75, 86, 89, 105, 107, 110, 113, 114, 122, 141, 143-46, 149, 190
"Big Three," 15, 29, 44, 48, 86, 106
Bloomingdale's Department Store, 139
Bochstahler, Peter, 13
Bohm, Ernest, 6
Bookkeepers, Stenographers and Accountants' Union, Local 12646, 4-9, 10-1, 53
  radicalism of, 7
Boston Mutual Life Insurance Co., 135, 138, 146, 192-203, 204
  strike against, 202-03
Boudin, Leonard, 121-22, 131-32, 134, 135
Boyer, Ralph U., 13, 14
Bradon, Jack, 12
Brennan, Ignatius, 113, 208
Brennan, William J., 188-89
Bridges, Harry, 55
Bright, Leonard, 6-7
Brisbane, James, 150, 159, 164, 167
Bristow, W. C., 13
Brooklyn Eagle, 17
Brooklyn Trust Co., 101
Brooklyn Y.M.C.A., 95
Brophy, John, 10, 11
Budenz, Louis, 8, 141

C

California Joint Fact-Finding
Committee to the 1948
Legislature, 101
Campbell Soup Co., 139
Canada, 29, 76
Churchill, Winston, 67
Clark, Tom C., 107
Clarke, Paul, 143
Cohen, Leo, 55
Collection service salary, x
Collective bargaining under
New York Law, 153-55
Collins, William, 9-10, 169
Colonial Life Ins. Co., 49
Columbia Broadcasting System, 139
Columbia Pictures, 139
Combination companies, 15
Commerce clause of Federal
Constitution, 78-9
Commission, agents', cf.
Compensation
Committee of Agents, 128
Commonweal, 102
Communications Workers Union,
130
Communism
C.I.O. expels U.O.P.W.A.
for, 130-35
C.I.O.'s interpretation
of, 132-34
Merrill's interpretation of, 98
U.O.P.W.A.'s, 64-8, 132-34
Communist 11, 195
*Communist Party Independent
Nominating Petition,* 127
Communist Political
Association, 101
Compensation, agents',
collection service salary, x
commission prior to 1933, viii-ix
first year commission salary, x
Hancock, 43, 76
intermediate monthly, 84, 154
Metropolitan, 43-8, 76-7
new method, ix-x

state laws regulating, ix, 153-57
Congress of Industrial
Organizations, 10-2, 54, 56, 57,
123-26, 129-30, 130-35, 140, 141,
143-46, 194-97, 209
expels U.O.P.W.A., 130-35
forms U.O.P.W.A., 12
forms Insurance and Allied
Workers Organizing Committee,
136-38, 147-49
C.I.O. Union News Service, 11
Condon, William F., 85
Condon-Crews Amendment, 85
Court of Appeals of the State
of New York, 24-8, 64
Cox, Guy W., 17
Cradle Will Rock, 110
Crews, Robert, 85
Cudahy Meatpacking Co., 48
Curran, Joseph, 125
Curtis Wright Corp., 48
Cutter Laboratories, 104

D

Daily Worker, 52, 53, 99, 125, 136
Debit
insurance, viii
splitting, 183-85
DeCaux, Len, 11
Depression insurance, 85-6
Dies' Committee, cf. House Un-
American Activities Committee
Discrimination, 106
Distributive, Processing and
Office Workers of America,
138-42, 143, 192
Distributive Workers Union,
138, 140, 146
D'Olier, Franklin, 35
Douglas, William O., 62
Dowling, Ralph, 70
Downey, John, 13
Dubinsky, David, 59
"due process," cf. New York
State Labor Relations Act

238

Durkin, James H., 9, 40, 68, 70,
85-6, 90, 91, 92, 93, 100-03,
104-08, 110, 114, 121, 122-29,
131, 134, 136, 140, 141, 142, 146
Dutch Mustard Co., 142
Dynamic Expansion, 180

E

"employee," cf. New York State
Labor Relations Act
Employees' Fidelity Organization,
19, 23
Equitable Beneficial Life, Health
and Accident Co., of
New Jersey, 29
Equitable Beneficial Life Insurance
Co. of Penn., 29
Equitable Life Assurance
Society, 100
Equitable Life Ins. Co., 79
Ervin, Charles W., 3
Eureka-Maryland Assurance Cor-
poration of Baltimore, 28, 29
"exclusively," cf. New York
State Labor Relations Act
Expense limitation, 153-55
Expense margin, 153

F

Far East Spotlight, 101
Farm Equipment Workers
Union, 104, 130
Fay, David, 41
Fay, Frank, 107
Federal Bureau of Investigation, 107
Federal Telephone and Radio,
95, 104
Federation of Architects,
Engineers, Chemists and
Technicians, C.I.O., 97
Federation of Jewish
Philanthropies, 51
Ferris, Joseph, 117
"50 and 10," 86-7, 91, 94, 99, 109
Financial Employees Guild,
UOPWA, 101

Fire and casualty companies, 30
First year commission salary,
cf. compensation
Fiscal quarter, cf. New York
State Insurance Law
Fiske, Haley, 7-8
Food, Tobacco, Agricultural
and Allied Workers Union,
138-40, 142
Forscher, Albert, 106, 107, 113
Frank, Nelson, 103, 105
Frayne, Hugh, 5, 6
Frey, John, 52
Fur Workers, 104, 110

G

Ganey, J. Cullen, 132
Garfinkel, Charles B., 3
Garvin, Victoria, 141
German Alliance Ins. Co., 80
Gillen, William A., 162, 166-67,
205-06, 208-09
Gimbel's Department Store, 139
Golden Eagle Life Assurance Corp.,
27, 29
Goldberg, Arthur, 132
Gompers, Samuel, 5
Gordon, Benjamin, 198
Green, William, 144, 172-73, 178
Grievance, definition of, 73
Groel, Frederick, 37
Growers and Shippers Association
of California, 139

H

Hancock, cf. John Hancock Mutual
Life Insurance Company
Hancock "Bargaining Committee,"
160-61
Hancock "Policy Committee,"
160-61
Hancock "Streamlined
Committee," 159-63
Hansen, George, 122
Harper, William, 190, 191
Hartley, Fred, 105

Hawley, Peter K., 54, 59
Haywood, Allan, 27, 37, 100, 118,
    125, 135, 137, 144, 148-52, 157
Heisel, Charles, 37, 100, 113, 114,
    125, 129, 135-37, 145, 147-50, 170
Helfgott, Simon, 137, 144, 149,
    159, 160, 166, 168, 205
Henderson, Donald, 139, 140-42
Higginson, Arthur H., 167-68,
    208-09
Hogan, Matthew, 36, 41, 170,
    178-80, 191
Hollywood ten, 109
Home Beneficial Association
    of Richmond, 79
Honest Ballot Association,
    34, 40-1
Hoover, J. Edgar, 107
House Un-American Activities
    Committee, 52, 64
Howell, Valentine, 84
Hurst, Fannie, 7

I

Independent Hancock Agents
    Association, 17, 72
Industrial and Ordinary Insurance
    Agents Council, A.F. of L., 30,
    38-9, 47-8, 69, 74, 79, 94, 109
Industrial debit insurance
    agent, vii, viii
    salesman, viii
    as "employee" and "independent
    contractor," cf. New York State
    Insurance Law
Industrial endowment insurance,
    viii, xiv-xv
Industrial Insurance Debit
    Employees Union, 12
Industrial life insurance
    described, viii
    lapses of, xi-xiii, xiv-xv
    sales of, xv
Industrial Workers of the
    World, 3
Insurance Agents International

Union, A.F.L., 173-75, 190-92,
    197-202, 203-07, 209
Insurance Agents Local Union,
    8676, St. Louis, 1-2
Insurance and Allied Workers
    Organizing Committee, C.I.O.,
    143-46, 147-52, 157, 174-75
Insurance Mutual Protective
    Association, 3
Insurance Worker, 167
Insurance Workers International
    Union, AFL-CIO, 209
Insurance Workers of America,
    C.I.O., 157-59, 191-92, 193,
    199-201, 203, 207, 209
Intermediate monthly premium
    insurance, 84, 154
International Harvester, 104
International Ladies' Garment
    Workers' Union, Local 22, 7
    58-9
International Union of Life
    Insurance Agents, 15, 30, 39, 71,
    72, 127-28, 190, 207
Interstate commerce
    life insurance in, 78-83

J

Jefferson School of Social
    Science, 99
John Hancock Mutual Life
    Insurance Co., xv, 1, 2, 9, 15,
    16-9, 28, 30, 31, 42, 43, 47,
    48, 54, 60, 73, 74, 76, 77, 78,
    83, 85, 119, 125, 135, 137,
    143-47, 159-63
    compensation of agents, ix
    lapses of policies, xii
    turnover of agents, xiii
    union shop, 74
Jordan, Robert, 112

K

Kampelman, Max, 99, 103
Kent, Rockwell, 66

Kenton & Campbell
   Associates, 29
King, Jerome, 56
Kline, Benjamin, 20, 21
Korean War, 136, 143, 153

L

Labor Leader, 101
Labor Relations Commission of
   Massachusetts, 18, 73, 75
Landix, Osborne, 122, 141, 142
Lane, Everett, 195, 196, 198-202
Lapse
   laws, ix, xii-xiii
   rates, xi, xiii
LaTourette v. McMaster, 80
League for Industrial Democracy, 8
LeFebvre, Eugene, 208
Lefkowith, Max, 141, 198-99,
   200-03
Leonard, Richard T., 149-50,
   158, 165, 166, 167
Lerner's Department Stores, 139
Levy, Joseph, 110, 113, 122
Lewis, Catherine, 56
Lewis, John L., 11, 12, 14,
   56, 131
Lewis, Richard, 122
Life Insurance Agents of
   Virginia, Detroit Local, 191
Lincoln, Leroy, 16, 19, 20, 24,
   27, 61, 105
Little Steel Formula, 40, 76
"Little Wagner Act," cf. New York
   State Labor Relations Act
Livingston, David, 142, 195,
   197, 199
Local 30, U.O.P.W.A., New York,
   16, 19-24, 33, 40-3, 58-9, 60-4,
   69, 71, 100
   accuses Lewis Merrill, 63-4
Local 1282, D.P.O., Boston, 194-98
Local union jurisdiction, 204
Lumpkin, Harry, 3

M

Maccabbees, 48
McCarran Act, 77, 82-3, 155-56
MacDermott, William S., 167-68,
   208-09
McDonald, John G., 13
Maintenance-of-membership
   Metropolitan, 73
   Prudential, 37
Manufacturers' Trust Co., 46
Margin, expense
   cf. expense margin
Marquard, O.W.G., 69
Marshall Plan, 109-110, 124
Maryland Prudential Agents
   Local union, 178-80, 191
Massachusetts Commission In-
   vestigating Communism, 194, 198
Massachusetts State Labor Board,
   cf. Labor Relations Commission
   of Massachusetts
Matusow, Harvey, 141
Meany, George, 144, 206
Merger of Insurance Workers of
   America, C.I.O. and Insurance
   Agents International Union,
   A.F.L., 203-10
Merrill, Lewis, 8, 9, 11, 28, 30,
   37, 42-3, 47, 52-6, 57-8, 59,
   60, 62-8, 73, 83-4, 86, 87, 89,
   97-100, 103, 146
   denies he is communist, 68
   evaluates communism, 98
Metro-Goldwyn-Mayer, 139
Metropolitan Life Insurance Co.,
   xv, 1, 2, 7-8, 9, 15, 16, 19-24,
   25, 26, 27, 28, 30, 31, 32, 42,
   43-8, 54, 60-4, 69, 70, 73, 75-6,
   77, 78, 85, 119, 135, 137
   accused of discrimination in
   housing and debit insurance, 106
   compensation of agents, ix-x
   Greater New York agents, 19-24
   lapse rate, xiii
   New York State Labor Relations

241

Act, 24-8
Temporary National Economic
Committee, 60-4
turnover of agents, xiii-xiv
Metropolitan Agents of Maryland,
local union, 191
Mine, Mill and Smelter Workers
of America, 110
Monthly intermediate insurance,
cf. intermediate monthly debit
insurance
Monumental Life Insurance Co.,
87-94, 99
cites communism of U.O.P.W.A.,
89-90
strike against, 92-3
U.O.P.W.A. loses Chicago
office, 94
U.O.P.W.A. wins contract, 93-4
Mooney, Bernard, 110, 122, 136
Murphy, John, 115
Murray, Philip, 100, 111, 114,
118, 121, 123-26, 127, 131,
132, 141, 147

N

Nashville Trade and Labor
Council, 2
National Association of Industrial
Insurance Agents, 13
National Association of
Manufacturers, 104
National City Bank, 6
National Committee of Office
and Professional Workers, 9
National contract
Prudential, 32-8
National Federation of Insurance
Agents Council, A.F. of L., 120,
121, 127-28, 144, 148, 169-73
National Insurance Agents
Union, 73
National Labor Relations Act,
20, 94, 102, 106, 134, 156
National Labor Relations Board,
16-7, 30, 31, 32, 39, 79-81,
83, 88-90, 106, 121, 122, 127-29,
179, 180, 187-89, 191, 192,
198-201

insurance firms subject to, 80-1
rules on appropriate bargaining
unit, 31, 34, 37-8
rules on U.O.P.W.A. as non-
complying union, 94
National Maritime Union,
56, 125-26
National Polish Alliance of the
United States of North America,
80-1, 83
National War Labor Board
compensation of agents, 34, 37,
44-7, 76-8, 84
Nation-wide contract
cf. Thirty-one state agreement
New Masses, 99
New York Association of
Federation Workers, 51
New York Credit Clearing
House, 9
New York Newspaper Guild, 110
New York State Constitution
due process clause, 26, 78
freedom of contract, 25
New York State Court of Appeals,
cf. Court of Appeals of the
State of New York
New York State Insurance
Department, ix, 46, 154, 155,
156, 177
compensation of agents, ix-xi
opposes changes in compensation
of agents, 85, 155-57
power of, ix
turnover of agents, xiii-xiv
New York State Insurance Law, 44,
84-5, 153-57, 160, 161, 175
industrial endowment, xiv-xv
regulates elections to board
of directors of mutual insurance
companies, 60
retroactive pay, 76-7
New York State Labor Relations
Act, 20, 24-6, 30
appropriates bargaining unit,
17-8, 24-8
employee, 25, 78
exclusively, 26
independent contractor, 20, 22

New York Court of Appeals
rules on constitutionality, 24-6
New York State Labor Relations
Board, 17-8, 19-28, 33-4, 64, 74
on the appropriate bargaining
unit, 30
New York State Supreme Court,
24, 155-56
New York Times, 5, 59, 120, 172
New York World Telegram,
103, 104
Newport Associates, 29
Nicholson, Robert, 159, 164
Noncommunist affidavit of the
Taft-Hartley Law, 95, 102,
106-07, 115-16, 117-18, 120, 122
North, Cecil, J., 46, 47

O

O'Dell, Kenneth, 159, 160, 161,
162, 163-67, 193, 194, 204
Office and Professional News, 98, 99
Office Employees International
Council, A.F. of L., 59, 80
Office Workers Union
cf. United Office and Professional
Workers of America, C.I.O.
Office Workers Union of the Trade
Union Unity League, 52
O'Gorman & Young v. Hartford
Ins. Co., 80
Ohio, Prudential election in, 38-43
O'Neill, Albert, 39
O'Reilly, Harry, 171
Osman, Arthur, 138, 139, 141,
193, 199

P

Packinghouse Workers, 110
Paley, Jack, 195, 199
Paperworkers Organizing
Committee, 125
Paperworkers Union
cf. United Paperworkers Union
Paramount Pictures, 48, 139
Parents' Magazine, 95

Part 1: Prudential contract, 35, 41
Paul, Samuel, 79
Paul v. Virginia, 79-80
Pegler, Westbrook, 105
Perkins, Frances, 131
Philadelphia United Mutual
Insurance Co., 191-92, 193
Pieper, Fred, 149
Pike, Sumner, xv-xvi
Polish National Alliance
cf. National Polish Alliance of the
United States of North America
Pollack, Joseph, 184, 185-87
Ponsi, Robert, 164, 208, 209
Portnoy, Julius, 7
Post War Depression, 83-7
Progressive Party, 104
Provident Home Industrial
Mutual Life Ins. Co., 49
Provident Home Life Ins. Co., 204
Prudential Insurance Company of
America, xv, 1, 3, 9, 15, 16,
28, 30, 32-42, 47, 48, 54, 60,
73, 76, 78, 83, 85, 111, 114-17,
119, 120-23, 125, 126-29, 175-78,
180-85, 187-90
appropriate bargaining unit, 33-5
compensation of agents, x
election, general, 32-8
election in Ohio, 38-43
lapse rate, xiii
mass disability in, 172-73
refuses to bargain on city-
wide unit, 33
strikes against, 3, 172-73, 175-78
thirty-one state contract, 32-8, 110
turnover of agents, xiii
Wisconsin, 33
Public Affairs Committee of
Philadelphia, 60
Public Workers Union
cf. United Public Workers
Pugh, Ernest, 128

Q

Quaker Oats Co., 139
Quill, Michael, 138

R

Raab, Joseph, 161-62, 208
Random House, 139
Rank-and-File Movement, 50-1
Retail, Wholesale & Department
 Store Union, C.I.O., 138-39, 140
Retroactive pay, 76-7
Reuther, Walter, 157, 195
Reynolds, R. J., 139, 141
Rice, Charles Owen, 123
Rice, Ed., 15
Rieve, Emil, 130, 131
Riesel, Victor, 141
Rock, Leo P., 89-90, 93
Roosevelt, Eleanor, 7
Roosevelt, Franklin Delano, 54,
 64, 67, 108
Russ, George L., 13-4, 69, 121,
 144-45, 170, 177, 187-89, 190,
 204, 205, 210
Rutenberg, Stanley, 132

S

Santos, John, 109
Saposs, David, 126
Sayre, Harry, 111-15, 130
Schaeffer, Oscar, 114
Schneider, Aaron, 110, 141
Seabury, Samuel, 24
Second Front, 66-7
Segal, Bernard, 141
Shanks, Carol, 37, 105
Shell Oil Co., 104
Sheet Metal Workers,
 Local 281, 52
Shine, Max, 103, 145, 209
Shore, Jerome, 39, 40, 92
Sickness and accident insurance,
 179, 181
Sidener, Charles H., 1
Siegel, Frank, 192, 193, 194-97, 199
 says he is not a communist, 197
"65 and 15," 109, 120
Slichter, Sumner, 57
Smith, Edward, 17

Social Service Employees Union,
 U.O.P.W.A., 55
South Eastern Underwriters' Asso-
 ciation, 77, 81-82, 83, 155
Southern Aid Society, 49, 129
Split debit
 cf. debit
Squirrel cage, xi
Stachel, Jack, 51
Stanley, John P., 30, 68, 110, 114,
 122, 125, 130, 141, 146
Steelman, John R., 34
Steering Committee, Prudential
 agents, 171-72
Steuer, Aron, 24, 26
Stipchic v. Metropolitan Life
 Ins. Co., 80
"Streamlined Committee"
 cf. Hancock "Streamlined
 Committee"
Subversive Activities Control Act
 of 1950, 141
Sun Life Insurance Company of
 America, 28, 29, 79

T

Taft, Robert F., 105
Taft-Hartley Law
 cf. National Labor Relations Act
Taylor, Charles B., 16, 27
Tehran Conference, 68, 133
Temporary National Economic
 Committee, xv, 21, 60-4, 87, 93
Textile Workers Union
 of America, 130
Thirty-one state contract
 cf. Prudential Ins. Co.
Thomas, Norman, 8
Thompson, Hugh, 195-97
Title Guarantee Co., 48
Trade Union Education League,
 5, 7
Trade Union Unity League, 52
Trager, Frank, 51
Transport Workers Union, 110, 126
Truman, Harry S., 107, 133

Turner, Eugene, 11, 55
Turnover among agents, vii,
xiii-xiv
Twentieth Century Fox, 139,
213, 153-57
213A, 153-57

U

United Artists, 48
United Electrical Workers
Union, 104, 110, 130
United Insurance Agents of
America, 145
United Mine Workers, 56
United Office and Professional
Workers of America, C.I.O.,
xvi, 9-12, 15-9, 20, 22-8, 31,
32-49, 50, 72-4, 88, 91, 95,
96, 142
Communism of, 64-71, 132-34
composition of, 10-1, 148
expulsion from C.I.O., 130-35
founding convention, 10-12, 54-5
infiltrates other C.I.O.
unions, 56
insurance division, 29, 59
membership figures, 29, 57-8
merger with Distributive Workers
and Food, Tobacco, Agricultural
and Allied Workers Union,
143-46
Second Front propaganda, 66-7
temporary constitution, 11
voting at 1948 convention, 105-06
United Paperworkers Union,
111-19, 124, 130
United Public Workers
Union, 110, 135
United States Supreme Court,
80-2, 187-89
U.S. v. South Eastern
Underwriters Association
cf. South Eastern Underwriters'
Association
Unity Life & Accident Co., 149

V

Van Camp, 139
Vannett, Louis, 55
Viking Press, 139
Virginia Life & Casualty Co., 13

W

Wallace, Henry A., 105,
108-09, 124
Wallace, Leo, 106-07, 110-11, 114,
129
Walther, Julius, 88-9, 92
Wayne Pump, 104
Weikel, Frank, 59
Westinghouse Salaried Employees
Union, 98
White collar employees, 147-48
Haywood's ideas on, 148
Whitman, Roy, 16, 27
Wholesale and Warehouse
Local 65, 138
Wilkie, Wendell, 65
Wisconsin State Labor Board, 33
Work without a contract,
173-74, 183, 184
Workingmens' Cooperative
Association, 20, 69
World Federation of Free Trade
Unions, 124

Wortis, Rose, 51

Y

Yanoff, Morris, 54, 55, 92, 110
Young, Horace C., 13

Z

Zam, Herbert, 51

245

BIOGRAPHICAL NOTE

Born in Yonkers, N.Y., in 1927, Father Harvey Clermont, O.F.M. Cap., entered the Capuchin-Franciscan preparatory seminary at Garrison, N.Y., in 1941. He entered the Order's novitiate in 1945 and the Capuchin junior seminary in 1946. Ordained in 1953, he entered the Catholic University of America the following year and received a Master of Arts degree from the University's Graduate School of Social Science in 1956. Fr. Clermont completed the necessary work for the doctorate at the Catholic University in 1959. At the present time, he is a professor of economics and philosophy at the St. Anthony Friary Seminary in Hudson, New Hampshire.